THE ENDTIME
MONEY
SNARE:
HOW TO LIVE
FREE

All Scripture quotations in this book are taken from the New International Version of the Bible unless otherwise noted.

The Endtime Money Snare: How To Live Free
Copyright ©2002 by Midnight Call Ministries
West Columbia, South Carolina 29170
Published by The Olive Press, a division of Midnight Call Ministries
P.O. Box 280008, Columbia, SC 29228 U.S.A.

Copy Editor:	Susanna Cancassi
Proofreaders:	Angie Peters, Susanna Cancassi
Layout/Design:	Michelle Kim
Lithography:	Simon Froese
Cover Design:	Michelle Kim

Library of Congress Cataloging-in-Publication Data

Hahn, Wilfred
   The Endtime Money Snare: How To Live Free
   ISBN #0-937422-55-7

   1. Christian stewardship

Printed in the United States of America

Dedication

*To Jesus Christ, Who has guided my experiences
and life path to the completion of this book
and the many who contributed to its message
through their input, advice
or teaching.*

*God is not without a sense of humor.
Perhaps signifying that money may be the Philistine
Goliath of today taunting His people, four-fifths of all
those unnamed helpers are christened with
the first name of David.*

CONTENTS

INTRODUCTION

Every Knee Will Bow

You may be surprised to learn that the greatest religious ingathering the world has ever known is underway right now. Everywhere we look, revival meetings are taking place. Already, massive conversions have taken place. The many evangelists of this faith are fervently preaching to the world, employing the latest technologies and techniques and scouring the outposts of the world for new believers. This faith is gobbling up the affections of untold numbers of humanity from different cultures, countries and religions. In fact, it may already have claimed close to four billion new converts in these past two decades alone.

What faith is this? Could it be a giant explosion of the Muslim faith? No. Neither has it anything to do with Christianity. I am referring to a massive global boom in a material-based faith: Mammon worship. To coin a word, we might call it Mammonism. The apparition of a great prosperity is sweeping the world. Many want to share in its spoils; they want the gods of gain and technology to shower them with their blessings and security. Along the way, the God of Abraham has been deposed and diminished.

I call this phenomenon the *Endtime Money Snare*. It presents some deep challenges to Christians. Many of us may not even be aware that we are serving at the altars of Mammon. Perhaps some of us have even opted to do so willingly. Sadly, I believe that much of modern-day Christianity is already caught in this endtime money trap. The number of its captives is increasing daily. It grieves God greatly that His children are falling for such a shallow sham, one so blatantly false and such a pale, shabby imitation of the great promises and eternal riches He has for us.

What is this snare? Why does it hold endtime significance? In my estimation, these questions call for some deep soul-searching and spiritual discernment. Above all, it requires a scriptural response. I am sure that you will be amazed to discover the message that God seeded into the Bible — guidance that I believe was meant specifically for our generation.

As sensational as the book's title may sound, I assure you that it wasn't chosen to scare anyone. Profit is not a motive in the production of this book. It would have been much more lucrative for me to stay in my job as an international executive. This book was written to relieve a burden. In the pages that follow you will indeed read about snares, money and endtime conditions. That is why this book is entitled exactly as it is —*The Endtime Money Snare:*

How To Live Free — no guile intended. These three elements — snares, money and the last days — are interrelated more than you may imagine.

Readers of this book won't find an "economic shock" story that closes with a pitch to sell gold coins or survival supplies. When our long-suffering God finally unleashes His judgment upon our deeply idolatrous world, we will not be able to rely upon any man-made financial instrument to provide a stable refuge. Not even gold will be safe from monetary corrosion. This book is about our trust in God, the affairs of the heart, the hooks and dangers of living in the endtimes as a Christian and the grave risks of falling into a grand snare that our enemy is setting for the last-days world. It is crucial that we know what form this trap will take. Yes, you may be shocked as you learn some of the facts. Your eyes will be opened to many of Satan's ruses and agendas operating today. However, my objective is not to make you anxious, but to equip you to live for Christ uncompromisingly in a world where it is becoming increasingly difficult to do so. My desire is that our Lord be reinstated as the God of everything in this world — not just the God of that which we cannot understand or of those last few remaining domains that mankind cannot control or influence. My desire is that every knee will bow to Him.

I have observed the encroachment of the *Endtime Money Snare* upon the world from a ringside seat as a senior executive in the global financial industry over a period of 20 years. In traveling the globe, I came into contact with many senior people and elites in the world's major financial centers. As a financial research director, global portfolio manager and head of a large investment management operation with offices strewn around the world's financial centers, I was in a privileged position. I had access to chief executive officers of major companies, central banking authorities, leading economic thinkers, financial strategists, and enormous amounts of information that the vast public would never see. I saw money in motion, people in power and avarice in action: billions of dollars on the loose around the world. With the advantage of my global perch, I read an enormous number of publications from around the world, scanning for significant trends in any area of human life, from religion to politics, technology to fashion, and industry to private households. I began to see common threads connecting these seemingly unrelated pieces of information. I saw that most world affairs marched to the tune of a mysterious, intelligent drummer. I perceived the rise of a number of very powerful false gods, more powerful than any before in human history. Moreover, I was amazed to learn that these developments are prefigured in the Bible — in great detail, no less. By the end of this book, I will have taken you behind the scenes and unmasked both the drummer and his triad of piedpipers.

During my research, the most important discovery I made was how closely the trends and conditions of a fallen endtime world relate to my own faith and actions. I soon realized that I had become a co-conspirator, an accomplice, a pawn and a captive of the *Endtime Money Snare*. Perhaps you, or someone you know closely, has also been ensnared unwittingly, unwillingly or even complacently, and has been taken hostage. If so, they will be no different than most of us, including me. Even though I penned this book, its message posed great personal challenges for me as it will for many others. I still grapple with these issues every day, a process that will undoubtedly continue indefinitely.

Though this book deals with aspects of the endtimes, it does not require that readers adhere to any prominent eschatological position — a Rapture or Christ's return occurring pre-, post- or mid-Tribulation. Having studied Scripture on these questions, I certainly have an opinion. However, the topic is immaterial to this book and would only cloud its central message. Whatever view you hold on these issues, I believe they have no impact on our relationship with Jesus Christ or our salvation. As such, this book's message is relevant to all believers. All of Christ's commandments to Christians living in these last days are the same whether we will live through the Tribulation or not. In nine different contexts throughout the Gospel accounts, Christ tells us to "watch." For example, *"Watch and pray so that you will not fall into temptation"* (Mark 14:38). Without detailing each of these nine commands, suffice it to say that all are relevant to the times in which we currently live.

Christ also warned us not to fall into a trap. In Luke 21:34–36 Christ made this point very clear:

"Be careful, or your hearts will be weighed down with dissipation, drunkenness and the anxieties of life, and that day will close on you unexpectedly like a trap. For it will come

upon all those who live on the face of the whole earth. Be always on the watch, and pray that you may be able to escape all that is about to happen, and that you may be able to stand before the Son of Man."

There can be no doubt that the world is facing an endtime trap. What form will it take? How can we avoid its grip? How can we prosper in the Lord's grace and live free of money's lure? This book attempts to answer these questions.

I could have chosen to write this book purely from the perspective of an economist or a global financial strategist to appeal to the secular world on some of its points. Though some encouraged me to take that route, I chose not to. Why? First, because I felt a primary burden for my fellow Christians, the Church of Jesus Christ. If the Church can't first overcome the wiles of an endtime snare that is essentially spiritual in its design, what hope can there be for those who remain lost? We must first lead by example. We know that *"...our struggle is not against flesh and blood, but against the rulers, against the authorities, against the powers of this dark world and against the spiritual forces of evil in the heavenly realms"* (Ephesians 6:12), and that the ways of God are foolishness to people of the world (1st Corinthians 2:14).[1] Therefore, those of us who have been given the Spirit can only fully comprehend the nature of this *Endtime Money Snare.* Though non-Christians may agree with many of the views expressed in this book, without a belief in the inerrancy of the Bible and godly discernment, much of the perspectives I present will not be compelling to those who do not belong to the Lord.

14

Yet, I have written it in a way that speaks and appeals to people from all walks of life. I wanted to be sure that fellow sojourners with little knowledge about arcane topics of investments, economics and finance, science and technology, or world affairs will benefit. I also wanted to speak to skeptics — people like me — who need lots of facts and documentation before faith gets its chance. To serve both groups, I present a format that uses extensive footnotes providing further in-depth explanations for those who desire them. They are not essential information to the reader. However, they ensure factual and fundamental rigor. This approach also seeks to avoid the stigma of being categorized as another sensationalist "future shock" work. In my view, too many speculative books have been published about the endtimes, world conspiracies and Christian "get-rich" formulas based upon unsubstantiated facts and weak analysis. I couldn't bear to bring discredit to Christ in that way, either deliberately or ignorantly. I hope I will not be caught in ignorance.

A few words about the layout of the book: Starting with a fictionalized story in the first chapter, we are then subtly pulled into the realm of the *Endtime Money Snare*. After alerting readers to the dangers of the times in which we live, we establish the urgency and importance of the snare by rolling up our sleeves and delving into the Bible. This lays a necessary foundation for the fascinating journey that follows. At this point, the snare will begin to be laid bare. The remaining chapters are self-explanatory.

I offer both spiritual and financial advice in this book — an uneasy pair, to say the least. I must be especially careful and humble with regard to stewardship advice. People are the least charitable about any error in this area. Early on in my profession I learned that financial recommendations can cost friends no matter how well meaning the advice. Even the best advice can go wrong given the unpredictable vagaries of financial markets. I have learned to only provide information and suggestions that will allow the advice-seekers to make their own stewardship decisions. I may even tell my friends how I have chosen to be a steward of the resources God has given me. My objective, however, is to encourage them to evaluate the facts and examine their values and beliefs for themselves before making these important decisions. After all, we are all called to be godly stewards individually. We can't blame someone else for our own situations.

In that sense, dear reader, I hope to both win and keep your friendship as we delve into the realm of the modern world in this book. I am going to give you information and new perspectives that will surely challenge you. Some of these viewpoints may open up entirely new vistas for you. Others may unintentionally cause pangs of fear. In the end, I hope that you will be able to make decisions based upon hope and will choose to make the most of everything you have that God has given you, including resources, skills and time. My desire is that it will result in a big pay-off of peace and contentment on earth and an eternal reward in heaven.

To conclude, my main mission is to alert my brothers and sisters to the present and coming challenges, and to give hope that we have nothing to fear if we put our trust in God. But, there is a price. We must choose to stand for eternal values and opt for timeless riches. We must break free from the control of a materialistic web that ensnares our thoughts and actions and enlists our labors and energies to serve false gods and a temporal realm. Therefore, this book is about purity of heart, as well as the guarding of our hearts.

Join me in this journey into the "maws and claws" of an increasingly secular and materialistic world.

By the end of this book I hope that you will be free from its slavery.

"There are not a few who believe in no God but Mammon, no devil but the absence of gold, no damnation but being poor, and no hell but an empty purse; and not a few of their descendants are living still."

–Robert South

ENDNOTES

1. *"The man without the Spirit does not accept the things that come from the Spirit of God, for they are foolishness to him, and he cannot understand them, because they are spiritually discerned"* (1st Corinthians 2:14).

CHAPTER 1

The Visit

An Invitation

The Hopes are about to be taken captive.

Albert fidgeted in the waiting room. He was ill at ease with people who held themselves out to be professionals, sitting atop pillars of knowledge, regally looking down upon him, their potential prey of ignorance. He was sure they would probe and invade his privacy with endless personal questions. He'd have to answer and submit. Yet, he did want their help. He consoled himself with the thought that if he were entirely truthful, they would better be able to prescribe advice for him. He was convinced it was the right thing to do. It would only be to his benefit. After all, Alice had insisted that he come for months now.

She was there with Albert. Alice sat across from him, separated by an expansive coffee table, its polished surface punctuated by a pile of technical-looking journals. She sat bracketed in a taut, polished leather wingback chair, its

19

protrusions like the epaulets on a general's shoulders. She didn't look comfortable, pressed rigidly against the upright leather seat back that rose up above her head. Yet her face was at ease. The rich ambiance of the room comforted her. She was infatuated with the dark mahogany woods, the Italian-marbled floor, the big oil canvas behind the reception desk and the two large Inuit art statues in the opposite corners of the waiting room. She breathed deeply. Instinctively, she knew that they had come to the right place. It smelled of success, competence and security. She was glad that Albert had given in after months of cajoling. They were finally here.

Albert and Alice had driven into the center of this large metropolitan city from the suburbs. It wasn't often that they threaded their way into this land of glass spires and row upon row of tall office buildings. Perhaps only on weekends to catch a cultural event, but certainly not during prime business hours. The cost of daily parking was enough to cover a fast-food meal for a small family. It would have been better had they taken the train. But the familiar cocoon of the family car was still preferable to facing the confusion of unfamiliar train schedules and masses of stern-looking commuters during the morning rush hour. Their trip could not be avoided, for it was only here in this district, shrouded inside buildings of impressive granite and glass, that one could access the brains and services that would provide the help that the Hopes were looking for.

They had arrived a full 20 minutes early. After announcing themselves to the receptionist, they had politely been invited to have a seat. Albert disinterestedly scanned the sumptuous surroundings of the room. Bored at the prospect of nothing to do for the remaining quarter hour, he looked for something that would occupy him. He loathed waiting. Albert leaned forward to scan the disheveled pile of journals on the coffee table. *Pension Fund Age* lay on top. It profiled a puckish looking character on the cover with his arms folded across his chest, posing like some conquistador ruling an unseen kingdom. The title of the related article was slashed diagonally across the cover: "The King of the Bond Markets: Atop $100 Billion in Assets." "*Boring,*" he thought. He rifled deeper into the shallow stack, hoping to find a copy of *People* magazine or a *Sports Illustrated.* No such luck. *Private Investor* was next in the pile. "The Growing Demand for Hedge Funds, An Alternative Investment Class" was its profiled feature. Ugh. Albert dug further. *Financial Analyst Journal...Money Magazine.* The theme of the titles was all the same. He scanned the side tables. A brightly colored travelogue promising pages of glossy pictures caught his eye. He bent over to reach it. Just then the reception room door swung open and Mr. Guinn entered the waiting room.

"*Amazing!*" Albert thought. He couldn't believe this fellow was actually going to see them early. Maybe an earlier appointment called to cancel, he speculated.

"Mr. and Mrs. Hope?" Mr. Guinn asked, addressing them both.

"Yes," Albert blurted, as he lurched to his feet.

"Hello, Mr. Hope. I'm Shane Guinn. I'm so pleased that

you could make it," cooed the professional clad in the requisite dark suit.

Glimpsing the man before him, Albert winced to himself: Just what he needed, he thought: a young whippersnapper, probably half his age. Shane barely looked 30 years old, probably in his late 20s, he guessed. Albert extended his thick hand and shook Shane's firmly, harder than usual. Albert resolved that he wasn't going to take much guff from this youngster. "Hi, Mr. Guinn. I'm pleased you could see us," he said engagingly.

Alice had also risen to her feet and smiled broadly towards Mr. Guinn. She extended her hand, exclaiming, "I'm so glad that we've finally come to see you. Our friends, the Gowiths, have said such nice things about you. They're so pleased with all the money you've made them."

Mr. Guinn gleamed. "It's a pleasure to meet you," he responded. "Yeah, I've had a pretty good run these past few years. That's really what our firm is all about. Creating wealth for our clients."

Shane Guinn was a financial planner—a certified financial planner.

"May I invite you into one of our meeting rooms?" he asked. Without waiting for a response, he announced, "Please follow me." *"This would be an easy sell,"* he thought to himself. The Hopes were virtually sold, thanks to the endorsements of the Gowiths. But he knew he couldn't be flippant. Mr. Hope looked like an imposing man. He wasn't going to risk blatant bluffs of any kind.

The Hopes found themselves in a small meeting room

with a round conference table and four chairs. A laptop computer was on the table, its screen illuminated with the random flickers of a screen saver. Mr. Guinn introduced his firm and reeled off its many fine qualifications. He briefly explained why the investment philosophy of his firm was so distinct. The computer screen continued to swirl with shapes and figures. He explained that his company's superior management, reporting systems and fund selection capabilities were the key factors to their success in providing superior advice and services to their clients. The combined market experience of over 50 years between the firm's seven financial planners testified to the company's deep understanding of financial markets. He mentioned the satisfaction of the Gowiths, the family friends of the Hopes, more than once.

"Over 600 hundred clients have put their trust in us," he stated, "accounting for a total of over $800 million in client portfolios. The reason they come to us is that we have been able to show a track record of consistent performance. Our investment returns have always been positive measured over the longer term. The main reason why we've been able to achieve this is that we strongly believe that all of our clients should have a very high equity content in their portfolio — that, and a disciplined selection process."

Albert began to warm up a little, although he was somewhat troubled by Mr. Guinn's last comment. Of course he liked consistency and positive returns, especially the high ones he had so frequently seen advertised in his local newspaper. Yet, he still had a deep-seated distrust of financial markets, particularly the stock markets. His brother had lost a fortune during the crash of 1987. He was flat busted after he finally settled his investment loans and broker's margins calls. Albert was nervous when it came to any kind of risk, let alone the seemingly casino-like stock markets. He didn't understand them. Yet, nervous as he was, he was intrigued. Stocks had been successful in making more than a few people rich in recent years. And some of these people were very unlike his "flash-in-the-pan" brother. They were ordinary hardworking people, a few of whom had racked up more capital gains in a year than their annual employment incomes. The Gowiths, friends from church they had known for over 25 years, were just such an example. They were a very conservative couple still living in their first house. Yet, they had recently purchased a $150,000 motor home. It sure was a beauty, loaded with every conceivable gadget of convenience. They often joked that it had cost more than 15 times the price of the house they had bought back in the early 1960s. Now, they were planning to take an early retirement, cash out the house and travel the open road for two years before settling in Arizona.

Albert and Alice were not yet in such a carefree position. After the drain of paying for two university educations, residence fees — one of them to graduate level — they had not yet built up a sizable nestegg for their retirement. Yes, they could rely on the payouts from Albert's company pension plan, but it would be subsistence. They would live on a tight budget when they retired. They'd tour the country in a compact car, not a luxurious motor home, if at all.

Shane's investment spiel again pierced into Albert's consciousness. He had drifted off in thought for a few moments. "We have a very different investment philosophy, one that is very client-sensitive," was the last comment Albert could remember. He again focused on what Mr. Guinn was saying.

"We like to give our clients what they want," continued Shane Guinn. "Just tell us what your return objectives are and we'll get you there."

As if programmed himself, Shane tapped a key on the portable computer. Its screen burst to rich hues of burgundy and gold displaying the logo of Mr. Guinn's firm and its slogan: "Your Financial Freedom is Our Goal."

Alice had been listening very attentively. She had no doubt as to why she was here. She wanted a comfortable retirement. And the truth be known, she was somewhat envious of the Gowiths. She wished the same for Albert and herself. How enchanting and romantic it would be to while away their retirement years like them. "Well, Mr. Guinn," she chimed in, "we're actually very conservative people. Our expectations are modest, really. We're quite happy and content. It's just that we'd like to know that we can retire comfortably, you know, to not have to reduce our standard of living very much from what we enjoy now." She felt little apprehension opening up to Mr. Guinn. Not only had the experience of the Gowiths over the past few years been assuring, but she was also comforted by the fact that his firm advertised on a local Christian radio station.

"Yeah, that's all we want," Albert nodded in agreement. "But I don't want to stake my future on the ups and downs of the financial markets," he qualified.

"It sounds like we may be able to help you," Mr. Guinn responded matter-of-factly. "May I suggest that I take you through our computerized planning package. It's really a fantastic program, the latest. We've spent years perfecting it, designing it to come up with the very best recommendations for our clients. We've fed in all the investment returns of various markets over the past 30 years, reliable numbers vetted by top-notch performance measurement agencies. It'll only take 10 minutes or so," he enticed. "If you will allow me, I need to ask a few questions about your state of financial affairs. But, please be assured," he quickly interjected, "we keep all of our client's information in the strictest of confidence. Your information never goes outside of our firm."

Albert looked sullen. The moment of truth had arrived, the exact thing he had been wanting to avoid. He'd have to reveal his most private of affairs: his financial condition. To him, a man who liked to play his cards close to his chest, burly and independent, this was like revealing his innermost secrets. He'd rather be talking to a female doctor about prostate cancer. "No problem. We'd be glad to answer a few questions," he breathed.

"Just what kind of a retirement lifestyle would you like, Mr. and Mrs. Hope?" began Mr. Guinn. "We need to first establish how much income you will require when you retire." Albert and Alice looked at each other. The process had begun.

Twenty-five minutes later, Mr. Guinn pressed the "enter" button on his computer for the last time. The computer was now processing the information, shortly to erupt its erudite, techno-perfect solutions to the light of its screen. The whole process had taken longer than the ten minutes he had initially indicated. That usually proved to be the case, though it didn't need to be. Clients always asked a lot of questions, and sometimes deliberated endlessly in responding to Mr. Guinn's queries. However, in the case of the Hopes, Alice's endless list of questions was what extended the whole process. Embarrassingly, she had asked as many of Albert as she did Mr. Guinn. Apparently, the financial condition of the Hope's household balance sheet was as unknown to her as it initially was to the financial planner.

Albert was feeling very warm. During the interrogation he had taken off his sport jacket and hung it on the empty chair. The whole process had been even more embarrassing than he had feared.

"Here, we have the answer," announced Mr. Guinn. "The computer, having carefully considered your personal preferences and risk tolerances, has suggested these recommendations. Let me see...," Mr. Guinn took a moment to focus on the computer screen, "...given your ages and retirement income requirements, we will need to begin with an 85% weighting in equities and 15% in fixed-income securities."

Albert felt a sudden pang in his gut — an anxious constriction. "Eighty-five percent in equities?" he stammered. He could see his whole future riding on a roll of the dice.

"Isn't that much in the stock market too risky?" he winced.

Shane responded without hesitation, betraying a practiced response. "Well, Mr. Hope, we actually think that it's a greater risk not investing that much in equities. When you think about it, how much financial security have you already missed by not conservatively investing in the stock market earlier? Our research shows that it's an unfortunate misconception to believe that equity investing — especially the way that we do it — is very risky," counseled Mr. Guinn. "You know, stocks always eventually go up. One just requires a conservative and disciplined approach."

The financial planner liked using the words "conservative" and "disciplined." The senior partners of the firm had carefully instructed all the firm's employees in the exact wording of their investment presentations. A believable and soothing presentation was key to the firm's success. In the space of five years, the firm's two founders — former stockbrokers — had seen incredible success. Already, they were receiving overtures from a local bank that wanted to expand its wealth management business. It was a growth industry everyone knew, and based on the latest purchase offer, each of their ownership stakes were already worth well into eight figures.

Albert now felt out of his league. He knew that the only counter-arguments he could come up with against Mr. Guinn's apparently-informed comments were all emotive, all feelings with little statistics and facts.

"May I show you some of our research?" Shane asked.

He had already clicked the mouse, and instantly a scientific-looking chart was poised upon the screen, ready to work its infectious propaganda.

Albert and Alice squinted, trying to locate a point of orientation on the screen. "Please move in a little closer," invited Shane. He repositioned the computer to allow the Hopes a better vantage. "What I'm showing here is the relative return of stocks versus a short-term interest rate over the past 20 years. You can see that stock markets have way outperformed — by almost 8 percentage points per year. To not have been invested in the stock market would have really hurt."

Even with this explanation, Albert and Alice were still not able to decipher the message from the chart. They would simply accept Mr. Guinn's verbal expositions. Already, the chart had morphed into the next one.

"Here we see the probabilities of a negative return from the stock market," he continued, pointing to a bar graph on the screen. "Over a 10-year period, the chance of a negative return is virtually zero as this research shows. It's based on the actual results over the past 30 years. So for folks such as yourselves, who are at least 10 years from retirement, there's really no reason for worry." Turning toward Albert, Mr. Guinn added, "Actually, I'd be concerned for your financial well-being and personal freedom if you weren't exposed to the stock market."

Mr. Guinn continued illustrating his firm's knowledge about financial markets and investing with an array of charts. The Hopes did their best to follow Shane's explanations and illustrations. Frankly, they understood very little. Yet, they felt comforted and impressed. The charts demonstrated professionalism and knowledge. How much, they did not know.

A few points did stick with Albert and Alice. They remembered that asset allocation — whatever that was — was important to time correctly. From what the Hopes could make out, the best thing to do was increase their equity mutual fund holdings "on dips" as Mr. Guinn put it. To invest globally was also important. The financial planner had stated that globalization was engulfing the world. Therefore, one had to be invested in some of the faster growing countries of the world. "Emerging markets," he called them. One series of charts particularly intrigued them. It showed China growing into a bigger economy than the US by the year 2025. If that was to happen — these predictions being supported by the World Bank — Mr. Guinn said that it was imperative to be heavily invested in Asian stocks. Albert couldn't recall seeing a local bank branch by that name. Whatever the bank, the projection sounded credible. Next, Mr. Guinn loftily explained how his firm selects mutual funds. He assured Albert and Alice that his firm only picked the best performers. As soon as these funds began to under-perform for a year or more, he always recommended selling them. It sounded like a sure-firm system.

Shane Guinn turned away from the computer and squarely faced the Hopes. He folded his hands on the table. The time had come for him to add his personal wisdom and convey a bit about what he knew as well as his own personal credentials. "You know, if I may share with you personally," he began, "in the seven years I've been in this business, I've been blessed by the fact that I have helped so many people build a better future. I really have been privileged. In fact, a testament to how strongly I believe in my advice is that even my parents are clients of this firm."

He continued, "When you think about it, just look at what's going on in America — this computer revolution, the Internet, and the superior strategies of the big multinational companies. There's no reason in the world why stock markets can't keep growing at 20% plus per year over the long-term. It's been that way since I've been in the business," he added proudly.

Albert studied Mr. Guinn's face. He couldn't deny that this guy was young. But he was impressed with his passion for doing good. And with such a reputable and apparently successful firm backing him up, his age might not be anything to be concerned about.

"The world is really in a new age of prosperity," Shane Guinn continued, waving his arms expansively. "You know, the Russians and Chinese were really smart adopting capitalism. They finally saw the light. Market economics is really the great hope for the world's future. Prosperity and freedom will eventually trickle down to even the poorest people on earth."

Albert and Alice were mesmerized. They soaked in this last burst of wisdom for a moment. It really was such an inspiring gospel. Wealth was seemingly a few keystrokes away. Why not relent and accept the sweet promises and security of secular financial markets and global trends?

Alice turned her head expectantly towards Albert, anticipating a response.

"Where do we go from here, Shane?" asked Albert.

He could already see himself playing bridge with the Gowiths in Arizona.

Little did the Hopes know that they had taken a step towards the *Endtime Money Snare*.

CHAPTER 2

Into The Whirlwind

History Beckons

Albert and Alice Hope, whom we just met, have taken a step toward danger. Why? What have they done? Their responses to Mr. Guinn were probably no different than most. Many of us have considered staking our future in financial assets. Yet, although the Hopes may not have done so knowingly, their hearts were subtly snared during that meeting. In a moment of spiritual blindness, they bought into a slew of questionable promises and world developments. In effect, they chose to stake their future retirement years upon the fragile rock of some deceitful endtime developments. They may soon discover that they have become spiritually entangled with a diabolically inspired last-days boom in financial wealth. It includes an agenda that involves a lot more than just money. Sound farfetched? In the chapters ahead, you will discover how and why to avoid this snare. The facts will speak for themselves.

An Agenda Lurks Largely Unseen

At this very moment, planet Earth as we know it, is being reordered more quickly and completely than ever before. The speed of these developments is literally too much for any one person to comprehend or follow. Already, these changes have had enormous implications for each of us — our families, jobs, values, incomes, investments, and even our health. Most of the world is welcoming these developments with open arms, entirely unaware of their future implications. By and large, many Christians are included in this number.

We all eagerly anticipate a future world of good things, complete with more comforts, deeper knowledge, greater freedom of choice, more wealth and prosperity, cheaper products, higher productivity, and improved prospects for the world's poor. Plenty of prophets today see a world of prosperity and peace ahead — in fact, as far as the eye can see. In part they are right, yet they are mostly wrong.

But, what's worrisome is that the ultimate impacts of the sweeping changes underway — the epic objectives that lie beneath — remain largely invisible to most individuals. Few sense the spiritual dangers and the approaching entrapment, or recognize the signs of the times. Shouldn't Christians be aware of what these will mean for the world, their faith and freedoms, for eternity? Their economic lives — decisions to buy, sell, save, invest, and raise families — increasingly challenge the fundamentals of their faith.

In the meantime, the world is definitely in a hurry. While humanity eats, sleeps, marries and increasingly gives itself over to amusement, a swirl of activity and initiative drives our planet toward a rendezvous. From out of this apparent chaos, a clear pattern emerges. There is an agenda behind the rapid and sensational trends of our modern age.

I call it the *Endtime Money Snare*. It represents the central development of our time. As already mentioned, it has made incredible advances in recent years, sinking its claws of influence into more geography and people than ever before. A worldly kingdom is being erected that seeks to eclipse God, denying the worship that is due Him. Instead, three powerful, false gods are given life by humanity just as the Bible predicts. The world has chosen to put its trust in them rather than the One and Only God. As we will see, this triad of false gods already exists. They are capable of entrapping us into deep bondage if we let them. It is already very difficult to escape their lures and deceitful traps. Sadly, much of humanity has already been entranced by their lures and trapped by their snares.

A Snare Is Being Set Very Quickly

What makes the topic of an *Endtime Money Snare* more urgent is the rapidity of its advance. Its pace has been breathtaking in recent decades, progressing faster and faster every year. In fact, the world has made more progress toward a common materialistic belief system in these past few years than ever before in human history. Global financial trends — one of many modern developments — play an integral and central role. Not only has monetary finance provided the carrot at the end of the stick—enticing participation through its hopes and promises of financial wealth but financial markets have also served as the blunt instrument that has extracted global compliance to this emerging, materialistic order.

"So what else is new?" some might ask. Haven't human progress, enlightenment and modernity been underway for a long time? Yes, their roots may go back a number of centuries. Yet, world history reveals how frighteningly quick these developments have crescendoed over the course of this past century. Looking across the span of time since Christ walked the earth, we can see that world developments have mysteriously only begun speeding up over the past few centuries, certainly so over the last 100 years. Almost any trend—population growth, new patents, the size of the world economy, financial wealth, the speed of communications, and countless other developments—plotted over two millennia all look the same. For almost nine-tenths of this duration of time, change has been virtually imperceivable. Then, suddenly, an enormous amount of activity erupts upon human history. Events and developments are speeding up its acceleration as well.

Different as well today is that new developments now envelope a greater part of humanity in a coordinated way and more quickly than ever before. Trends that affected only a small number of countries fifty years ago, accounting for less than one-sixth of the world's population, now apply to as much as two-thirds of the world and more.

To gain a sense of the incredible pace of change, consider a few examples applying to just one century, the last 100 years.

- **Radical Change in Livelihoods** – At the beginning of the last century, 68% of Japan's labor force worked on the land, 44% of America's and about 20% of Britain's. Today, agriculture accounts for only 7% of workers in Japan, 3% in America and 2% in Britain.[1]

- **Technology** – Today the processing power of all the semiconductors made each year, including the transistors in microprocessors, and the bits of memory in information storage devices, roughly equals the total thinking power produced in all the previous years since the beginning of time.[2]

- **Economic Output** – The total amount of goods and services produced in the twentieth century is estimated to have exceeded the cumulative total output over the preceding recorded human history. Between the years 1900 and 2000 world economic output at constant prices has increased about 19-fold.[3]

- **Money and Finance** – Between 1915 and 1995, the economic activity — buying, selling and income — of the average human being in the world valued in financial terms has increased by a factor of 4.6 times. For thousands of years prior to this time, this advance of the world of money trend was almost unnoticeable.[4]

- **Communications** – Technological progress has literally exploded, particularly in the communications field. The speed of telecommunication has multiplied by over 100 trillion times during the past century.

These are just a few examples that provide a sense of the rapidity and sudden eruption of change upon our generation. Is it possible that all these massive developments are a cosmic accident with no design or plan? Are they all meant for good? Is it possible that many of the new conveniences of our modern age carry a spiritual danger? And if so, does it raise a specific agenda against Christians — to diminish or snatch away their faith in God and in the imminent return of His Son, Jesus Christ? The answer is an emphatic yes.

Sorting Out Fact From Fiction

I have chronicled global trends for years and can only say that their pace has been stupendous. My office file cabinets are bulging with information — hundreds of files — that I have collected in my travels and research in an effort to document the trace and direction of major world trends. In my view, an endtime agenda is at work. It is like a large octopus, with many arms, faculties and branches. Each tentacle represents a development that is moving independently, yet progressing on a path of global convergence. All of these paths intersect with each other at an ultimate objective: a system of world domination and individual entrapment — a world with little want or need for God.

Many of these endtime developments intersect with money — a world state of affairs ruled by a "free-market" financial system and a headlong pursuit of prosperity. In the past 15 years alone, more than 4 billion more people have come under the influence of such a system. This has happened because many countries have begun to pursue prosperity by opening themselves to "free market" economics.[5] As a result, a massive wave of deregulation has taken place. Barriers of all kinds — to foreign investors, cultural values, language and commercial trade, personal liberties, to name a few — have toppled. For example, in the past fifteen years over 135 countries have made significant changes to liberalize and integrate their financial systems with the rest of the world.[6] The convergence of values and beliefs that such rapid change represents is simply unprecedented in the history of the world. As such, more than two-thirds of the world's people (soon, probably many more, if not the entire world's population) will stand in the crossroads of a potential money snare. The elements and dangers of this snare will become clearer in later chapters.

But how can we unveil this master endtime agenda and capture the scale and essence of the change swallowing up the world? More importantly, how can we discover its true essence — the identities of the spirits behind this whirlwind? What complicates it for the untrained eye is that this lightning advance of a materialistic world religion is buried under a thundering cacophony of statistics and technical words. Few of us have the time to sort out the truth from the statistical lies and worthless sound bites. The truth be known, a large part of society has been conditioned to blindness and complacency. For them, discernment is inoperative. Musing has given way to amusement. Even when confronted with organized evidence, many would rather choose complacency and settle back into their lives of Western comfort.

Though we may face an avalanche of change and information in our day, sorting it all out is not as difficult as it appears. God has already provided us with the necessary framework to more easily understand our times — the Bible. Looking through the window of its pages, we are able to clearly see an intelligent structure and plan in progress. Therefore, in our search to understand our advanced technological age and the spiritual challenges it presents to Christians, it is only logical that we begin with God's Word. A brief examination of some of its predictions about our day will prove to be highly illuminating in unveiling an *Endtime Money Snare* against the faithful. It will set the stage for the remainder of this book.

Bible Prophecy Provides The Best Hand-Guide To Understanding Our Times

The Christian faith is the only major world religion which concerns itself with prophecy — the foreknowledge of things to come. The prophetic Scriptures are worth consulting in our quest for two important reasons: First, they unquestionably speak about the events of our time. Second, prophecy has always proven to be reliable and accurate. All prophecy, with the exception of the portions which refer to the last days, has reached fulfillment. So far, we can know that the accuracy of God's prophets have been 100% perfect. Given the proven exactness of the Bible, we are sure to gain important insights into our times through its prophecies referring to the last days.

The prophets of the Bible provide some views about our time which are very different from the visions of the popular secular prophets of today.

∞

Jacques Delors, one of the key visionaries behind the European Union and former president of the European Parliament, once admonished, "We must hurry. History is waiting." Just what is this history waiting to be fulfilled? Apparently, the world must meet a deadline with destiny. What are the implications of humanity's destiny?

I believe that these are the most urgent questions of our time. To answer them, Christians must consult the Bible. In the next chapters we will lay a brief foundation before further unveiling the *Endtime Money Snare*. It is absolutely vital that we remain free of its traps, choosing courageously to live free for Christ.

∞

"Why do the nations conspire and the peoples plot in vain?"

–Psalm 2:1

"How long will mockers delight in mockery and fools hate knowledge?"

–Proverbs 1:22b

ENDNOTES
1. Organization of Economic Cooperation and Development.
2. *Financial Times.*
3. International Monetary Fund, "The World Economy in the Twentieth Century."
4. Ibid. Quoted from *Globalization and Growth,* Nicholas Crafts.
5. Crossborder Capital, *The Age of Global Capital,* 1998.
6. International Monetary Fund.

CHAPTER 3

A Different And Deceptive Age

The Bible Speaks About Our Day

D oes the Bible give us any indication about an *Endtime Money Snare*? Is a role prefigured for money, financial markets and economics, and if so, will they be in the service of a benevolent or malevolent force? Scripture provides some answers in surprising detail. The Bible warns us of an era in which an ensnaring commercial system will emerge, working in concert with three false gods — gods that have been erected by humanity. These endtime gods play key facilitating roles in leading much of mankind into a money trap, an endtime idolatry with a boom in wealth and promises of prosperity, a great new world religion of Mammonism. It is a devious snare that is both subtle and brutal. Many people are entirely unaware that there is an underlying agenda behind these developments, let alone that the Bible speaks about this very subject.

According to God's Word, what should we expect to see happening in world affairs, financial markets and economies during the endtimes? To find out, we first need to examine what the Bible says about the world regime of the last days. Therefore, a brief understanding of prophecy is necessary. A biblical foundation will be most helpful to us for more than a few reasons. First and foremost, it establishes that the Bible makes an ordained and direct call to Christians living in modern times. In doing so, it seeks to forewarn us against falling into a trap during the endtimes. Repeating Christ's call to us mentioned in the foreword, *"... that day will close on you unexpectedly like a trap. For it will come upon all those who live on the face of the whole earth. Be always on the watch, and pray that you may be able to escape all that is about to happen, and that you may be able to stand before the Son of Man"* (Luke 21:34–36). Lastly, as already mentioned, I believe Scripture gives us many indications as to what form this trap will take.

A Brief Look At Prophecy

In looking at Bible prophecy, our main goal is to present what the Bible says about the emerging world system of Mammonism — an *Endtime Money Snare*. I do not intend to provide a detailed, comprehensive presentation of endtime developments. Why? For one, this book is mainly about identifying modern-day financial and economic developments, not a general exposition on prophecy. Many excellent resources are available to those who wish to delve into prophecy in greater detail.

Yet, knowledge of the Bible and the workings of the modern-day world won't be enough to unveil the spiritual and physical strategies behind a potential endtime money trap. Mere human intelligence is no match for the endtime deceptions and temptations that the world and its Christians face. After all, we are dealing with the end of days, the last chance that Satan has to overcome the saints and cap his insurrection against God. All the stops must be pulled out in executing the final chapters of a satanic cosmic agenda. All the pistons of his master strategy must fire simultaneously. The "father of lies"[1] as Jesus Christ called Satan, will be lying and deceiving at the very top of his form. And, an element of surprise will serve as a helpful tactic too.

Therefore, it is absolutely paramount that we begin with a balanced and clear foundation properly rooted in Scripture. Otherwise, we are bound to lose our way and risk error in discerning the nature of any traps of our age.

The Identity Of The Last Day's Kingdom

In Daniel chapter 2, we read the interpretation of Nebuchadezzar's dream of a large statue: *"...an enormous, dazzling statue, awesome in appearance"* (Daniel 2:31). Quoting Daniel 2:32-33: *"The head of this statue was made of pure gold, its chest and arms of silver, its belly and thighs of bronze, its legs of iron, its feet partly of iron and partly of baked clay."*

God enabled Daniel to interpret this dream. He revealed to Daniel that each section of the statue corresponded to successive world kingdoms. Nebuchadnezzar's kingdom — the wealthy and powerful Babylon — was represented by the head of gold. The lower sections then prefigured later kingdoms. Briefly described according to the generally held view, the chest and arms of silver portrayed the Medo-Persian Empire stretching from 539 B.C. (the approximate date that the Babylonian Empire fell) to the beginning ascendancy of the Greek domination established by Alexander the Great. This old world power gave rise to a number of successive dynasties including the Ptolemies and Seleucid kings, right through to 63 B.C. under the Hasmoneans. This whole era is considered of Greek origin and together is represented by the statue's belly and thighs of bronze. Next came the Roman Empire, an age of iron-like power. Roman rule superseded the reign birthed from the Greeks. The legs of iron portray the military might of Rome and its emperors, with the feet of iron and clay symbolizing a following extension of this kingdom that remains related in character. Parts of it are made of iron, just as the legs.

In considering this vision, it is important to recognize that the described kingdoms do not necessarily refer to nations headed by all-supreme kings. Though this is certainly true in the case of Babylon, the term "kingdom" simply implies the identity of the dominant, world-ruling regime of the times, whether autocratic, democratic or a multilateral collection of nations or other entities.

This last kingdom in Nebuchadnezzar's dream symbolizes the world regime that would exist during the last days. It is also the one that witnesses the return of Jesus Christ. This is the kingdom that God will wipe away in order to set up a new eternal kingdom that will never be destroyed. These events are portrayed by the words, "...*a rock was cut out, but not by human hands...It struck the statue on its feet of iron and clay and smashed them ... But the rock that struck the statue became a huge mountain and filled the whole earth"* (Daniel 2:34b–35). The rock symbolized Christ and His returning reign over a new world.

This last earthly kingdom is the focus of our analysis. The more we can learn about the nature and characteristics of this kingdom, the better we can assess the dangers to the world and its Christians living at that time — this present generation.

A Time Of Great Vagueness And Deception

An important distinction of the last kingdom is its vagueness and confusion. This endtime regime is very different from any that have gone before it in several ways. Daniel's next dream about four beasts — the second of four — reveals more useful information in this respect. This account is found in Daniel 7:2–8 and 11–12:

"In my vision at night I looked, and there before me were the four winds of heaven churning up the great sea. Four great beasts, each different from the others, came up out of the sea. The first was like a lion, and it had the wings of an eagle. I watched until its wings were torn off and it was lifted from the ground so that it stood on two feet like a man, and the heart of a man was given to it. And there before me was a second beast, which looked like a bear. It was raised up on one of its sides, and it had three ribs in its mouth between its teeth. It was told, 'Get up and eat your fill of flesh!' After that, I looked, and there before me was another beast, one that looked like a leopard. And on its back it had four wings like

47

those of a bird. This beast had four heads, and it was given authority to rule....Then I continued to watch because of the boastful words the horn was speaking. I kept looking until the beast was slain and its body destroyed and thrown into the blazing fire. (The other beasts had been stripped of their authority, but were allowed to live for a period of time.)"

Careful examination of this vision reveals that it is another version of the one given to Nebuchadnezzar. Dealing with the very same topic — about the kingdoms that are to come — this time it highlights very different themes.

The first of the four beasts — the lion — again represents Babylon. The second, described as looking like a bear, again portrays the period of Medo-Persian rule. In turn, the leopard with the four heads foreshadows the rise of the Greek kingdom founded by Alexander the Great, the next phasing into the four separate divisions (symbolized by the four heads) under his four generals following his death. The last beast revealed in Daniel's vision is the one that we are studying closely.

Daniel was puzzled by this last beast. Actually, he was terrified and frightened by it. Significantly, it was the only beast that prompted him to ask for further clarification. Upon doing so, he received the information found in Daniel 7:23-24:

"... The fourth beast is a fourth kingdom that will appear on earth. It will be different from all the other kingdoms and will devour the whole earth, trampling it down and crushing it. The ten horns are ten kings who will come from this kingdom."

Most illuminating is that we see a world system very different from any that has gone before, one that cannot be easily recognized by the definitional standard of previous kingdoms. It is not an obvious one. Rather than lending itself to crystal clear identification, it is opaque and divisive.

We are repeatedly told that this last kingdom will be different. Three times in this vision we are informed that this beast is a strange and puzzling creature: *"It was different..."* (Daniel 7:7); *"...which was different from all the others..."* (verse 19); and *"...will be different..."* (verse 23). In no uncertain terms are we told that it was strange.

Therefore, this point is extremely significant. It beckons us to sharpen our senses and to take off any blindfolds that may exist due to our preconceived notions and perceptions of the world and its systems. The accepted norms of our lives during these days, whether social, political or commercial, must be set aside lest they bias our thinking and eternal perspectives.

The Real Power Behind A New World Regime

In Daniel 8 we see another spotlight on the endtime world from a different angle. This is the third time Daniel was allowed to peer into the future. This additional picture adds new perspectives to his two earlier visions.

Daniel is shown two animals: First a ram and then a goat with one horn between its eyes. The ram is widely believed to depict the reign of the Medo-Persians. The goat, which then vanquishes the ram, prefigures the lightening-quick rise of Alexander the Great.[2] At the height of the goat's power, we are told that its horn is broken off and four others grow in its place. These scenes prefigure the seceding of Alexander's power to four separate generals. Out of one of these succeeding horns (we are not told which), a smaller horn grows that would ultimately reach to the heavens. This small horn signified the beginning of the next kingdom; the regime that would lead to the end-times. This is the same kingdom earlier portrayed as the feet of iron and clay and the beast with four heads. In Daniel 8:9-12 is found the prophet's initial written impressions of this vision concerning the kingdom of the last days — the small horn.

"Out of one of them came another horn, which started small but grew in power to the south and to the east and toward the Beautiful Land. It grew until it reached the host of the heavens, and it threw some of the starry host down to the earth and trampled on them. It set itself up to be as great as the Prince of the host; it took away the daily sacrifice from him, and the place of his sanctuary was brought low. Because of rebellion, the host of the saints, and the daily sacrifice were given over to it. It prospered in everything it did, and truth was thrown to the ground."

Daniel had great difficulty understanding this vision. Then, an angel-like person named Gabriel, who appeared like a man, was instructed to tell him its meaning. He made it clear to Daniel that this vision had to do with the endtimes, *"...I am going to tell you what will happen later in the time of wrath, because the vision concerns the appointed time of the end"* (Daniel 8:19). Gabriel then interpreted the entire vision. Further information about this last kingdom, which spans to our generation in the new millennium, is found in Daniel 8:23-25. There we read:

"In the latter part of their reign [the period of Greek rule] *when rebels have become completely wicked, a stern-faced king, a master of intrigue, will arise. He will become very strong, but not by his own power. He will cause astounding devastation and will succeed in whatever he does. He will destroy the mighty men and the holy people. He will cause deceit to prosper, and he will consider himself superior. When they feel secure, he will destroy many and take his stand against the Prince of princes. Yet he will be destroyed, but not by human power."*

Some important details about this kingdom not provided in the earlier visions are revealed here. I believe that they help unlock some important points of preparation for us living in modern times.

The most significant revelation is that the power behind this kingdom is not human. We learn that the source of its power is something apart from this earthly regime. As such, it is a significant differentiation from the earlier three kingdoms—Babylon, Medo-Persia, and Greek. These realms became strong through their own power, through military might or superior human strategy. But in the case of this last kingdom, we find that a different type of power has taken interest in the affairs of mankind. Apparently, a new inspirational force has descended, lurking behind the din and clang of human history as it grinds its way to the time of the end.

Just Who And What Is This Power?

Further study of this passage leads us to a clear conclusion as to its identity. We are told that this king (representing a world regime) would be a *"...master of intrigue..."* (Daniel 8:23) and that *"...he will cause deceit to prosper..."* (Daniel 8:25). Daniel 8:12 also says that *"...truth was thrown to the ground."* Deceit is obviously the very essence of his character. What spirit could inspire such a king? Could it be the same power that is the very personification of deception?

Jesus Christ Himself provides the answer to this question in John 8:44 by saying, *"...He was a murderer from the beginning, not holding to the truth, for there is no truth in him. When he lies, he speaks his native language, for he is a liar and the father of lies."* Christ was talking about the devil.

Satan's character of deception, lies, secrecy, intrigue and mystery are well identified elsewhere throughout Scripture. There is no higher power than Satan who can claim paternity of the lie. Certainly, no other can claim the title of "master of intrigue." Intrigue is the domain of darkness, only existing without the light. Therefore, intrigue must be against truth. The liar is the master strategist behind the advance of the endtime kingdom. And advance it will. In fact, it will rise up to the very heavens, as we will see and as Scripture indicates. It throws some of the *"...starry host down to earth..."* (Daniel 8:10), this ruler considering himself superior (verse 24), and standing against the Prince of princes (verse 25).

The Grand Architect Of An Endtime Snare Has A Purpose

Just when and why did Satan decide to become so directly involved in the march of human history? We know that he already was in command of the kingdoms of the earth at the time of Christ.

The devil tempted Christ when He went into the desert to fast for 40 days and nights. He took Jesus up to a very high mountain and showed him all the kingdoms of the world and "...*their splendor*" and said, "...*All this I will give you,*" he said, "*if you will bow down and worship me*" (Matthew 4:8).

Christ is not recorded as having refuted Satan's ability to deliver on this proposal. Instead, He chose to respond to the implicit idolatry. Christ rebuked him saying, "*Worship the Lord your God, and serve him only*" (Matthew 4:10).

Apparently, Satan was already busily orchestrating mankind's organizational affairs. Here we learn of one of his most effective tactics: puppeteering. He tempts everyone. Better yet, he tempts leaders and centers of influence into accepting his enticement to worldly power. This temptation serves as an effective stimulant to legions of the world's leaders, movers and shakers, driving them to a state of hyperactivity on the global stage.

Clearly Satan was actively coordinating an agenda at the time of Christ. Writing perhaps 30-40 years after the Resurrection, the apostle Paul mentioned that "...*the secret power of lawlessness is already at work*" (2nd Thessalonians 2:7). The secrecy of this power identifies it as the same as the "...*master of intrigue....*" The apostle John also expressed the view that this "other power" was already present saying, "...*This is the spirit of the antichrist, which you have heard is coming and even now is already in the world*" (1st John 4:3).

The conclusion is that the grand strategist behind the

endtime kingdom is none other than Satan, the spirit of the Antichrist. He inhabits the affairs and developments of mankind's last kingdom acting as its architect. A carefully crafted plan is masked behind the confusing turmoil and strangeness of the world affairs of this kingdom.

The construction of this last kingdom is driven by a purpose. The king who symbolizes its reign is shown as one with a stern face. A stern face implies serious determination, or the weight of a grand undertaking. And it is indeed. His mission is to wage war against the saints and to set himself above the Most High; to bring the whole world under his domination. That's no small undertaking for a creature that is neither omnipresent nor omniscient.

The success of this mandate — if there is any chance of success — must depend on effective strategy and organization. There must be a shrouding of its advance, a dependence on secret agendas, camouflage and intrigue.

Conclusions From Bible Prophecy

To this point, we have discovered some important characteristics of the endtime era. The whole world order is unlike any power structure that ever existed. It will be very different. We recall that Daniel was mystified by its form. Above all, we must remember that the main characteristics of this time is one of deception, untruth, and strangeness ... an era in which *"...deceit will prosper."*

In short, the *Endtime Money Snare* that this book proposes to reveal depends on a grand diabolical enterprise of deception and surprise. After all, it is revealed as a system that will crush and destroy the entire earth. It cannot be allowed to be easily evident to the world nor to Christians who are deeply engaged in its cares. We must uncover a few more clues about this great diabolical agenda before we connect it to events of our day.

Predictions About Modern-Day Money And Economics

The book of Daniel makes some solid connections to the present financial and organizational structures of the world. You may be surprised to learn that a modern-day boom of false wealth is foreshadowed by his words. While Daniel couldn't have used the terminology that we are familiar with today, he certainly predicted the types of conditions that are currently giving rise to a boom in wealth and world-wide materialism, an endtime phenomenon that ultimately comes to a sorry end. Many people will be snared into slavery and complicity with this system, lured by promises of financial security, prosperity and modernity, unable to escape the destruction that follows.

Financial systems may control their lives through investments, debt or the love of money. Others may simply be involved in this system by misplacing their faith. Though they may be good stewards, avoiding some of the more obvious worldly traps, they may still place their hope in other gods beside the true God. To do so is spiritual infidelity. Either way, whether this may happen to individuals through voluntary spiritual idolatry or involuntary enslavement, it leads to an *Endtime Money Snare,* the consequences of which have an impact for eternity, not to mention the here and now.

You may be wondering where all these connections to money, an endtime boom in wealth and materialism can be found in the Bible. Albert and Alice Hope, the couple we met in the first chapter, certainly have no inkling. However, we will see that the evidence is not hidden as we continue our foundational search of Scripture.

In Daniel 11, we find more key revelations about the nature of the last kingdom. Verses 36–45 contain an account of another vision Daniel was given — his fourth and last concerning the last-day kingdom and regime. Here emerges an enormous list of tell-tale characteristics of this period, and for the first time, we begin to see a foreshadowing of economic and financial dimensions. It seems that his fourth vision of the fourth world kingdom is specifically meant for those of us who are alive today.

"The king will do as he pleases. He will exalt and magnify himself above every god and will say unheard-of things against the God of gods. He will be successful until the time of wrath is completed, for what has been determined must take place. He will show no regard for the gods of his fathers or for the one desired by women, nor will he regard any god, but will exalt himself above them all. Instead of them, he will honor a god of fortresses; a god unknown to his fathers he will honor with gold and silver, with precious stones and costly gifts. He will attack the mightiest fortresses with the help of a foreign god and will greatly honor those who acknowledge him. He will make them rulers over many people and will distribute the land at a price."

Many strange clues are given in this passage. Some of the implications are truly astounding, striking right into our generation.

What could be meant by the fact that this endtime king — meaning a regime, system or kingdom — has no regard for the "gods of his fathers" or "the one desired by women" (Daniel 11:37)? Who are the "god unknown," the "god of fortresses" and a "foreign god"? We shall attempt to identify them all.

ENDNOTES

1. John 8:44.
2. In this vision of the future of human history and the endtimes, there is no image of the Babylonian Empire as there were in the earlier two visions of Daniel 2 and 7. This may be because Babylon was on the verge of being conquered by Darius the Mede (also sometimes identified as Cyrus) at the time of this prophecy.

CHAPTER 4

Out With the Old Gods

Chasing After New Gods

You shall have no other gods before me." This was the first of the Ten Commandments that Moses brought down from the top of Mount Sinai. And it is precisely here — at the start of the list — where mankind's road toward the endtime and final judgment begins. Refusal to heed this command has shaped a human history of massive upheaval and endless sorrows. An epidemic of vain imagination and curiosity has spawned a pantheon of other gods — numbering into the tens of thousands — that have been chased after and worshipped through the ages. The preoccupations and vital energies of countless millions of human bodies have been sacrificed to their pleasure.

Yet, the Bible predicts that most of these false gods will eventually either disappear or fall out of popularity. We learn that in the endtimes there will be a great convergence of false gods. Strangely, though it was prophesied that the number of false prophets will multiply during the last days,[1] the number of gods will actually see the reverse trend. Even the gods themselves will not be immune from the threshing machine of globalization. Just as in the corporate world, they face consolidation and mergers of their domains. Yet, even though there may be fewer false gods, those remaining are destined to be much stronger, as shown in Scripture. These last-day gods will have a global following of worshippers, and moreover, will play an overarching role in the endtime agenda.

According to Daniel, three major false gods will exist in the endtimes. Just who and what are these gods? Are they already among us? These are critical questions. We must discover the answers if we are to earnestly follow Christ's command to watch and know the season of His return — to continue living knowledgeably and righteously.

Let's take a closer look at the text found in Daniel 11:36–45, quoted at the end of the previous chapter. To recall, a man dressed in linen, with a belt of finest gold, explains the nature of the last king of the endtimes to Daniel. This king prefigures the last world kingdom, the same one that is portrayed by the feet of iron and clay, the terrifying beast, and the small horn of the goat in the earlier revelation of Daniel chapters 2, 7 and 8.

Three "endtime" gods are revealed in this passage. Two are found in verse 11:38: *"...he will honor a god of fortresses; a god unknown to his fathers he will honor with gold and silver, with precious stones and costly gifts."* This verse counts two gods — a god of fortresses and an unknown god. Since one of them is already identified as the god of fortresses, it cannot also be considered the unknown god.

Additionally, in verse 39 we see that another god plays a role in the endtime dominion of this last kingdom. We are informed in this verse that *"He will attack the mightiest fortresses with the help of a foreign god."* Here emerges a helpful and powerful "foreign god" for the world regime of the last days. We now have conclusive evidence that three major gods will play a significant role in endtime developments.

Discovering The Identity Of The Three False Endtime Gods

Just who are the three new gods of the endtimes? A quick word of caution before we continue on our investigative journey: The conclusions I reach are referenced to the knowledge of our age and, of course, my own understanding, which is limited. It is possible that two decades from now the perspectives provided by Daniel may allow for different interpretations. While we must remain open to that possibility, I still believe that the identifications made of these three false endtime gods in this book are profitable ones: They can still help today's Christians lead lives that are separate and apart.

We can begin searching for the identity of these gods by using the process of elimination. We are given clues as to what they are *not*. Some gods will disappear or decline in favor of these new ones. The last kingdom has no regard for the gods of his fathers and the one desired by women. The influence of these "old" false gods will fall away, superseded by new gods that will be worshipped during the last days. Who could these "old" gods be? Let's begin with the single god mentioned specifically: The god desired by women. Who is it?

It would be difficult to conclude that this god desired by women could mean anything other than a fertility god. The Bible mentions several: Artemis of the Ephesians, Baal of the Canaanites, Asherodoth of the Hittites, Tammuz and others. Of course, many more have also been worshipped down through the different cultures and religions of human history. Is it possible that the god referred to in the book of Daniel is Tammuz, a prominent fertility god worshipped during that time? We cannot be sure. However, according to Daniel's vision, whatever pagan god may have been represented by the term "god of women," he will no longer be worshipped during the last days. The prominent role of a fertility god will have been deposed and superseded by new ones. But why?

Throughout history women have regarded bearing as many children as possible as a virtue. To be cursed with a barren womb has traditionally carried a humiliating social stigma, as it struck the very foundation of economic health and a nation's power. Wealth and prosperity have been directly equated with large families, huge populations and big armies. Having many children has been considered an enrichment and honor. A large family represented a storehouse of labor and real wealth, and above all, a comfortable retirement for the parents. The worship of fertility goddesses, therefore, played a large role in all pagan societies. Women and men have worshipped them in the hopes of being favored by the gods with many sons and sizable families.

Consider how dramatically these perspectives have changed today. Contrary to the attitude about child birthing in the past, a large family nowadays is regarded as an impoverishment. Many people believe that the more children a family has, the more stresses placed upon Mother Nature: More pollution, greater depletion of natural resources, etc. In the consumer society of the 21st century, another mouth to feed is seen as intruding upon the resources and lifestyles of those who are already living. Most people in the modern-industrialized world — North America, Europe and other high-income countries — consider a large family a throwback to olden times. "They replicate like rabbits," people may snidely deride parents of large families, implying a lack of responsible behavior. A similar attitude is reflected in the case of the higher birthrates experienced in lower-income countries. Attributed to illiteracy and irresponsible policies, this condition is considered to be the direct cause of the relative poverty that many of these countries suffer. Some even go so far as to suggest that these are sufficient reasons to cut population growth in any way possible. As a consequence, organized population control is promoted by the highest institutions and non-governmental organizations (NGOs) of the world. A number of wealthy individuals have bequeathed their fortunes to this cause.

We do know that, according to the book of Daniel, the old-time god of women has been deposed by new ones. This old god is history. What has happened is that the promise of prosperity of an old god — the god of Tammuz, through the veneration of high fertility — has become barren. Instead, the world now worships at the shrine of new prosperity gods. These new deities have nothing to do with the imagined impoverishment of the old god of women. Rather, they represent the new, modern-day givers of prosperity and are appeased if there are fewer mouths to feed on earth. We will learn who they are.

Massive Changes In Population Growth Predicted

If women and society no longer desire to have large families in the last days, it is only logical that this must be evident in world population dynamics. A decline in population growth should be a characteristic of the endtimes. At the very least, we should see birth rates falling during those days.

If that conclusion is correct, then there can be little doubt that Daniel's prophecy clearly dates our generation as the one of the endtimes. World population trends of the last century are simply unprecedented. For example, population aging is unprecedented, without parallel in the history of humanity.[2] The present world generation is the first in human history to voluntarily promote a decline in the earth's population. This has never happened before on such a wide scale. Widespread abortion, voluntary and mandated birth control could very well be among the practices foreshadowed in the Bible that lead to this result.

Not so long ago, the world witnessed a massive population explosion unlike any before. Over the last 40 years of the previous century, the global population has doubled to 6 billion people. During the prior 40 years (between

1920 and 1960), the number of humans jumped by 75%. This rapid population growth of the 20th century contrasts sharply with earlier eras. For example, the world population was estimated to be approximately 300 million people at the time of Christ. It would take another 1600 years before the earth's population would double to 600 million inhabitants. By comparison, the earth's population doubled at a rate 40 times faster during the middle of the 20th century.

However, since the mid-1960s, the world's population growth rate has declined substantially, falling from a rate of over 2.0% per annum to an estimated 1.13%[3] in recent years. The average number of births for each woman has almost halved from a rate of five births in the mid-1960s to 2.82 in 2000. Birth and fertility rates are expected to continue slowing with fertility rates falling by as much as half again.[4] In fact, it is predicted that the number of human beings on earth will actually begin declining in perhaps 30 to 40 years once population momentum has peaked. It is possible that this reversal could happen even sooner.

A New Gospel Of Prosperity

The population boom of this past century — though unparalleled in human history — is not entirely surprising. The major reason for this occurrence is the modern-day advance of health and medicine. As a result, the 20th century experienced a dramatic decline in the infant mortality rate and a lengthening of the average human lifespan. Today, people in high-income countries can reasonably expect a life span of 75 years or more. The average longevity for the world overall has increased by more than 50% to 65 years since the turn of the last century. Infant mortality rates have fallen by two-thirds over this same period. Such advancements are joyous developments to celebrate; however, the rapid changes in world population growth — first a rapid acceleration and then a voluntary decline — such as never recorded before in human history are a key development of the endtime that holds many implications for our generation. It is important that we understand these connections. They have direct links to the financial trends of our day.

Freedom Of Choice: Children Or Portfolios?

That we all retire in comfort and good health is everyone's sincere hope. That is exactly why Albert and Alice Hope sought the advice of Sean Guinn. Yet, it is very possible that most people will be sorely disappointed with Mr. Guinn's advice. The reality is that anyone who will be of retirement or working age over the next quarter decade will have cause for concern. The world's population faces an aging trend, as already mentioned. If so, then believe it or not, our pensions — in all forms, corporate, government, or individual IRAs, RRSPs and others — have a prophetic role. Sound far-fetched? As I will explain, pensions play a facilitating role in creating an apparition of great financial wealth in the last days, a condition that produces the "maddening wine" which figures prominently in the rise of a great commercial colossus.

A World Retirement Crisis Just Around The Corner

In recent years, policy-makers around the globe have sounded alarms about an approaching world retirement crisis. They are concerned that there will be too many old people and not enough young workers. The feared consequence is that many pension systems — particularly those of governments — will go bust, leaving retirees out in the cold.

Is it a hoax or a genuine cause for worry?

Actually it's both. I believe its a cause for concern because there most likely will be a general retirement crisis that will be very tough on the lifestyles of the present baby boom generation of the Western world. And yes, there's also a hoax in the works. The specter of a retirement crisis is being used to encourage the acceptance of several financial solutions that are both bogus and misleading. Millions of North Americans and other world citizens are systematically encouraged to pursue financial and economic behavior that will come up empty. Interestingly, these developments fit hand-in-glove with the diabolical strategies of the *Endtime Money Snare* as this book lays out. An endtime boom in massive pension funding helps create a financial market boom.

Many Studies Support The Conclusion Of Massive Pension Problems

Exactly how serious is this supposed retirement crisis? Countless studies, reports and essays alerting readers to a potential retirement problem and its possible solutions have been published over the past decade. Among the more prominent ones are several studies commissioned by the United Nations. In the opening paragraph of one of them it reads, "...it is generally accepted that most existing pension regimes may be financially unsustainable, and that, as the population ages, they will require substantial reform to forestall the emergence of large public sector deficits...".[5] In plain English, what the researchers are saying is that government budget deficits will soar in some countries and many public pensions systems are likely to go bust if they continue their present course. The World Bank published a heavy tome on the same topic and opened with this comment: "Systems providing financial security for the old are under increasing strain throughout the world...the result is a looming old age crisis that threatens not only the old but also their children."[6] Later, the International Monetary Fund (IMF) and the Organization for Economic Cooperation and Development (OECD) also chimed in with a thorough study offering similar views.[7] Countless reports have followed from these august organizations. In the "speak" of these transnational agencies, the above quotations betray a high level of concern. They are obviously worried, but what is their solution?

Facts Suggest That Studies Are Correct

The issues that these studies have raised — I have cited only a few of them — are real and largely correct. The world is definitely headed for a retirement crisis. While this realization is troublesome enough, what's worse is that the widely accepted solutions being pushed forward to avert this crisis lead to much more serious problems and complications. Not only will these solutions fail the hopes of many future retired people (probably most of those reading this book), but they play a direct role in instigating an enormous endtime financial delusion — one which will involve large transfers of wealth, as well as mad financial booms and busts. I believe that the threat of a crisis is being used as a lever to prompt the inappropriate responses of mainstream citizenry, while simultaneously advancing an *Endtime Money Snare*.

The Pension Problem Explained

Before we can be more certain about these conclusions, we first need to understand the nature of the problem. The average age of the world's people is definitely increasing. In 1990, slightly more than 9%, or one half-billion of the world's population was over 60 years of age. The World Bank estimates that this proportion will double to 18% by the year 2030. The aged will increase even faster in the higher-income countries. In the case of the OECD countries, (the thirty members of the Organization for Economic Cooperation and Development), the percentage of the population over 60 years of age is expected to increase to 31% in the year 2030 from only 18% in 1990. That's an unprecedented development.

It's worth reviewing the causes of this phenomenon in greater detail. These predicted trends have two main causes: First, people are living longer; and second, birth rates are falling substantially. Today, we see that fertility rates (the number of children born to an average woman during her lifetime), for industrialized countries have already fallen to levels that are generally below 2.1, the rate required just to maintain a stable population. For example, Italy and Germany have a low fertility rate of 1.3; therefore, their country populations (excluding immigration inflows), are declining. The fertility rate in the United States is now estimated at 1.9. With birth rates in many countries falling below maintenance levels, it follows that the proportion of youth versus the aged will fall. Further, this trend is expected to accelerate, according to the latest estimates.[8]

The looming problem is that eventually there will be fewer working people to support the living requirements of the aged. Economists and demographers gauge this trend with a statistic they call the "elderly dependency ratio." This measure compares the size of the population over 65 years of age versus the population between 15 - 64 years of age (what's considered to be the potential working population). Needless to say, this ratio has been rising and is expected to sharply increase over the next decades as the world's population ages. For example, in the United States, the elderly dependency ratio jumped from 19.2% (at the end of 1995), and is expected to climb to 27.6% by the year 2020 and 38.4% in 2050. In other words, over 38% of the US population at that time will not be employed and will have to be supported by the 62% who are of working age. This population shift is even more dramatic in other countries. Italy will have an elderly dependence ratio of 37.5% in 2020 and will be as high as 60.0% in 2050. Imagine! If this prediction proves correct, there will be three retirees for every five people of potential working age.

Though the predictions we have reviewed relate to the distant future, this already spells serious financial trouble over the short-term, given the current state of pension systems. Paying for the living requirements of this burgeoning retirement class will prove to be a very heavy burden on both the present and future work force. Pension deductions from the paychecks of workers in some countries 25 years from now will become very large. It will be as much as 40% to 60% of income if the promised retirement benefits are paid out to the retirees of that day. Alternatively, saving for the future by laying aside sufficient funds now would require incredibly massive amounts of money. Either approach — transferring income directly from future workers or saving the money now [9]— eventually comes up short in meeting the income requirements of future retirees if world birth rates decline sharply.

Though both approaches stand to be unsuccessful, they have a very different impact on the world of money and finance. The former leads to a gradual and realistic economic downturn. The latter solution of laying aside money today, one that is being eagerly pursued these days, is leading to a massively corrupt environment which I believe will ensnare and enslave many people. But before I explain how this could happen, it will be helpful to first take a look at how the retired were cared for in the past.

The Pension Plans Of Yore

A little over a century ago, a person's retirement did not

solely depend on savings levels and the ability of financial markets to act as storehouses for future spending requirements. Retirement needs were the responsibility of extended families. Retirement prospects were bleak for those who had no children or relatives. On the other hand, the more children you had, the higher the comfort level you would enjoy in old age. Many of today's societies still rely on extended families to care for their aged. For example, 83% of China's over-60 population live with their children or relatives.[10] For the 85% or so of the world's population living in lower income countries, more than 75% of people over the age of 60 live with their children. In these lands, perhaps only 5% of the aged live on their own. The contrast with high-income countries such as Canada, the US, UK and Australia is stark. In these developed countries only 23% of the elderly live with their children. It seems that as countries become wealthier, birth rates drop and parents either choose, or are sent off to, retirement homes. The important point is this: By and large, the quality of retirement in these lower-income societies depends on the number and quality of children. That seems obvious enough.

Apparently, in today's heavily financialized world, the experts would have us believe that this is no longer true. In fact, they propose that the world's prosperity is no longer dependent upon children. They would also have us believe that modern-day pension systems and booming financial markets have liberated humanity from the burden of the created order; reproduction, toil and labor. We can choose to have fewer children — even to the point of

allowing a declining population growth — and yet expect
to have comfortable retirements and lifestyles. Supposedly,
we can expect to rely upon the wonders of wealth-creating financial markets to sustain us instead of the fruits of
our labor and that of our children. But can this really all
be true? Something doesn't make sense.

I discuss these ideas at the risk of being misunderstood.
I only wish to illuminate some of the fallacies of financial
markets. They are not gods who are able to create matter,
real wealth and income. They cannot work for us. They do
not liberate us from the physical order of creation. We
must continue to live off of the fruits of our own labor as
well as the collective labor of humanity. We are free to
decide whether we want fewer children, or perhaps none
at all. However, there are consequences to these decisions
that cannot be ignored. Simply put, if the world chooses
to have fewer children, resulting in a population decline,
then not only will the retired members of our societies be
worse off, but our societies will be less prosperous. There
is no escaping this fact. The consequences are dictated by
our choices.

The Ticking Time Bomb Of An Aging World

As already mentioned, most global government pension
systems are in danger of going bankrupt at some point
over the next 20 – 35 years. The liabilities of some of these
systems, and what they promise to pay future retirees, are
enormous. In fact, they are so enormous that there is little prospect of ever meeting these obligations. Therefore,
many poor retirees will go unfed.[11]

How should this potential problem be solved? It is surprising how little debate there is over this question. According to professional literature, strong momentum has been built in the direction of recommending solutions to the emerging world retirement crisis that focuses action on increasing investment in stocks and bonds and other real assets.[12] Overwhelmingly, the solution widely endorsed is to increase financial investment today, so as to store up income and capital for the needs of future retirees. Even the United States and Canadian governments are promoting the acceptance of similar solutions for its national social security and pension systems. In professional parlance, this means a move to funded pension systems around the world, a movement that has gained much momentum already.

Of course, saving today for tomorrow's retirement needs is definitely a good idea. There is no contesting that advice for almost any individual. We must all strive to do this diligently and intelligently; yet, seen in the aggregate, investing in financial assets cannot avert a financial crisis nor provide for reasonable retirement lifestyles for the broader society if population growth rates slow substantially.

A Hoax Perpetrated By The Vested Interests

The real issue of concern is the financial solution being widely promoted as a means to overcome the problems of slumping birth rates is being done without any admission to the fact that it cannot work. Then why is it offered and accepted as a viable solution? We don't have to look very far to find our answer: Greed. It is no surprise to discover that the most enthusiastic supporter of this idea is the financial services industry at large: Banks, brokers, financial planners, mutual fund companies, accountants, actuaries, pension fund consultants, and the list goes on. The prospect of a retirement crisis presents a delightful specter to the financial industries of the world. They like to promote the idea that if governments, corporations, and individuals started putting money aside today and investing it in financial markets, a retirement crisis could be largely avoided. They salivate at the very thought of how much money might come into financial markets — an area under their domain. All of this new money, which is mostly financed through debt, would no doubt be invested in financial securities. As such, it would fan the demand for stocks and bonds. Both private and government investors panicked at the prospect that a looming retirement crisis will chase financial gains in securities markets. This bogus financial solution to declining birth rates promises enormous profits and a huge boom in financial markets around the world. In so doing, the whole ruse plays to the greed of the public who likes to pursue gain, even if only momentary, at whatever the ultimate cost. Financial markets would continue to thrive and so would the profits of the financial services industry.

Private investors are acting on the same conclusions and directing their investments more than ever into securities, particularly stocks, around the world. And, indeed, at the time of this writing, this process has already been long underway, albeit facing an interruption. There's no telling how intense this phase may become, or how long it may continue, though it could end at any time.

∾

"Children's children are a crown to the aged, and parents are the pride of their children."

Proverbs 17:6

ENDNOTES

1. *"Watch out that you are not deceived. For many will come in my name, claiming, 'I am he,' and, 'The time is near.' Do not follow them'"* (Luke 21:8).

2. World Population Aging 1950-2050, Executive Summary, 2001, United Nations Population Division (UNPD).

3. *Population, Environment & Development: The Concise Report.* United Nations, New York, 2001 Forecasts of the United Nations Population Division (UNPD).

4. Ibid.

5. United Nations.

6. Source: *Averting the Old Age Crisis,* a World Bank Policy Research Report, 1994.

7. International Monetary Fund, Occasional Paper, *Aging Populations and Public Pension Schemes,* 1996.

8. World population growth is expected to continue slowing, according to the latest report of the United Nations Population Division. After a period of high growth — unparalleled in human history — the world's population will shrink 30 – 40 years from now. Already, the fertility rate (births per female), has nearly halved to 2.7 from a mid-1960s rate of over 5.

9. There are two main ways of providing benefits to retirees — Funding and Paygo (pay as you go). Funded pensions systems are prevalent in the private sector — virtually all companies in North America take this approach — which invests monies today in proportion to the expected retirement benefits that they anticipate paying out in the future. On the other hand, Paygo systems do not lay aside any investment. Rather, these systems simply levy payroll premiums on present-day workers and transfer these proceeds to retirees. Most gov-

ernments employ this method to meet their pension liabilities. However, both approaches ultimately exact a heavy cost on workers if the retired population becomes very large relative to the number of workers. The two approaches have a very different effect upon financial markets.

10. Source: *Averting the Old Age Crisis,* a World Bank Policy Research Report, 1994.

11. Italy's predicament is a good illustration of this dilemma. In order for this country to be able to pay future retirees their promised retirement benefits, its national pension system would need to fund its pension system — lay aside savings today and invest them. In other words, by an amount more than five times its Gross Domestic Product (GDP). Imagine. That's an impossible liability. While Italy is one of the worst examples, it is true that virtually every major government in the world faces similar challenges. Gross pension liabilities of the major industrial countries are estimated at nearly three times their collective GDP.

12. Even the IMF (International Monetary Fund), in a December 1996 report entitled, *Aging Populations and Public Pension Schemes,* concludes that funded pension systems are the best course of action.

CHAPTER 5

The Emergence of Three False Gods

An Unholy Triad

The kingdom of the last days has little thought for the gods of antiquity. A triad of new gods emerges to replace them. The god of women — a god of fertility — is no longer revered. But also the gods of his fathers, signifying a group of gods other than the fertility god, will no longer be regarded. This is significant: One god — perhaps two or three — has replaced many. How is this possible? Has there been a merger and acquisition binge in the pantheon of false gods? How can a few emerge to assume the domain of perhaps thousands of other gods?

To discover the answer, let's next uncover the identity of the other "gods of his fathers" mentioned by Daniel that are being so unceremoniously deposed. Who are these other gods? The Bible only mentions them in a generic sense. Although many are unnamed, the prophets of the Old Testament repeatedly castigated the Jewish nations for worshipping them. The Bible often speaks of gods made of materials such as gold, wood, bronze and stone. However, this description mainly referred to the man-made images of these gods such as figurines and statues. The influence and domain of their supposed powers is not mentioned.

Many of the references to the worship of false gods — or idolatries as they are also referred to in the Old Testament — allude to the influences of other pagan religions upon Jewish society. A study of the pagan beliefs of people in neighboring countries to Judah and Israel uncovers a large assortment. For example, the early Semites of Mesopotamia worshipped trees, mountains, springs, blocks of stone and other inanimate items. The gods of Babylon and the Egyptians had a particularly strong influence upon Jewish society as well. After all, the Jews lived in Egypt for more than 350 years and under Babylonian rule in exile for another 60 years or so.

Of course, this does not provide a comprehensive survey of all of the false gods of the various tribes and nations mentioned in the Bible. Indeed, humanity may have worshipped tens of thousands of false gods throughout the ages. Mythology textbooks are crammed with accounts of many false gods, either animistic (taking the form of objects or animals) or in human form (anthropomorphic gods). The fact is that a belief in such types of gods has been the primary form of religion throughout history. Any natural phenomenon or physical law that could not be logically explained according to the understanding of the times, had a god assigned to the task of governing its behavior. Each animal might have had a representative patron god. Different religions would have different gods for the same phenomena or animal. No global convergence of pagan belief systems had yet occurred. There was yet no global transnational organization meeting in Geneva, Switzerland (the headquarters for more than a few global organizations) seeking to harmonize the names and domains of the false gods. Collectively, I believe this myriad of gods is representative of the gods of the fathers.

Modern-Day Gods Of Wood And Stone

Few educated people in the world today would seriously consider worshipping gods of the types mentioned. For instance, why would anyone today believe in Ra, the god of the Nile, the reputed source of Egyptian life and prosperity? We think Ra is laughable today. Modern science has destroyed him. We know today that the sun powers the earth's climate. Water is pulled from the surface of the earth through the processes of evaporation and transpiration, to return to it again in the form of rain or snow. Rivers collect these waters back to the sea. Knowing these facts, mankind no longer has a need for the Nile god. Rivers are now explainable scientifically. Faith has been transferred to the physical sciences. Therefore, it would have made more sense to put faith solely in the sun god. But this god is now dead too. After all, it is now widely believed that the sun is the product of the cosmic "Big Bang" theory. Apparently the universe was randomly flung into creation out of primordial anti-matter billions and billions of years ago. For agnostics, no god is required to believe in this phenomenon.

Away with the old gods! We need no god other than the god of reason, science and technology.

Apparently the new god of science and technology has replaced the many gods of the fathers.

A God Of Science And Technology?

Surely, science and technology cannot be a modern-day god. After all, its explanations and claims are not fictional. The hypotheses of science are tested by verifiable observations. Though electricity itself is unseen, its properties are well documented. It can propel a large 25-ton ore truck, illuminate television screens and power global telecommunications systems; therefore, its existence is not mythical.

Indeed, this is true for the most part. Yet, the crucial fact is this: The new reliance on the modern-day ingenuity of science and technology leaves little room for the One true God. In fact, with the advance of modern technology, the world arrogantly no longer sees a need for the sovereign God, the One who created the heavens, the earth and mankind in His own image. Even the unknown frontiers of the future no longer require a belief in God. Modern probability theory has taken care of that too, and in the process has given rise to enormous financial service industries such as insurance and securities markets. As such, though modern science has superseded perhaps tens of thousands of mythical false gods, it has itself become a new one. It alone has replaced many others, including the One and Only God. That makes it a false god.

Could this be one of the three new false gods named in the Bible?

More Evidence Of SCITE's Existence

Could the modern-day faith in the new god of science and technology be the same as the god of fortresses found in Daniel 11:37? There are more than a few possible connections. Fortresses are fortified structures, as their name implies. By design, they are strategically defensive and play an important role in the balance of wars and conflicts.

In Daniel's day, the design of strong fortifications and the implements of warfare demonstrated the leading edge of technology just as today. Fortresses needed to be intelligently constructed. Not only was their location critical; equally important was an effective layout. Lookout towers needed to be strategically placed; wall heights and thicknesses were specifically designed; building materials needed to be flame-proofed as best as possible; every physical advantage calculated to survive a long siege if necessary. In this sense, the science of fortress construction is related to the modern god of fortresses otherwise known as "science and technology."

People with advanced technology will tend to have strong fortresses and defenses. Countries with leading-edge armaments and early defense systems will feel secure and invulnerable. Impenetrable fortification speaks of independence. It sets itself up as a bulwark against outside intervention. Who will attack a strong city-state that is ruled by a god of fortresses? It represents a society that is insulated against all enemies – natural or human.

However, the true God of Fortresses is someone else. Psalm 18:2 says: *"The LORD is my rock, my fortress and my deliverer; my God is my rock, in whom I take refuge."* In fact, God is referred to as our "fortress" on at least 20 occasions in the Old Testament. He is also referred to several times as a "tower." For example: *"The name of the LORD is a strong tower; the righteous run to it and are safe"* (Proverbs 18:10). On the other hand, the god of fortresses worshipped by the kingdom and people of the last days is another god. He is a counterfeit and causes mankind to trust in the works of their hands through knowledge, science and technology.

Let's call him SCITE — short for science and technology. In reality, this god is nothing more than the faith of humanity in the knowledge of science and technology. Science and technology is not evil in itself, of course, but mankind has turned it into an idol.

Searching For The Unknown God

What about the unknown god? Though Daniel may not have been able to recognize him, I believe some clues are given which allow us today to attempt an identification. What we do know is that he is new. He didn't exist in Daniel's day. If that were not so, Daniel wouldn't have referred to him as "unknown." Therefore, the faculties or capabilities that he represents were not evident 2500 years ago, but would become known at the time of the end. Also, as was the case with the god of fortresses, the new unknown god must fill a void left by the other gods — the gods of the fathers and the god desired by women that are regarded no more — who will no longer hold influence over mankind. We also know that the "unknown" and "fortress" gods are not the same as they are mentioned separately in the same verse. Therefore, the unknown god must represent something entirely distinct from science and technology, yet something that is also new.

There are more clues. The unknown god is also one that the king or kingdom of the last days *"...will honor with gold and silver, with precious stones and costly gifts."* This is an illuminating piece of information. Here he is a god honored in a very different way than the other gods of the fathers. The former gods and the god of women were not generally honored with such precious gifts. Their images may have been constructed out of gold and silver, yet it was not gold and silver that were offered to them. Rather, the types of things offered to these gods were drink libations, animal and meat sacrifices, the practice of various rituals and even human sacrifices. However, in the case of the unknown god, all the items used to honor him are of an extremely high value — gold, silver, jewels and other unknown costly gifts.

What kind of god accepts gifts such as these? Surely, an inanimate god would not be able to consume these donations. If these were charitable gifts offered at a shrine of the unknown god, surely the priests of this temple would be mobbed with job applications. Precious gifts such as these given to a god that cannot consume them? If so, these honorary gifts would find their way into the pockets of the priests no sooner than they were donated. This belief system would quickly turn into a religion of kleptocracy. Who, in our modern day, would serve such a self-serving faith? Clearly, this type of god is both impractical and improbable. The god must then be either figurative or take on a true, physical, living form. The latter alternative isn't possible either. There simply is no other living god beside the God of the Bible and if this were meant, Daniel would have been shocked. His whole life is a huge, joyous testimony to the existence of the One, true, Living God that shouts a message of hope across 25 centuries. It was the Living God who bound the mouths of the lions when he was thrown in the pit. Therefore, the unknown god can only be a figurative one, unassociated with any organized religion or system of donations.

There is more significance in the fact that the honorariums given to the unknown god are all of very high monetary value. In fact, each of these — we cannot know if this is true for the other costly gifts as we do not know what they exactly are [1] — may also have served a monetary function. Certainly this is true for the commodities of silver and gold. Most struck coinage was made of either substance throughout early history, though not exclusively. There are at least two common characteristics to each one of the identified gifts that were true even in Daniel's day. Each served as a storehouse of wealth or an object of adornment signifying wealth. This leads us to a safe conclusion about the character of this unknown god: It is a god closely related with wealth. But, as it is an unknown god of wealth, it must refer to a modern-day god of wealth.

MOFI — The Magical God Of Money

I propose that this new unknown god very likely prefigures the rise of a massive idolatry with modern monetary finance — the new high religion of globalized economics and markets. Other evidence we will yet examine suggests that it is the very seat of sorcery that's behind the "magic" of Babylon the Great. He is a great monetary financial monster that rears up to take on a life of its own. Ennobled with great powers and arrogance, this god could not exist as easily were the god of Tammuz (the god of women) still around. It is necessary that the god of women be cast aside in order for this new god to stride the global stage. An endtime boom in wealth and the emergence of a giant global financial/economic system would not be otherwise possible. We will explore these important connections in the next chapters.

Mankind's confidence in this new god even rises up to eclipse a reliance and belief in God. Who will need God when Mammon shows itself able to provide all the economic and material sustenance mankind desires?

So, here is the second false god: Let's name him MOFI — short for monetary finance.

Daniel could see MOFI in his vision but not recognize him; most people in the world today also do not see this god though they may be able to name his parts. He lurks behind much deception and camouflage. I will strip away his cover in Chapter 9 and pull him out into the light for you to see him more clearly.

The Third And Final False God Revealed

Next, let us attempt to identify the third god—the foreign god — who emerges as another very powerful force. Again, referring to Daniel 11:39, we read that the king of the last days *"...will attack the mightiest fortresses with the help of a foreign god."* We know that he will overcome even the strongest fortresses on earth — a feat that would not be possible without the assistance of this god of foreign origin. But just what does the word "foreign" mean in this verse? The word can imply something unknown or strange, or something that is non-domestic, pertaining to something having to do with another country. In my estimation, a careful study of all the clues in this passage lead to the conclusion that this god finds its power outside of a country.

The reference to a foreign god seems to have much to do with the sovereignty of countries as it relates to the conquest of fortresses. After all, fortresses are almost always associated with the defense of a sovereign nation. Therefore, the mightiest fortresses represent actual sovereign countries. Even the strongest and most powerful of nations will be attacked and overcome with the aid of the foreign god. How can something that is itself foreign — the other sovereign fortresses — simultaneously be attacked by something foreign? Yet we see foreign countries are being captured by something foreign. This is indeed strange. Just what is this foreign god?

We can know that it is not an unknown god in the same way as the second god we identified — MOFI — there again proving that it is a god having to do with foreign countries. We also know that it isn't a foreign god in the generic sense, as is sometimes used in the exhortations of the Old Testament prophets. Why? Because all of the three endtime gods we are examining qualify as foreign gods in this sense. Therefore, it is not logical that only one god would be identified as "foreign" and the others not. We are left with the only definition that can apply. The riddle, wrapped in an enigma, is this: It is a god that cannot be a single country, yet it is something pertaining to a foreign nation, though stronger than a single nation. It must be collective: Something greater than the whole, yet different from its parts.

I propose that it is a god of globalism.

Welcome to GLOBO.

GLOBO — The Most Powerful Modern God

Can globalism be a god? Indeed, I believe that GLOBO is the single most powerful weapon of the spirit of the Antichrist in our time. GLOBO is an immensely powerful god that is incredibly vicious and indescribably brutal. Working together with the unknown god — the god of monetary finance (MOFI) — and science and technology (SCITE), they are literally smashing the very mightiest fortresses of sovereignty around the globe. Even the United States and other strong nations are being immobilized by this god of globalism, its ramparts being stormed by a flood of foreign values, influence and mobilized money. We will track this new beast in Chapter 11, identify its footprints, and examine its prey.

We may finally have uncovered the unholy trinity that

fosters the misplaced worship of the world and aids the spirit of the Antichrist — the creature that commandeers the final last-days kingdom from under the cover of deception and darkness. They are mankind's self-sufficiency based upon globalism, monetary finance, and science and technology — GLOBO, MOFI and SCITE.

Alarmingly, these three false gods have only risen to power during the last 250 years or so. That is an extremely short period in relation to human history. Their advance has been rapid. Not one of them existed in their present form during Daniel's time. What he foresaw over 2500 years ago has all come into existence in the last tenth of this period.

This points to an urgent question: Are we indeed living in the last days — during the time of the last king? And if so, can we conclude that we are in the very season of Christ's return?

The answer becomes evident as we take a closer look at each of these new gods and their implications, great and small, in the next chapters.

Moving ahead, we will need to stoke our lamps with bright-burning oil. As Christ Himself repeatedly exhorted us — four times alone in Mark 13:33–37 — we must watch carefully and remain alert.

The false gods of GLOBO, MOFI and SCITE may be displeased. They have lost some of their anonymity.

ENDNOTES

1. A similar reference to the gifts mentioned here is found in Revelation 18. The very same order is used describing the commodities being traded with Babylon the Great.

CHAPTER 6

Modern Booms Told From Afar

The Rise Of An Endtime Commercial System

The people of the last kingdom are crazy about their three gods — GLOBO, MOFI and SCITE.

In fact, they are proud of them and raise them up to challenge the very primacy of the heavens. God is now obsolete. Yet in reality, in its self-professed wisdom, the world has given itself over to the service of three new tyrants. Though mankind gives rise to them by basing its self-sufficiency upon these gods, no longer does it have dominion over them. As we will see, a greater part of the world becomes captive of the three false gods, patrons of the *Endtime Money Snare.*

As we already know, technology, money, and the foreign world are not evil in and of themselves. They have existed in one form or another since the dawn of civilization. It is only our wandering affections that have given life to these gods. These idolatries, along with the anti-Christian objectives of the great diabolical strategist behind an endtime kingdom, are the things that are evil. Technology, finance and globalism are not the first things that evil has personified.

However, the three gods of the last days are different in several key respects from the false gods of the past. They have global realms and are capable of touching all the people of the world. They have great power. Even the strongest — whether countries, people, or individuals — are no match for them. For the first time in creation, false gods have the ability to take all of mankind into captivity, under their harsh rule, not just one culture, one religion or one country.

But isn't this sheer speculation? All this business about an evil force challenging God, the end of the world, isn't it just another mythological tale like any other? What differentiates it from other great literature and myths such as Homer's *Odyssey* or the Greek tales of the gods of Olympus, Osiris and Isis? The movie cinemas these days are filled with improbable supernatural plots. Their scripts are entertaining, yet do not beg belief. Why would educated, modern people believe that the ideas we are discussing here would hold even a shred of reality?

For one, this supposed endtime fairy tale we have been developing is documented in the Bible. Therefore, the story stands on the truth of the Bible. If you choose to accept the stated objectives of Satan's endtime manifesto as fable, then implicitly, you are not regarding God's Word.

This book will not spend much time proving that the Bible is the Word of God beyond saying this: Every prophecy in the Bible has come to pass other than those having to do with the endtimes. Many prophecies that might have been considered either fable or incomprehensible during the time of Daniel, Jeremiah, Isaiah, Christ and others, all have come to pass in full Technicolor, to be recorded in the annals of human history as fact. All that is left to fulfill of what was foretold in the Bible are the things of the last days: Events leading to Christ's return, the coming Millennium and the Judgment. That being the case, we are compelled to seriously consider the prophecies about the last days, to make our best attempt at understanding its meanings and to discern the times. To do so, we must first discover two other important features of the endtimes revealed in the Bible. They play an integral role in the *Endtime Money Snare*.

An Endtime Boom In Wealth

A prominent financial characteristic of the last days is clearly revealed in the book of James. The statement: *"You have hoarded wealth in the last days,"* charges the prophecy to the rich in James 5:3. *"You have lived on earth in luxury and self-indulgence. You have fattened yourselves in the day of slaughter,"* he goes on to say in verse five. It is a development that is well underway. Wealth has virtually exploded during the past century.

Total world wealth has multiplied by approximately 40 times over the past 100 years. Never before in mankind's history has wealth accumulated so quickly and to such an enormous level. Of course, a big reason why wealth has jumped so dramatically is rapid population growth throughout much of the past century. All the same, per capita wealth (the average wealth for each person in the world) has multiplied by at least 10 times over this same period.

One type of wealth—financial wealth—is surely booming. Much of what society regards as wealth today finds its expression in the form of stocks, bonds, deposits or other types of financial instruments and securities. Given society's fixation with financial markets, the boom of securities markets is very interesting. Advances in this area have been exponential during the past century, especially in the past two decades. We can track this development by measuring the increase in their total market values. The world's pool of securities is now worth an estimated $65.5 trillion. That's double what it was just 10 years ago (measured in US dollar terms), despite the financial crashes of emerging markets and Japan during that period. Had these markets participated in the general upward trend during this time, the total value of global securities wealth would have risen by a factor of 10.

What we find is that wealth in the form of financial securities now amounts to more than twice the value of all the annual income of every person on earth. Imagine wealth having been created this quickly and easily. Obviously, a lot of this increase in value is not real wealth. It couldn't be, as it isn't supported by commensurate increases in the underlying savings or incomes of the earth's wage earners. Wall Street (a cover-all term for the world's financial service industries), may spin any kind of story to justify clients' investment activities as they may wish. The fact is that much of this explosion in financial values in recent years is based upon nothing more than bubble economics and fanciful idolatries (the evidence for this statement is yet to be explained in Chapter 13). All the same, it is certainly true that wealth has boomed over the last century, speeding its advance at a more rapid pace in recent decades and years. As such, it definitely marks a condition or a process of the endtimes. It also means that the temptations of wealth have become much more perilous and pervasive. Christ's admonishment that "... *it is easier for a camel to go through the eye of a needle than for a rich man to enter the kingdom of God*" (Matthew 19:24), is not an empty threat. A world whose heart is burdened with the cares of its burgeoning financial and economic edifices and its material temptations will not easily find its way to God.

Sadly, many Christians share in the spoils and complacency of this endtime boom in wealth. Therefore, it is hardly unlikely that attitudes of worship will not have been affected. The idols of material wealth will certainly have found their way into the inner sanctuaries of Christ's modern Church.

Interestingly, in the book of Revelation, Laodicea — the last of the seven churches addressed by the apostle John — is one that has become fat, wealthy and content, one that has fallen asleep. Its attitude is complacent and smug. This church says "... *'I am rich; I have acquired wealth and do not need a thing'*" (Revelation 3:17). If this church is intended to serve as a foreshadow of the Church in the endtime, it parallels the explosion of wealth foretold of the last days.

Strikingly, the attitude of this church is also similar to that of Babylon the Great described in Revelation 18 who says *"...I sit a queen; I am not a widow, and I will never mourn"* (verse 7). Is there any connection?

The Emergence Of A Commercial Colossus

In Revelation 18 we found the account of Babylon the Great. What is it? There are more than a few interpretations. Let's look at the large number of identifying clues found in verses 2–24.

"And he cried mightily with a strong voice, saying, Babylon the great is fallen, is fallen, and is become the habitation of devils, and the hold of every foul spirit, and a cage of every unclean and hateful bird. For all nations have drunk of the wine of the wrath of her fornication, and the kings of the earth have committed fornication with her, and the merchants of the earth are waxed rich through the abundance of her delicacies. And I heard another voice from heaven, saying, Come out of her, my people, that ye be not partakers of her sins, and that ye receive not of her plagues. For her sins have reached unto heaven, and God hath remembered her iniquities. Reward her even as she rewarded you, and double unto her double according to her works: in the cup which she hath filled fill to her double. How much she hath glorified herself, and lived deliciously, so much torment and sorrow give her: for she saith in her heart, I sit a queen, and am no widow, and shall see no sorrow. Therefore shall her plagues come in one

day, death, and mourning, and famine; and she shall be utterly burned with fire: for strong is the Lord God who judgeth her. And the kings of the earth, who have committed fornication and lived deliciously with her, shall bewail her, and lament for her, when they shall see the smoke of her burning, Standing afar off for the fear of her torment, saying, Alas, alas that great city Babylon, that mighty city! for in one hour is thy judgment come. And the merchants of the earth shall weep and mourn over her; for no man buyeth their merchandise any more: The merchandise of gold, and silver, and precious stones, and of pearls, and fine linen, and purple, and silk, and scarlet, and all thyine wood, and all manner vessels of ivory, and all manner vessels of most precious wood, and of brass, and iron, and marble, And cinnamon, and odours, and ointments, and frankincense, and wine, and oil, and fine flour, and wheat, and beasts, and sheep, and horses, and chariots, and slaves, and souls of men. And the fruits that thy soul lusted after are departed from thee, and all things which were dainty and goodly are departed from thee, and thou shalt find them no more at all. The merchants of these things, which were made rich by her, shall stand afar off for the fear of her torment, weeping and wailing, And saying, Alas, alas, that great city, that was clothed in fine linen, and purple, and scarlet, and decked with gold, and preciious stones, and pearls! For in one hour so great riches is come to nought. And every shipmaster, and all the company in ships, and sailors, and as many as trade by sea, stood afar off, And cried when they saw the smoke of her burning, saying, What city is like unto this great city! And they cast dust on their heads, and cried, weeping and wailing, saying, Alas, alas, that great city, wherein *were made rich all that had ships in the sea by reason of her costliness! for in one hour is she made desolate. Rejoice over her, thou heaven, and ye holy apostles and prophets; for God hath avenged you on her. And a mighty angel took up a stone like a great millstone, and cast it into the sea, saying, Thus with violence shall that great city Babylon be thrown down, and shall be found no more at all. And the voice of harpers, and musicians, and of pipers, and trumpeters, shall be heard no more at all in thee; and no craftsman, of whatsoever craft he be, shall be found any more in thee; and the sound of a millstone shall be heard no more at all in thee; And the light of a candle shall shine no more at all in thee; and the voice of the bridegroom and of the bride shall be heard no more at all in thee: for thy merchants were the great men of the earth; for by thy sorceries were all nations deceived. And in her was found the blood of prophets, and of saints, and of all that were slain upon the earth."*

Many obvious connections to wealth and commerce are presented in the above passage. Observe the heavy use of economic terminology. No less than 45 terms of commercial relevance are used in this passage, some of them numerous times. Many references are made to luxuries and precious items. By my count, 28 commodities and products are mentioned.

There is much more to learn about this commercial/economic entity called "Babylon the Great." First, it is both a source and distributor of great wealth. The merchants of the earth *"...grew rich from her excessive luxuries"* (verse 3), and *"...gained their wealth from her"* (verse 15), yet they also are identified as being part of this system. In verse 23 they are referred to as "your merchants."

Furthermore, this Babylon is the very embodiment of riches. Though it is called a "great city" (verse 16), it is dressed like a person in the most expensive clothes, and glitters with gold and jewelry. Her luxuries, "maddening wine" (verse 3), and "magic" (verse 23), prove to be intoxicants for the world's kings and merchants. Every nation and king has relations with it, committing "adulteries." One might wonder why it is called a city if it is dressed like a person. Perhaps it is a called a "city" because it is the nucleus of this system, or simply as an indication that it is an organized entity, not necessarily implying that it has a single address.[1]

Clearly, what is being described in Revelation 18 is both commercial and global in reach — an aspect of the end-time regime. At the very minimum, Babylon the Great appears to embrace an economic colossus that underpins the nations and power structures of the world.

It is a system that will totally collapse at some point.

Intriguing is the fact that the *"...merchants were the world's great men"* (verse 23), at the time of this network's fall. This confirms an interesting phenomenon of the last kingdom. Apparently the world's greatest men are no longer kings, priests and political leaders. Here, they are now shown to be merchants — business people, in other words. When has this ever been true in human history — at least on a global scale? The accounts of Tyre, given by Ezekiel and Isaiah, bear some similarity, describing a major seaport city *"...whose merchants are princes, whose traders are renowned in the earth?"* (Isaiah 23:8). Actually,

Tyre's reign and fall makes for an interesting parallel to the account of Babylon the Great. However, historically, many cultures actually despised the merchant classes. Businesspersons were usually considered among the lower castes since they were concerned with material gain and earthly matters. The pursuit of truth and virtue were held as the highest calling in these religious cultures. If anything, the heads of sovereign states or religions were considered among the greatest of people. Yet, in this endtime system, it is merchants who are the heroes and great men of the world.

Why would being a successful businessperson offer a candidacy for the status of world-class greatness? Obviously, a globalized economic and financial system must have emerged during the last days. If this were not so, merchants could not be world "greats." The leaders of this commercial economic system accumulate enormous luxuries, are given high visibility, and are honored and idolized. The adulation that the world and its news media pours out on the world's business titans today surely fits this image.

Corroborating evidence for this perspective in Revelation is again found in the book of Daniel. One parallel emerges in the list of the 28 commodities or "costly gifts" mentioned in Revelation 18. The first three — gold, silver and precious stones — are the very same (even in the same order), as are found in Daniel 11:38. Daniel tells us that the last world regime and its leaders will honor a god unknown to his fathers — the "unknown god" — with *"...gold and silver, with precious stones and costly gifts."*

Nowhere else in the Bible are these same precious metals and jewels mentioned together, let alone in the same order. Is this a coincidence? Perhaps. Earlier, we had proposed that it could represent the collective faith of mankind in modern-day monetary and financial systems — a god we dubbed MOFI (monetary/financial). Whatever the case, we see that wealth and luxury are the rewards of conspiring with this endtime system prefigured by Babylon the Great.

More Evidence Of An Endtime Colossus

This interpretation of Babylon the Great embracing commercial colossus does not disagree with the Lord's Word spoken through Isaiah. He spoke of the various conditions of the world at the time of the "day of the Lord," the term he used for the last days. In Isaiah 24:1–3, we again discover a heavy emphasis upon commercial activities.

"Behold, the LORD maketh the earth empty, and maketh it waste, and turneth it upside down, and scattereth abroad the inhabitants thereof. And it shall be, as with the people, so with the priest; as with the servant, so with his master; as with the maid, so with her mistress; as with the buyer, so with the seller, as with the lender, so with the borrower; as with the taker of usury, so with the giver of usury to him. The land shall be utterly emptied, and utterly spoiled: for the LORD hath spoken this word."

One half of the 12 "inhabitants" that represent the people living at the time of the "day of the Lord" are directly involved in an economic or financial activity. Specifically identified in this way are sellers, buyers, borrowers, lenders, debtors and creditors. It is likely no coincidence that the subject of debt is mentioned four times in one form or another. A creditor is the same as a lender; a borrower the same as a debtor. Therefore, it would hardly be surprising to discover that a debt-based financial and economic system might play a prominent role during the last days. While this passage does not provide conclusive evidence of this last statement, it certainly offers an interesting alignment.

A System With A Global Realm

Evident from the Revelation 18 account is that Babylon the Great is part of an endtime regime that will be global in nature. Its reign over the entire earth parallels the global reach of the fourth future kingdom that Daniel foresaw in his four separate visions. The three previous kingdoms or kings that Daniel saw were indeed leading world powers, yet they were not global. Only the last one is stated to have a world-wide reach. *"All the nations"* (Revelation 18:3, 23, and 14:8); *"...kings of the earth"* (verse 3, 9); *"...merchants of the earth"* (verses 3, 11); *"...world's great men"* (verse 23); and *"all ... on earth"* are part of it.

Represented in this case is the hub of a coordinated international trading system. It will be different from all the other kingdoms and *"...will devour the whole earth, trampling it down and crushing it"* (Daniel 7:23). In order for a single regime to overcome and devour the whole earth, global interconnection and worldwide mechanisms of coordination and influence are required. In short, there must be a globalization of the world — a convergence of belief systems and values. A world that consumes Big Macs and Coca-Cola from Nairobi to Taipei and participates in a seamless global financial market and economy is not incompatible to this development.

Something More Than Trade In Goods And Services

I believe that the endtime trading system associated with Babylon the Great must involve more than just a system of commerce for goods and commodities of the nature mentioned. Simple manufactured and agricultural items such as those listed in the Revelation 18 account and its marine transportation would not intoxicate the world's merchants and kings with "maddening wine" (Revelation 18:3). There must be something else — something "magic" (verse 23) — involved in this system that leads the world astray. What could it be? Nowhere in the prophetic Word is there any specific indication as to what it might be other than in a generic sense. Yet something clearly is enervating this whole system. Something is giving rise to "adultery" as all of the kings of the earth *"...are committing adulteries"* with Babylon the Great. Wealth and money may be intoxicating, but are not magic. The love of money is definitely a powerful motivator of human actions, but also is not magic. Perhaps the "magic" and "maddening wine" of this endtime system is found in the corrupt means it employs to produce effortless wealth?

I can suggest one identity of this magical intoxicant. Of course, as a global investment economist, my interpretation will probably tend to fall close to my reference point.

You, the reader, will have to keep that thought in mind as you read further. By the measure of the present times, I would regard the workings of the modern-day monetary and financial systems and the interplay of the love of money as the magic referred to in Revelation 18. It is the alchemy and deception that springs out of our current monetary/finance systems that bring on the type of madness that is talked about here. Financial markets and monetary systems are indeed magical in one sense. Wealth can be spun out of thin air; fabricated with no cost. Great riches can be transferred easily, even though they may not be much more than paper. I will briefly explain some of these mechanisms in Chapter 9.

Another significant support to this financial/monetary interpretation may be found in the fact that Babylon the Great can come to a halt within an hour: *"In one hour your doom has come!"* (Revelation 18:10). And again: *"In one hour such great wealth has been brought to ruin"* (Verse 17). This presents a puzzle.

What can possibly span the globe and collapse so quickly, yet leave the world standing? Apparently, whatever is being destroyed during that hour presents no bodily danger to humans. People will witness the destruction of this city or system from afar. These and the many other clues certainly do not disagree with the view that Babylon the Great could represent the world's commercial/monetary/economic system of the last days. What other possible interpretation does not conflict with all the other descriptions of the endtime kingdoms also found in Daniel? How can international trade come to a sudden halt?

It is no secret that nothing can be ruined as quickly as an inter-linked, debt-leveraged financial system. Though it may amount to trillions times trillions of dollars in wealth, and touch every living person on earth economically, the speed of its destruction can be very quick. The banking and financial markets systems of the world actually hang on thin threads of human confidence. Without faith they would collapse instantaneously. The concepts of a fractional-reserve monetary system and free-market economics are fundamentally immoral, though functioning fairly if tightly regulated to limit the impulses of greed. These systems can only work if people believe in their continued existence. The slightest fears can trigger financial markets crashes. In that respect, the market tremors of the past few years around the world are a clear reminder that this possibility is more than just an idle theory.

It is interesting that Babylon's "doom" (verse 10), and "...*great wealth has been brought to ruin*" (verse 17), are the result of a much shorter span of time than the plagues pronounced upon her. The plagues take place over a day, a period that may be open to a number of interpretations. "*... in one day her plagues will overtake her: death, mourning and famine*" (verse 8). However, the doom and destruction of wealth is pronounced in a matter of one hour. At the very least, this differentiation supports the view that the demise of the world's financial/commercial system will be very sudden.

I am persuaded to believe that Babylon the Great involves not only a commercial/economic, but also a monetary/financial system — a vast, integrated, global colossus

enervated by the love of money and material, perched upon humanism and confidence. I can find nothing in Scripture that directly refutes the view. The evidence strongly
suggests that it is or is in complicity with a wealth-creating
system of money and trade. We also can safely conclude
that Babylon the Great does not represent the United
States,[2] or New York City, as others have suggested. Pictured
here is a system greater than any single country or city.

A System In League With Three False Gods

The apparition of Babylon the Great intertwines tightly with the rise of the three false gods of the endtimes. It
represents a human, materialistic triumph combining
monetary finance, globalism and technology. The "unknown god," "foreign god," and the "god of fortresses" of
Daniel 11:37–39 — MOFI for monetary/finance, GLOBO
for globalism, and SCITE for science and technology — are
in a league with this last-day system prefigured by Babylon
the Great. We will yet unveil the modern-day existence of
each of them. In spirit, they are all connected in the form
of self-sufficiency and boastfulness. She says: *"I sit as queen;
I am not a widow, and I will never mourn"* (Revelation 18:7).
This endtime system considers itself secure and unassail-
able for as far as the eye can see. The trinity of
the three false gods, energized by the fallen choices of
mankind and the love of money, define and propel this
world-ensnaring system represented by Babylon the Great.

The Spiritual Challenges To The Faithful

Reviewing the evidence so far, you may already conclude that Babylon the Great — a world-spanning com-

mercial system — is in her prime today. Imagine: Twenty five hundred years ago, Daniel forecasted the underlying conditions that would lead to a booming, global financial and economic system in the last days. Approximately 500 years later, the apostle John, incarcerated on the Isle of Patmos, provided additional, illuminating prophecies about this last-days regime that align with Daniel's accounts.

A pause for reflection: Revelation 18:23 says that Babylon the Great will lead *"...all the nations... astray"* with her magical spell. This observation should immediately put Christians on guard. Could the magic spell of this endtime financial manifesto be leading Christians off the narrow path as well? Are we steering our lives to the siren call of the luxuries and false wealth of this idolatrous endtime commercial system?

These are serious questions because a dire warning is given. God's people are admonished to come out of her so that "[you] *will not share in her sins...for her sins are piled up to heaven"* (verse 4). Even though the Church may already have been raptured away before the great catastrophic collapse of this endtime commercial system, we will still be held accountable for our complicity and the participation of our hearts while this system took form and world dominance. Whether or not the interpretation of Babylon the Great presented here is correct, the warning it presents to Christians today surely remains relevant.

Babylon the Great does come to ruin. In fact, it comes to a terminal end. It will harbor no more workmen or trade ever again. It *"...will be thrown down, never to be found again."* I am persuaded that this collapse will take place no later than the Great Tribulation. And, as with many endtime conditions, the processes that lead to their eventual occurrence can be seen well in advance. Could it be that the financial market troubles of the past few decades, already unprecedented as the International Monetary Fund has often warned,[3] are the early tremors of this ultimate crash?

The last endtime kingdom, a global regime partly reflected by Babylon the Great, is inhospitable to believers. *"Rejoice, saints and apostles and prophets! God has judged her for the way she treated you,"* says verse 20. *"In her was found the blood of prophets and of the saints and of all who have been killed on the earth"* (verse 24). It trades on the *"...bodies and souls of men"* (verse 13). Not only are the idolatries, humanism and love of money underlying the advance of this global commercial/financial system — Mammonism, as I call it — potentially deadly to Christians, they have been at the root of all world genocide and murder.

ENDNOTES

1.   Estimating world wealth is a hazardous exercise in the best of times. My estimate is only intended to be indicative, if not approximate. I use world estimates of World Gross Domestic Product (GDP) from J. Bradford DeLong of the Department of Economics, U.C. Berkley as the base figure and then multiply by five to reach an estimate of total wealth. While this surely is a gross underestimate, it is nevertheless based upon some rigor. Using the "Flow of Fund" statistics of the US Federal Reserve as a proxy, a multiple of five times GDP is a very conservative estimate. At the end of 1999, the Federal Reserve estimated total US wealth market value in excess of $55 trillion. As US GDP

for 1999 was estimated at little more than $9 trillion, this implies an actual GDP/wealth multiple of approximately 6 times.

2. Sources for this estimate include the International Monetary Fund, Bank of International Settlements, Morgan Stanley Dillon Reed, and others.

3. No geographic indications are given in chapter Revelation 18 as to where this "great city" of Babylon the Great may be located. This is unlike the Mystery Babylon described in Revelation 17 *"...who sits on the many waters"* and *"...on seven hills."* A study of these two chapters suggest that the Mystery Babylon of chapter 17 and Babylon the Great of Revelation 14:8 and chapter 18 could not possibly represent the same part of an endtime system. One is commercial, the other spiritual in nature.

4. *The United States in Prophecy* by Edward Tracy, Convale Publications, 1969.

5. In a recent Trade and Development Report entitled "Towards Reform of the International Financial Architecture: Which Way Forward?", the International Monetary Fund makes many alarmist comments, including: "The increased frequency and virulence of the international currency and financial crises, involving even countries with a record of good governance...suggests that instability is global and systemic."

CHAPTER 7

Maddening Magic

The New Role of Money

A giant war is recorded in the heavens: *And there was war in heaven. Michael and his angels fought against the dragon, and the dragon and his angels fought back. But he was not strong enough, and they lost their place in heaven. The great dragon was hurled down – that ancient serpent called the devil, or Satan, who leads the whole world astray. He was hurled to the earth, and his angels with him. Then I heard a loud voice in heaven say: Now have come the salvation and the power and the kingdom of our God, and the authority of his Christ. For the accuser of our brothers, who accuses them before our God day and night, has been hurled down. They overcame him by the blood of the Lamb and by the word of their testimony; and they did not love their lives so much as to shrink from death. Therefore rejoice, you heavens and you who dwell in them! But woe to the earth and the sea, because the devil has gone down to you! He is filled with fury, because he knows that his time is short"* (Revelation 12:7–12).

One question that we haven't yet examined fully is why Satan is orchestrating a grand endtime manifesto. As we have already proposed a great commercial/economic/monetary-financial colossus takes form — a fiefdom in cahoots with the endtime gods of GLOBO, MOFI and SCITE. Why is he so busy crafting a massive, global-possessing strategy in order to lead the world astray? As the above verses indicate, it is a story that begins sometime earlier in the cosmos and that has everything to do with the affairs of the world today.

It is recorded in the book of Revelation that Lucifer is deposed from the heavens. He is hurled to earth and is now bent on revenge. He is extremely furious and has a few scores to settle. Trounced by his former fellow angels, some of them no doubt past compatriots that he probably thought were inferior to him, he wants revenge. He needs to justify his arrogance. And to top off his indignation, he has been put in a position of great disadvantage. The humans on earth have been given a great offer of protection against him. They can elect to receive a membership to the kingdom of God even while they are still living on earth. All they have to do is to accept the Lordship of Jesus Christ. In return, they have been absolved from the sting of sin — spiritual death — and are promised to be delivered faithful and righteous,[1] guaranteed a certain place in heaven no matter what. It seems implausible that these humans might want to be part of any plan that will challenge God.

The deck looks stacked against Satan. Think of the challenge! Now reigning as the prince of the air on earth, how could he possibly mount an offensive? What are his capabilities in doing so? He is not omnipresent; therefore, he can only be in one place at a time. He cannot broadcast his influence over a worldwide telecommunication system such as is available to God through His Holy Spirit. He is not all-knowing, and similar to humans, he doesn't know the exact time of the Second Coming of Christ.

However, he is not without his resources. He possesses supernatural abilities and an intelligence level many times that of the smartest human being. He is able to outwit every one of us — if not often, at least some of the time. He is a master of falsehood and deception. In fact, the very essence of his character is the lie. Also, he has the aid of his cronies. A third of the heavenly host was evicted from heaven along with him. Critically, he has an intimate understanding of the human being, our insecure psyche, our fleshly weaknesses, our innate need to worship a god. He also has the advantage of time, possessing a memory and base of experience that spans much of the cosmos. Lastly, all the resources of the earth are available for him to commandeer.

It is with these resources and knowledge that Satan must construct a domain on earth that will be successful in seducing humanity to turn away from God and worship an image of Satan instead. Most of Christianity accepts Satan's objective as a fundament of its beliefs. Theologians don't argue this point very much.

The bottom line is this: Somehow Satan must fashion a false heaven from the ether of the material world. That's no small task.

But, he is doing so with embarrassing success.

Second-Guessing A Satanic Strategy

Let's briefly consider the central challenges in achieving the world's full and voluntary worship. How could the earth's population, now exceeding 6 billion, potentially all be brought under subjugation or complicity to this satanic scheme? And, is it possible that even Christians, who are supposedly aware of the devil's schemes, could fall for any such agenda?

If we considered Satan's position, what plan could we devise in order to attain his objectives? The scheme must mandate a means, or find a way to control and direct the actions of individuals, and the affairs of mankind. These tactics must be both deceptive and alluring so as to not unnecessarily alert the world to its miserable end-game conclusion.

Of course, it is highly speculative and vain to assume that Satan's grand strategy of the last days will be fully comprehensible by man. After all, he is the master of deceit and the father of lies. The characteristics of this time that were very clearly outlined in Daniel's prophecies were deception and strangeness. All the same, Scripture does give us sufficient information to be forewarned against at least some of his tactics.

Taking Advantage Of The Enemy's Weaknesses

What role do human strengths and weaknesses play? It would be tactical negligence if the great evil strategist didn't take advantage of them if there were any. Similar to the martial arts, it is an essential technique to use the strengths and weaknesses of your opponents against them.

According to the Bible, man has three main weaknesses. The apostle John summarized them by saying: *"For everything in the world — the cravings of sinful man, the lust of his eyes and the boasting of what he has and does — comes not from the Father but from the world"* (1st John 2:16). He identifies three worldly weaknesses attributable to innate man — craving, the lust of the eyes, and boasting. Would it be a surprise if these may represent the main buttons on Satan's control panel of both the world and individuals alike? After all, they are the worldly affections which all of us potentially harbor in our hearts that can potentially snare us into complicity with his diabolical endtime plan or as one of its unwitting pawns.

Just exactly what are these three worldly predispositions that open us up to defeat? The weakness of craving is almost self-explanatory. It's the endless, unquenchable desires of physical want — things, food, drink, sex, etc.

To appreciate what is meant by the "lust of the eyes" requires some explanation, since it is not a commonly used phrase. Briefly, it refers to the desire for power, to own and possess, to have dominion. King Solomon recognized this danger saying, *"Death and Destruction are never satisfied, and neither are the eyes of man"* (Proverbs 27:20). No amount of influence is guaranteed to satisfy. No kingdom can be too big to satisfy the potentially endless lust of the eyes.

Boasting, the last of the three vices, is the human tendency to seek personal glory and self-significance. A familiar way of doing this is to puff up one's skills and strengths, or attribute one's accomplishments purely to personal effort. The boasting of humanity effectively claims an independence from God, establishes self-sufficiency and demands self-worship.

In short, the three buttons on Lucifer's control panel of humanity are the quests for satisfaction, dominion and ego. Pursued independently, they all lead away from God. That's precisely why Christ rebuked Satan when He was tempted by him in the desert.[2] Satan tested Jesus in these exact same three areas of innate human weakness. When Christ was hungry to the point where He would be most vulnerable to physical craving, Satan tempted Jesus to step outside the will of God by suggesting He make bread from stones. Next, atop the highest point on the temple in the Holy City, he enticed Christ to throw Himself down upon the rocks below to prove his powers and exalted position with God. In effect, He wanted Christ to boast of His greatness by tempting him to act independently of God's will. Lastly, taking Him to a high mountain, he tried to buy off Christ with the promise of *"...all the kingdoms of the world"* if He would only bow down and worship him. Imagine. Satan promised him no less than the whole world. There could be no greater appeal to the lust of the eyes. Christ both resisted and overcame all of these temptations. Satan's three great levers of power, the primal weaknesses of mankind, did not work against Christ. Yet, these very same tactics would be used by Satan to snare the world into an endtime insurrection against Christ, deceiving the world into worshipping the Antichrist.

Man's Major Weakness Is The Love Of Money

As powerful as these venal human weaknesses may be in Satan's arsenal, one stands alone as even greater. It is the love of money. It lies *"...at the root of all kinds of evil"* (1st Timothy 6:10). The love of money plays an integral and inseparable role in Lucifer's endtime agenda. If the desire for money were not such a human vice, Satan wouldn't make much progress in his plans. In fact, the advance of the endtime kingdom would either be stillborn or still floundering in its infancy if humanity were not so smitten by the love of money. It is the very antithesis of Christ. He Himself made this clear, saying, *"No one can serve two masters. Either he will hate the one and love the other, or he will be devoted to the one and despise the other. You cannot serve both God and Money"* (Matthew 6:24). It follows then that as God is love, the Antichrist is the very embodiment of the love of money.

If the love of money is indeed the root of all kinds of evil, and if evil is to wax worse in the last days, it follows that the world can expect to witness a money orgy, a real or imagined explosion in wealth, a boom in monetary activity. Some of these conditions have already been documented in earlier chapters. In this sense, the financial and economic trends of our day can serve as an accurate barometer of the times. We will investigate these connections further.

Choosing Money And Numbers Instead Of Eternal Truth

Which master does the world despise today? Certainly

117

not money. The people of the high-income countries of the world are head over heels in the pursuit of money. Gain and increase have become a fixation. Today, greed is considered a virtue and institutionalized as never before.

The Hopes, who have been lured into accepting the materialistic perspectives offered by Shane Guinn, have no idea that they have been invited to place their faith in an apostate, endtime system. It's not that investing is wrong. Of course, proper stewardship is required. The real issue here is the object of their faith. The Hopes' expectations of a comfortable lifestyle may happen, but then again, it may not. We don't know because we cannot know the exact timing of the collapse and destruction of the endtime world or any event for that matter.

It's something to think about while we track this real-life endtime beast of Mammon and take a closer look at each of the three false gods. But before we do so, it is helpful to discover how numbers and money have come to be new representatives of truth in the world. We'll be better equipped to gain a clearer perspective of the *Endtime Money Snare.*

Life Before Modern Money

We take our money and credit cards for granted today, as if the world had never been without them. With these inventions we can buy anything; satisfy every material want and insecurity. Whatever our urge, we can find satisfaction by ordering over the Internet, ducking into the corner store, or searching it out in the Yellow Pages. We can soothe our anxieties or fan our desires for wealth by transacting in the financial markets. As is often said, money indeed does make the world go round.

But just where did our modern-day financial system come from? How did it come to be a god, the source of pride and self-sufficiency? It wasn't always this way. At one time, both wealth and prosperity had different definitions. Yes, money has always existed in one form or another; yet, only in recent centuries has it taken on a form that is captivating and motivating all human action. It is even guilty of transforming our very thought lives into values that can be expressed monetarily. The role of money has changed in such a way that it intersects life at almost every turn. Who can ever escape this man-made creation?

Given the usefulness of this human invention we call money, as well as the conveniences it allows in our lives as consumers today, could it have ever been different? Before we investigate the modern world of money and its necessary role in an endtime snare, a contrast with the times of long ago will be instructive.

Consider a family living on an Oklahoma homestead in the year 1850. Let's call them the Bilfries. Money to them was mostly a transaction tool. It played a relatively small role in their lives. Perhaps only every other week Mr. Bilfrie would need to purchase goods and services that he and his household couldn't provide for themselves. After feeding his horses some oats that he may have harvested on his own farm, he would ride his wagon into town. First, he would head to the hardware store. Perhaps this week he was in need of a shovel or some rope, things he was not able to fabricate in his woodshed. Another week, though not very often, his wife may have requested some sections of canvas or other material so she could sew clothes for her family.

Home economic studies suggest that less than 20% of the Bilfries' physical needs were met from outside their immediate family — their household unit, as economists say. Looked at another way, we can say that over 80% of their living requirements did not involve an external transaction with someone outside of their extended family. Very few trading activities were required to obtain what was needed for the daily living requirements of the Bilfrie family.

Of course, it is quite different today. Economists estimate that over 80% of the value-added of the services and products that the average household now uses are purchased from outside their home. The other fifth of these services and products are sourced from within the household. After all, most of us still shave our own beards and wash our own floors.

A significant change has taken place. More than three-fifths of the physical needs and activities of our lives have moved into the path of money over the past 200 years. In other words, the role of money and economics has increased its share of mankind's physical activities by over three times in this period. We will discover why this change can be both good and bad in the next two chapters.

⤬

A thousand years ago the average income of every person in the world was only $160 dollars[3] in today's dollars. Today, the average income per person in the world is approximately $6,500. (By comparison, income per person in the United States is much higher at an average of $29,000.) In the space of one millennium, the role of money has multiplied its influence in terms of the world's daily human activities by a factor of 40 times. How is it that money has been able to expand its role so much in our lives?

The role of money has expanded even more than is implied by the above statistics. So far, we have only mentioned incomes, the monetary income or equivalent that is the product of our labor. However, money has many other roles than just facilitating our remuneration. It can serve as a storehouse for wealth — as a jar full of pennies or a bank deposit. In this sense, money combined in all its various forms is today fives times larger than total annual world incomes. On average, people have a net worth that is significantly larger than one year's income. Importantly, money is also used for the trading of existing things — assets such as houses, stocks, mutual funds or anything else that is tradable or buyable. Here, the role of money has boomed even more. Using the United States as an example, the annual volume of transactions to support these types of financial activities now amount to 80 times that of annual income.

Compared to life on the homestead only 150 years ago, the invention of money has come a long way. The Bilfrie family had need of it infrequently. The instrument of money, though very important, mostly provided a utilitarian service in their lives. Today, human lives have become a utility for money rather than money serving as a utility for people. Society wants us to work hard — more and more hours every week — in order to support the world's burgeoning mountain of financial wealth. Man serves money.

If we are to be free of this slavery, we must understand how so much of mankind has become a slave of the new god of MOFI.

In the next chapter I will explain how this false god has built his edifice. To understand the full enormity of an endtime snare and the spiritual dangers that it holds, we first understand the recent revolution in the use of numbers.

∞

"The thing that differentiates man from animals is money."

–Gertrude Stein

ENDNOTES

1. Romans 5:1.

2. *"Then Jesus was led by the Spirit into the desert to be tempted by the devil. After fasting forty days and forty nights, he was hungry. The tempter came to him and said, "If you are the Son of God, tell these stones to become bread.' Jesus answered, "It is written: 'Man does not live on bread alone, but on every word that comes from the mouth of God.' Then the devil took him to the holy city and had him stand on the highest point of the temple. "If you are the Son*

of God," he said, "throw yourself down. For it is written: "He will command the angels concerning you, and they will lift up their hands, so that you will not strike your foot against a stone?"' Jesus answered him, "It is also written: 'Do not put the Lord your God to the test.'" Again, the devil took him up to a very high mountain and showed him all the kingdoms of the world and their splendor. "All this I will give you," he said, "if you will bow down and worship me." Jesus said to him, "Away from me, Satan! For it is written: "Worship the Lord your God, and serve him only.'" Then the devil left him, and angels came and attended him" (Matthew 4:1–11).

3.   J. Bradford De Long, Estimating World GDP, One Million B.C. 1998 Draft. I will use these Gross Domestic Products (GDP) estimates as a proxy for real money income. While this is a reasonable way to interpret these statistics, a very small portion of GDP is actually an imputed estimate and does not really involve money transactions.

CHAPTER 8

Safety in Numbers

Precise Deception

N umbers play a very important role in our day. We must understand how before we fathom the end-time role of money. Please review the statistics that follow. Though they may seem like a jumbled assortment of trivia, they are all connected in an important way.

• The Canadian government estimates the average cost of every suicide in the Province of New Brunswick at $849,877.80. An official stated that the study was done to show the importance of measures to prevent suicide, and that economic studies are the way to raise awareness of health problems.[1]

• Having a successful marriage is enormously important to happiness — it is worth the equivalent of $100,000 a year in income, calculates Professor Andrew Oswald of Warwick University.[2]

• Abolishing all trade barriers in the world could boost global income by $2.8 trillion and lift 320 million people out of poverty by 2015.[3]

• Tuesday, February 29, is expected to have added about $25.3 billion to US Gross Domestic Product in the year 2000.[4]

• Middle East violence has cost the Israeli economy $2.9 billion, or about 4 percent of business output, since the Palestinian intifada began in October 2000.[5]

• It is estimated that the cost of complying with federal rules was $668 billion in 1995. Employing conservative estimates, federal regulation costs the average American household $7,000; more than the average tax bill of $6,000.[6]

You will probably have guessed the connection between these statistics. This collection of anecdotal information isn't any different from what might ordinarily be found in a daily newspaper. However, that's not their connection. What is common to all of them is that they are related to money. Every one of these trends or conditions, no matter how abstract or unquantifiable, has been expressed as a value in terms of a currency.

Your first reaction, like mine, may be this: Just how were these estimates made? What techniques could possibly have been used to convert all these unrelated phenomena to a common language of money? Some of these facts aren't really suited to being expressed as a monetary value. As such, this practice of relating facts to monetary value can be crude and inappropriate. After all, can human life be valued in terms of money? What's the value of a liver transplant? What's the real, monetary value of truth? These are difficult questions. The answers are immeasurable. Yet, estimates like these are printed daily about almost everything and anything.

It hasn't always been this way. What happened?

These items reveal the new common language of the *Endtime Money Snare* — the numbers of money.

A World Colored With Hazardous Statistics

We live in a world of numbers. They shape our world in numerous ways. Most of them are obvious. For example, all of today's computer data systems are based on a numerical language. Networks, digital communications systems, and anything controlled by a microprocessor or integrated circuit are driven by numerical formulas and codes. The organization of our entire world centers around numbers. Phone numbers, street and house numbers, passwords, bank accounts and investment accounts are all expressed in numerical digits. But, let's not get hung up in a detailed account of the new mathematical theories and digital technologies sweeping the globe. We are more interested in the application, interpretation and influence that numbers have upon our beliefs. Importantly, we want to better understand their endtime role.

Numbers shape and form statistics. That allows statistics to be considered as the representatives of truth. But what if numbers lie?

Numeracy is the practice of documenting news, opinions and trends with numbers and it is an activity highly valued today. News reporters and researchers practice it carefully. If I did not exhibit some numeracy in writing this book, peppering its pages with statistics and footnotes, you, the reader, would surely find my views less credible. If I didn't document trends by expressing various changes over a given period in terms of percentages, or by counting the growth or decline in the units of something, and referencing this information to reputable sources, you would be less able to assess the validity of my conclusions. Therefore, numeracy is very useful when used in good measure.

Yet, an excessive fixation with numeracy can lead to some dangers — ones that are extremely hazardous to Christians who seek to understand the times. How can something that is innately useful lead to peril? Numeracy serves as a springboard for three negative developments in our day: 1) as a mechanism for widespread deception and misinformation; 2) as a bridge to a world totally defined in terms of money; and 3) to a world which chooses to accept numerical systems and mathematical theories in place of God.

How A World Language Of Money Has Emerged

In my estimation, monetary numeracy, or a common world language of money, has developed in several stages. It begins with a fixation in quantification. Every trend and development is expressed in numerical terms, documented and captured in a statistical quantification. That in itself is not overly worrisome. But the danger really lies in the fact that our focus moves from the event to the statistic itself. The statistic now serves as a numerical image of the thing being quantified. Just how accurate is this picture? Can numbers really capture all of the nuances of something that is real? Three apples on a table may be exactly that. But what does it mean when we say that the annualized rate of inflation has fallen to 2.0% over the past month? Or, what is implied by the statistic that the teenage birthrate is declining by some percentage from the year before? These types of statistics require a more sophisticated interpretation. The image that these types of numbers portray can rarely be accepted for their face value. More often than not, the real truth lies underneath this neat veneer of statistical precision. Though the numbers themselves are accurate, the truth can be very different from what seems obvious from the statistical profile.

To illustrate, let's briefly examine the statistic about inflation. What does it really mean that inflation has fallen to 2.0%? To know this requires an understanding of inflation. Very few people really do. Alarmingly, very few financial professionals do either. Most accept the convenient and sanitized statistic of the Consumer Price Index (CPI) that is issued by the US Bureau of Economic Analysis (BEA) for its face value. The same applies to similar measures reported by other national statistics agencies around the world. As it happens, real inflation is actually something very different. The CPI has grossly misrepresented real inflation trends this past decade. Yet, the CPI statistic is followed slavishly, accepted as truth. Subsequently, people are being misled.

What about the statistic indicating that the teenage birthrate is declining? Yes, indeed, the teenage birthrate is declining. That appears to be a good development. But, why is it declining? To be able to accept this statistic as either good or bad, we need to get behind the number to discover its causality — its cause and effect. Are teenage births declining because of a decrease in sexual activity, more effective birth control or both? Or have births declined because abortions have increased? These are all relevant questions that require resolution in order to interpret the real meaning of the top-line statistic. As the case may be, the main contributing factor for the reduction in teenage births in recent years is a rise in abortions. What seems like such positive news actually disguises a disquieting trend. As such, we see that the real causes and effects can be overlooked, and in fact, hidden by statistics.

What George Orwell said about words has now happened to numbers. In 1946, in an article called "Politics and the English Language," Orwell decried the deliberate misuse of words, writing that people craft their words "...to make lies sound truthful and murder respectable and to give an appearance of solidity to pure wind."

Numeracy isn't the danger. The peril is found in the blind acceptance of numbers as the image of truth with no further critical analysis. That's the vulnerability of our age — that we allow statistical numbers to reign as reality and truth. It's very easy to allow this to happen. We live in a society bombarded by data. People lead harried lives. There is too little time for critical analysis and too many statistics to process. It's easier to accept the "sound bites" of the statistics just as they appear.

Deliberate Manipulation of Numbers

Benjamin Disraeli made this famous quip: "There are lies, damn lies, and statistics." The comment strikes to the heart of a potentially serious issue. If perceptions are allowed to rule with careless reference to truth and reality, then statistics become very powerful. Now, they can hide more than they reveal. And, if that's the case, then why wouldn't they be deliberately manipulated in order to create a certain desired perception? This manipulation is an important step toward the endtime role of numbers.

Are statistics deliberately manipulated? At times, definitely. But, this sounds like the stuff of conspiracies. Not really. I believe that it is just human nature at work. Consider these anecdotes of statistical tampering:

As of November 1991, the US Department of Commerce decided to switch its reporting on economic growth to the measure of Gross Domestic Product (GDP) from Gross National Product (GNP). There is a significance between the two that might not have been noticed by most. Roughly explained, the former does not include earnings from foreign sources, while the latter does. Since America is running large deficits with the rest of the world, GDP will appear bigger than GNP. This statistical sleight of hand can boost reported growth by over 1% in some quarters. There have been subsequent numerous other changes to the statistical methods of tracking GDP. One recommended in late 1996 held an equally large impact. It was proposed that the method of estimating inflation should be changed. The effect? Not surprisingly, a twenty-year record of inflation was lowered by 1.1% per annum, and the growth of the economy was boosted significantly...all at the stroke of a pen.[7]

In Britain, few economic statistics have been more mistrusted than the government's measure of unemployment. Between 1979 and 1995, some 30 adjustments have been made to the way that this statistic is calculated. Apparently, in violation of the law of averages, 29 of these caused "unemployment" to fall.[8]

I could recount many more examples. Strangely, the definition of these statistics tends to only change in one direction — that which leads toward a more advantageous perception. Invariably, what's favorable is any revision that seems to be positive for prosperity, gain and wealth. Is a diabolical conspiracy behind the above-mentioned statistical shifts? Yes, in a way. But not necessarily in the sense that there is a great, organized scheme devised by the government or other group to delude the public. Rather, the conspiracy exists in the sense that these types of subtle orchestrations are part of the great diabolical *Endtime Money Snare*.

But numeracy can lead to even worse abuse. Not only can numbers make us vulnerable to deceit and manipulation, but they also set up an all-important interface that allows the love of money to wreak its corruption upon the endtime world. We have already discovered how common this new language of money has become. Statistics expressed in terms of money somehow seem to be more illuminating to our imaginations. Once we know the cost or price associated with a piece of information, we are better able to frame its reference. It strikes a common chord. For example, a million bushels of wheat is more difficult to conceptualize than the price of a million bushels of wheat on the open market — probably around $2.5 million. The more we can express things, trends and values in terms of money, the easier will be the transformation to a world which is given over to the worship of wealth and material. That, too, is another subtle step toward the *Endtime Money Snare*.

Worst of all, is that numbers and their application can even replace a need for God. Believe it or not, many have made numbers their god. How has this happened? It's a development that's been fostered by the new false god of SCITE.

Numbers Rail Against God

Peter L. Bernstein wrote an excellent and informative book entitled *Against the Gods*. Essentially, the book's unstated thesis is this: With modern mankind's mastery of mathematics and the understanding of probabilities, gods are no longer necessary. He writes this in his introduction to the book:

> The revolutionary idea that defines the boundary between modern times and the past is the mastery of risk: the notion that the future is more than the whim of the gods and that men and women are not passive before nature. Until human beings discovered a way across the boundary, the future was a mirror of the past or the murky domain of oracles and soothsayers

who held a monopoly over knowledge of anticipated events.[9]

Mr. Bernstein is saying that mathematics enable us to look into the future and cross the boundaries of the unknown which, to mathematicians and financiers, is called "risk." Not knowing what will happen in the future is a risk, especially to those who have much money to lose.

The concept underlying this definition of risk is very simple. You can better know the future by looking into the past. While that thought carries some truth, it assumes that tomorrow will always be like today. And, if tomorrow can be counted upon to be like today, then God is no longer necessary. Though it's a simple notion, it has taken humanity many thousands of years to develop the mathematic and computational skills needed to capture the past with numbers, then to launch them into the future across the boundary of risk. It makes for a fascinating story. Today, there are a lot of sophisticated applications of this idea such as chaos and game theory, optimization, probability theory, portfolio theory, mortality tables and so on. But, taken too far, these applications can lead to the unfortunate delusion that a sovereign God no longer rules the affairs of creation.

The Bible ridicules and condemns this "rear-view mirror" concept of risk. *"Do not boast about tomorrow, for you do not know what a day may bring forth,"* said King Solomon in Proverbs 27:1. Isaiah scorns the idea also, caricaturing the culture of his day by saying, *"... let me get wine! Let us drink our fill of beer! And tomorrow will be like today, or even far better"* (Isaiah 56:12). James thinks it is outright evil.

"Now listen, you who say, "Today or tomorrow we will go to this or that city, spend a year there, carry on business and make money." Why, you do not even know what will happen tomorrow. What is your life? You are a mist that appears for a little while and then vanishes. Instead, you ought to say, "If it is the Lord's will, we will live and do this or that." As it is, you boast and brag. All such boasting is evil..." (James 4: 13:16).

Would Solomon, Isaiah and James think differently had they been schooled in the business schools and statistical mills of our day? Would the great tool of mathematics cause them to dispose of their belief in God?

Not likely. God and mathematics can co-exist. After all, God is the author of order. Mathematics is useful, but can only be a partial and pale imitation of God's order and will. He indeed remains sovereign.

The Root Of Statistical Fallacies

It is not my intention to provide much detail about the modern-day application of math to the field of economics and finance. That task could require countless volumes, boring ones at that. My objective is simply to show how numbers — perhaps even prefigured by the 666 of Revelation[10] — coupled with the love of money interplay in the great *Endtime Money Snare*.

Wherein lies the falsehood in the popular belief that the veil of the future has been lifted through the sophisticated use of numbers? The delusion is that risk has been lessened or eliminated. The fact is that the unknown exists as it always did. The consequences of this risk have simply been expressed in the form of money and transferred to someone else.

Let's look at just one illustration of the fallacy in this thinking that God can be replaced by numbers: the insurance industry. Does life insurance lessen the risk of anyone dying? Of course not. All that life insurance accomplishes is a transfer of the risk of the unknown — in this case, something that is fairly improbable over the short term — to the insurance company. The company agrees to accept this risk in return for payment of monthly insurance premiums. Is the insurer foolish to take this risk? No. It has used mathematics to figure out the probability of untimely death. To do so, it looks into the past and studies all available data about previous death patterns by age, occupation, sex, smoking habits, etc., to produce mortality tables. Then the company prices premiums accordingly, making sure to include a profit margin for their service. Customers still don't know when they will die; however, the insurance company has agreed to spread the cost of your early death across all of its customers. Economists call this the "socialization" of risk. It's a very useful service, but it doesn't change the unknown. God is still in control.

The concepts of calculating future risks by modeling the past through numbers and sophisticated math, then transferring it to other people through financial products are behind virtually all of today's financial innovation. Yet, at the surface, it can seem very confusing. The number of these types of services has exploded.[11] As such, the role and use of financial markets has substantially changed.

By now it should be very clear that numbers, expressed in monetary values, are a necessary device in the success of the *Endtime Money Snare*.

Before we move on, consider these thoughts: While we live in an age filled with more statistics and knowledge than ever before, there is less truth. People seem to know the price of everything, but the value of little. Instead, wisdom — past, present and future — today tends to be found in the belly of some financial model or spreadsheet.

Just what is the real value of truth and wisdom? This is what Job said:

"But where can wisdom be found? Where does understanding dwell? Man does not comprehend its worth; it cannot be found in the land of the living. The deep says, 'It is not in me'; the sea says, 'It is not with me.' It cannot be bought with the finest gold, nor can its price be weighed in silver" (Job 28:12).

Job is effectively saying that wisdom is priceless; therefore, we should not look for it in numbers and prices.

We live in a dangerous world where prices without value abound and costs are only measured in prices. In such a world, the price becomes the value and values are separated from actual costs. The common denominator of what is right becomes the price.

A world ruled by price? That is the exact characteristic

of a world that is quickly globalizing[12] and financializing.[13] Price then becomes the world's judiciary determining what is right and good. That's a concept that ideally suits the juggernaut of globalization, a process leading to a world system in which all human actions are governed through the incentives of wealth and prosperity. And if wealth and prosperity are the only worthy objectives, then whatever increases wealth will tend to be approved and considered good and right.

Of course, it's a satanic concept that prices and wealth can be used as a measure of truth. This thinking is most obvious in the world's money industries — investment management and brokerage or any business dependent upon trends in market prices. To financial professionals, price is effectively truth. As one financial service ad says, "The moment of truth is when the best price is yours."[14] How does this happen?

Allow me to use the illustration of a stock market investor to explain how price has become truth. Let's assume that a portfolio manager has decided to buy an investment, and then suffers losses. The "market" has judged his opinion that the stock would rise in price to be wrong. The inverse applies as well. If a portfolio strategist reduces his investment in the stock market on the belief that stock prices are too high, it will be left to the future direction of the stock market to determine whether he is correct. In the competitive wrangle to squeeze wealth out of financial markets, the market is never wrong. Only investors can be wrong. It doesn't matter that a stock market may be in the midst of a huge mania that will some day end up in a sorry bust. The price is the truth, and truth depends on the trend.

Christians Are Not Immune To The Deception Of Numbers

This subtle shift of thinking about truth hasn't just affected financial professionals, but extends to our whole society, including Christians.

A number of prominent Christian investment managers have assumed this posture. Their opinions about what drives world markets and trends, no matter how ill-founded and baseless, are arrogantly assumed to be right simply because "the market," in retrospect, has judged them as correct. That's perverse thinking. Markets represent the judgment and vanities of the world. The truth is not contained in markets, prices, money, or gold; they are all denominated in a currency of man's making.

We must not let prices determine our values. Our values — biblical standards and eternal objectives — must determine our conduct. Of course that imperative demands that we continue to be good stewards, work diligently and manage our resources faithfully. That is not the same as staking our hope and faith in the values of earthly wealth. Nor does it mean that the correctness of our living can be judged by how much wealth we accumulate, how much we earn, or how successfully our portfolios out-perform the world's financial markets. Yet, this monetary measuring rod, which can be likened to the idolatrous Asherah poles[15] worshipped during the times of the Old Testament prophets, is standing on many of the high places in the church today.

For Christians caught during the times of the great *Endtime Money Snare*, living apart from the rule of numbers and markets will carry a cost. The measuring stick of price should not be allowed to be arbiter of truth and what is right in our lives. And undoubtedly, for most of us, that will mean we may not accumulate as much wealth here on earth as the secular world thinks we should.

Actually, we have great reason for joy. In one sense, living to God's standard during the present upswing of the great *Endtime Money Snare* is hardly costly at all. We have the greatest money manager of all at our service. He promised that He would reward us 100-fold[16] for every one of our sacrifices, with payment in an eternal currency that will never rust or corrode.

With an eternal guarantee like that, there's absolutely no need to invest by the numbers!

"The world is naturally averse to all the truth it sees or hears. But swallows nonsense, and a lie with greediness and gluttony."

–Samuel Butler

ENDNOTES

1. Reported in the *Globe & Mail,* 1999.
2. *Financial Times* of London, February 3, 2000, "Why happiness is priceless."

3. World Bank, November 1, 2001, *Financial Times*.

4. LeapSource as reported in *The Wall Street Journal*, March 2000.

5. Bank of Israel estimate (January 2002).

6. Thomas Hopkins of the Rochester Institute of Technology. Reported in the *Economist*, July 27, 1996.

7. *Financial Times*, December 5, 1996; *Economist*, September 21, 1991.

8. *Economist*, April 1995.

9. Bernstein, Peter L., *Against the Gods: The Remarkable Story of Risk*, John Wiley & Sons, 1996.

10. *"This calls for wisdom. If anyone has insight, let him calculate the number of the beast, for it is man's number. His number is 666"* (Revelation 13:18).

11. Some examples of these types of financial products, to name a few, include stock options, money market swaps, financial futures, equity-indexed bonds...etc. There are now literally thousands of different types of financial instruments that, in essence, calculate various types of financial risk, transferring this risk or converting one type of risk for another. Many of these have proprietary names — SPYDERS, TIPS, CAT BONDS...etc. — and involve extremely sophisticated mathematics. An alarming amount of these new types of products and securities are so complex that it is impossible to predict how they may perform during periods of financial crisis.

12. See Chapter 11 for a broader review of globalization.

13. See Chapter 9 for a review of financialization.

14. Advertisement for INSTINET, *Barron's,* August 2, 1999.

15. Quoting *Compton's Expert Commentary:* Asherah poles became a regular feature of Judah's landscape for hundreds of years. They were dedicated to a mother-goddess and often erected alongside altars on the high places devoted to God. They came to represent Judah's slide into idolatry.

16. *"I tell you the truth...everyone who has left houses or brothers or sisters or father or mother or children or fields for my sake will receive a hundred times as much and will inherit eternal life"* (Matthew 19:28–29).

CHAPTER 9

MOFI – The Unknown God

Faith in Monetary Wealth

Earlier we estimated that total wealth per person in the world has risen 10-fold this past century. Economic output for each person on earth, measured in terms of money, has multiplied 40 times in the last millennium. We also discovered how the role of money has dramatically increased in our lives. Where once it was required for only about 20% of our economic activities, today money intersects our lives four times as much. Only one-fifth of our activities remain hidden from the monitoring eye of money.

Who can doubt that money has become a behemoth — a Philistine Goliath? It used to be that big business meant money. Today, it is the other way around. Money is big business. Given the huge boom in its role, it is no surprise that many are in its employ. Today, two out of every 13 people in the North American workforce labor in a financial service industry of some kind. Despite the great advances of technology — automatic teller machines (ATMs), internet banking, e-trading ... etc., — a 10% greater share of workers is occupied in some type of financial services job today than a decade earlier. Imagine! For every 6.5 people, one person makes a living shuffling around the financial wealth of the others. This may include insurance, stockbrokering, banking, investment management, leasing, and many other financial industry specialties. Money has assumed an enormous place of domination to keep so many people busy. At this pace of growth, were it to continue, the ratio of financial workers will be one in four only 50 years from now. Stranger things have happened. And it is not just a North American trend. Twenty-eight of the 29 OECD[1] countries experienced an increase in their financial services employment share between 1986 and 1996.

Doesn't it seem unimaginable that an inanimate thing like money, which at one time served only as a medium of exchange, should become something so large and complex, requiring legions of people to manage the myriad arrangements of who owes it and who owns it? Even with today's powerful and inexpensive computing capacity, many people are still required to administer the rights and privileges of owners and debtors. This whole phenomenon is evidence of just how controlling the monetary system has become. It signifies that there are many, many layers of financial relationships — obligations and enslavements in other words — that hang as millstones around the necks of humanity.

Of course economists cite all of the above-mentioned

statistics as evidence of human progress. But is it really? If it is, what must we sacrifice, and what vulnerabilities must we risk, in order to gain its conveniences? As we will discover, this progress does not come without dangers.

How Money Has Become A Measure Of Human Progress

Why has the role of money expanded so sharply? Where did all this thinking that more money means progress begin? It will take some effort to answer these questions. But let's not get bogged down in reviewing the whole history of economic thought. Otherwise, if we do, simple truths will get fogged up with high-sounding words.

The best way to understand how money has come to play a crucial endtime role is to use the example of a machine — a six-cylinder engine. To run it requires both fuel and lubrication. Knowing how this machine works will help us understand how the world's financial system captures the actions and motivations of humans. Only then will we see how this system has come to live so close to our souls, even defining our very existence and ascending to a position of controlling dominance.

Let's begin by examining the mechanism. To help explain, allow me to construct a simple model of how this money mechanism functions. My apologies if the illustration appears too technical in any way, but it is important that we understand how money has invaded our lives, leading to our potential financial captivity during the endtimes.

The Six Pistons Of The Money Machine

Six pistons make up the thrust of the world's engine of money and wealth. Each is connected to the crankshaft. Each piston represents a factor or trend that can grow and increase the measure of the world's wealth defined monetarily — the realm of Mammon, in other words. When all fire simultaneously, the advance of the *Endtime Money Snare* can be lightening quick. As we will see, that's exactly what has happened over roughly the past two decades. All of a sudden, each of these six pistons has been stimulated to rapid speed, as if some unseen pituitary gland has triggered them all to a state of hyperactivity. Together, this rack of pistons drives the structure of a great money system, like a modern-day Tower of Babel that virtually reaches up into the very heavens. We will briefly examine these pistons one by one.

Money Piston #1: Human Activity And Consumption

Simplicity and utility ruled in earlier days. Who would have believed centuries ago that the volume of consumption promoted today in the Western world would have been necessary or possible? In fact, our own grandparent's generation can hardly acclimatize to the consumer culture of today. More is always better. Eight pairs of shoes are better than two. A 4,000-square foot house is more desirable than 1,000. If a vacation home can be afforded, it must be owned. Conspicuous consumption is idolized in TV, movies, books and magazines. The push for more consumption extends into every human activity ranging from

146

entertainment, to leisure, to possessions and to our stomachs. More consumption means faster economic growth. More economic growth means that more wealth can be supported, its presiding politicians become more popular, and the masses become more content. At least that's the general philosophy that broader society endorses, though it's riddled with false assumptions and questionable values.

Yet, it's a philosophy being adopted by more and more countries and cultures around the world. The roads to freedom, higher development and progress all lead through the holy ground of higher consumption, production and trade. Quite a number of agendas are served by that objective. Most governments endorse it. Greater economic size is attached to higher tax revenues and greater world prominence — a greater influence around the negotiating tables of world institutions like the United Nations, the World Trade Organization (WTO), and a host of others. As sales and revenues grow, business people see greater profits; consumers enjoy a wider selection of products and services catering to their every whim, enticing them to increase their purchases, to borrow and labor even more.

It's a gospel with no shortage of evangelists. The knees of economists and business strategists turn to rubber when they think of the potential business and profit opportunities that could be realized if the whole world adopted the Western world's religion of materialism. They salivate at the thought that such populous countries as China and India might adapt to the Anglo-Saxon definition of prosperity and progress. Imagine the possibilities in China: If every household had one automobile, it would represent a car market almost four times the size of that in the United States! A consumer-crazed China could alone double the annual demand for cars in the entire world. Just think of the profits for the globe's automotive industry and suppliers. Think of all the new wealth. And, if the business strategists can ever devise an effective way of eradicating the hindrances of the Hindu and Muslim belief systems, India could be another gold mine for the owners and elites of the world's economic and mone-tary/financial system. Consumption in these countries would boom.

Who Pushes For A World Of Mass Consumption?

The globalists and the wealthy of the world have a dream. They imagine that every human being on earth would become a full-fledged, card-carrying member of the "free market" consumer society of the Anglo-Saxon world. What if the whole world attained the same standard of liv-ing enjoyed by the high-income countries of the world? World economic output would be five times the level it is today.[2] The financial wealth that this global economy could support would be at least 5 times greater as well. Wow! If so, how can we gain a big share of these riches the world's policymakers ask? Along with them come worldly power and influence.

While the numbers may seem exaggerated, the illustra-tion is true. This process of so-called progress is indeed ad-vancing upon the world. Many institutions around the globe are dedicated to its cause. As such, a world financial behemoth of truly gigantic proportions has emerged in the past century and accelerated its growth in recent decades. If the rest of the world can be fully convinced to follow this beast, it is believed that world monetary wealth can continue to surge in leaps and bounds. The rich and elite of all stripes would then become even greater lords. After all, they hold the strings that control the movement and action of the money marionette, whether they do so knowingly or not. And, as we have already proposed, the puppet image of the MOFI — monetary/financial god — will be worshipped by mankind as the source of prosperity.

To conclude, the first piston at the very front of the machine is the human being. It all begins and ends with the human consumer. The more products and services we consume, the more possible and effective the rule of a governing financial regime becomes.

Today, the average person living in the world's high income countries consumes 6 times more resources — energy, commodities, water, etc — than at the beginning of the century. Can the three false gods of the endtimes be summoned to help increase this another five, perhaps even 20 times? Some globalist observers think so. "Come," they say, "let us see if we can build a mountain of wealth so that we can worship it."

Money Piston #2: Trade With Others

The Bilfrie family whom we met in a previous chapter, sourced very little of their requirements from outside of their household. As long as they consumed only goods and services produced on their own homestead, this family had little influence with the commercial world outside. They could consume as much as they wanted and it would still have little consequence for their neighbors, provided they weren't living downstream and polluting the creek. Only when they begin trading goods and services with other households does a commercial economy begin to take form. Once they begin to do so, the ownership of goods and obligations are exchanged and transactions take place. Transactions require that the ones exchanging goods place a value on what they are receiving and offering.

The more the Bilfrie family relies on the outside world for its items of consumption and for the sale of the goods and services that its own household members produce, the greater the world of transactions becomes. Of course, there are numerous advantages to exchanging goods with other households. The Bilfrie family may have a big forest, and have the ability to supply firewood to those who do not. Another family may have built up a flock of sheep and a number of productive spinning wheels. The Bilfries would obviously want to exchange firewood for the wool. This makes good sense. Economists call this concept "comparative advantage."

Not only can trade bring advantages to two individuals, but also to companies and countries as well. In this way, countries like Japan who have few natural resources can still have the second largest economy in the world. They can trade their advantages of high productive investment and desirable consumer goods with other countries for currency in order to buy the resources they need. And so this process of trade and transactions expands.

Progress Taken To Extreme Has A Heavy Cost

What has happened to the Bilfrie family as they began trading with others is this: A greater part of their private livelihoods have become transactions, things that now require valuation and exchange. This is not bad in and of itself because it brings many advantages. The downside is that it also increases vulnerability.

However, the great idea of comparative advantage can be extended to extremes, so much so that it destroys the very household that began this entire process. No longer does the modern Mrs. Bilfrie churn butter, boil lye, or can turnips in the summer. The local pizza shop now supplies a portion of their diet. Most of their clothes come from the textile mills in China. New and exotic tastes have been acquired for piquant meals at the local bistro, winter Caribbean sunsets, the easy leisure of video, and a four-wheel-drive SUV. Their children may now be latch-key kids while mom and dad work to pay for the pleasures that were purchased on credit yesterday or perhaps even years ago. Mrs. Bilfrie now needs to work outside of the home. Both she and Mr. Bilfrie are stressed by the continuous increasing demands for efficiency and profitability at their places of employment. They work long hours. When a few minutes can be spared for a well-deserved family time, they are now spent sprawled out on the couch watching a movie, exhausted from the demands of serving MOFI, GLOBO and SCITE.

Money Piston #3: The Flow Of Money

There has been no mention of currency up to this point. Technically, it is not necessary for human existence. A world could exist without it. The barter of physical goods would be sufficient to sustain human life, as is still the practice is some remote corners of the world. The obligations of an extended family or clan could provide for needs of the retirement years. In this case, no monetary store of value would be necessary. Admittedly, while it is all possible, it would be an austere world, hardly recognizable to those living at the dawn of a new millennium.

Money is a great invention, possibly the greatest of mankind's advances since the mastery of fire. The history of currency is fascinating, evolving from simple seashells to what we think of as money today — cyber blips stored on magnetic media, sent through communications lines and airwaves across the world. Currency offered an obvious convenience. It was divisible into smaller quantities. People no longer needed to trade a whole cow for one thousand roses in order to purchase the twelve they wanted for that special person on Valentine's Day.

Yet, this invention laid the foundation for its misuse. The advent of money introduced two new developments. For one, it opened the door to the practice of valuing everything in terms of currency units. The value of goods and services could now be appraised in a common coin. In turn, the activities of all this buying and selling could also better be counted. Without this possibility, there could not be anything such as Gross Domestic Product (GDP), the capturing of all this human activity — both

152

imagined and real — in the form of a monetary quantity to be monitored by regimes and governments.

Another consequence of the invention of money was that it could now be used as a storehouse. A pile of seashells hoarded today could be stored for expenditure in the far future. Seashells could be stored much longer than eggs, milk and honey. It wasn't like manna, which had to be gathered and consumed on a daily basis or it would not last. Therefore, a big hoard of seashells could be considered a source of security. It also opened up the possibility of more easily accumulating riches; serving as an instrument conducive to controlling the obligations and resources of other people.

We'll leave this discussion of money without any deeper analysis. Suffice it to say that the properties of money make it a very important and strategic object. Whoever or whatever controls the creation of money or facilitates its flows — financial institutions, governments or central banks, for example — stand to become extremely powerful.

To conclude, the more that all transactions are expressed in monetary terms, the greater the growth of this piston in the creation of a financial behemoth of wealth. The greater the number of financial transactions, the larger the volume of money flows.

Money Piston #4: Capitalization Is A Big Multiplier

Capitalization. What does it mean? It is one of those technical terms often thrown around by financial professionals. Actually, it is a big word that buries the meaning of a very small concept.

The idea is this: Money is valuable. But, it is even more valuable if it is in motion. Money, like water, is important. But both are much more powerful when they flow. The more money that flows, the more valuable it can be. How does this work?

Suppose we open a store that sells eggs. It becomes well-known as the best place to buy large, fresh eggs. Soon it attracts a large number of customers, which increases our daily intake of money. Since our store has priced these eggs above their cost, our daily profits also rise. Two valuable things have occurred: First, a fairly reliable daily flow of money has been established; second, this flow is one that shows signs of growing bigger.

What would this business now be worth? If the daily profit flow of our little egg business amounted to one dollar, how much would you be willing to pay to own the right to receive this dollar every day from this point forward? Would you pay $365? At that price, you would earn your original investment back in one year. But that would be too cheap of a price. For $365 the buyer would be earning a 100% return on his original investment and at least that every year thereafter. By the standard of stock and bond prices today, we shouldn't sell this business for anything less than $10,000. That would amount to nearly 30 times the annual income of this business. In recent years it has not been uncommon for stocks to sell at more than 30 times their annual earnings. That's capitalization at work, establishing a value for the ownership of a flow of money.

However, $10,000 would probably still not be enough

to buy our egg business. Remember, this business is growing. After having inspected our egg business, the buyers have concluded that it will continue to grow at the same pace as before, doubling its sales and profits every year. Now how much would you be willing to pay? This business would certainly be more valuable than a business that was not expanding. Perhaps the ownership of this company is now worth $15,000, or even $30,000.

Do you see how this piston block of capitalization works? Without it, the activities of the world and mankind cannot be mobilized into movable wealth, riches that can be exchanged or stored in financial terms. Instantaneously, the human consumption activities that had become transactions valued in money terms as we saw in the first money piston have now catapulted into expressions of value that are many, many times the underlying flows of money.

The *Endtime Money Snare* has now taken a big step toward its ultimate endtime application. Yet, the act of capitalization itself is not evil, bad or wrong. It's the human weaknesses of craving, the lust of the eyes and boasting, that carry the ultimate blame for allowing financial wealth to tantalize us into serving it.

Money Piston #5: Sharing The Wealth Through Securitization

Securitization is another buzz word that hides a very straightforward concept. Like most other technical terms, they are barriers to simple understanding, shielding professionals behind curtains of apparent knowledge. Securitization is simply the turning of ownership (for example, the value of a flow of money) into discreet bits of stocks and bonds also known as securities. They are very handy things. Any one of us who owns a mutual fund or participates in a pension fund will be a beneficiary of securitization.

To briefly illustrate the role of securitization in the world's money systems, let's return to our egg business. Suppose it is has grown so that it is now worth $200 million. The trouble now is that no single individual or company can afford such a large price. Then why not attract many buyers of this company instead of just one? To do this, we divide the ownership of the company into equal portions called shares. We declare 20 million shares, register them with a government agency that regulates this process, and then sell them at a price of $10 each. Importantly, we also list them on a stock exchange. That way these shares can be more easily bought and sold every day. We must attract many buyers to sell our business for $200 million. It'll be a lot easier to do so if these buyers know that they can easily sell the shares to someone else any time they choose.

Tradable Stocks And Bonds Play An Important Role

The invention of securities is very significant. Not only does it make ownership of large businesses and huge loans more possible, but it also breathes life into wealth. Represented in securities form, wealth is now highly transferable. Buying and selling now becomes very inexpensive. Enormous quantities of securities can be bought and sold every day. In fact, today, some countries experience buying and selling activity in its stock markets equivalent to an entire change of ownership in less than six months.[3] Without a doubt, securities markets put wealth in motion.

Securities markets also give high visibility to financial wealth. The prices of stocks and bonds can go up and down daily, and can even fluctuate by the minute. Sometimes these fluctuations in price can be quite large. What happens is the gain and loss of wealth now has a very high profile. This whole mass of fickle wealth then becomes vulnerable to manipulation on a grand scale and highly sensitized to the emotions of fear and greed. Wealth is now alive. It has entertainment value.

Not all wealth in the world is represented by securities — stocks or bonds or various other derivative types of ownership. Perhaps no more than half[4] of all wealth is still held in a private form. The equity in our homes (value, less the mortgage owed) is private, as well as our physical possessions. Not all businesses are owned in the form of securities, nor are they all listed on stock exchanges. Yet the advance of securities markets has been extremely rapid. The value of all securities wealth has boomed in recent decades, even to the point of doubling almost every ten years or so.

Though securities markets offer great convenience, they also greatly aid the advance of the *Endtime Money Snare*. Securities facilitate the easy transfer of wealth and its manipulation. They encourage the preoccupation with gain. After all, what is it that causes such a high rate of buying and active selling of securities around the world? Necessity, fear or greed? In my estimation, securities play a necessary role in an endtime financial agenda. Without them, wealth would not be so tantalizing or mobile.

Does that mean securities are evil? No, of course not. We are free to own and buy them. But, we need to be mindful that the primary tactic in the arsenal of the endtime beast is to lure us into misplacing our faith. Once deceived in this way, enslavement is sure to follow. When buying securities, we must try to avoid complicity in these endtime roles of financial markets. I will lay out just such an approach at the end of this book.

Money Piston #6: The Eye Of The Beholder

What is something worth? What is its value? Though we ran across the concept of valuation in the course of reviewing the previous five pistons, it really deserves an engine cylinder of its own. Why? Because like beauty, value is in the eye of the beholder. An oil painting can be worthless to one individual and priceless to another. The same with financial securities and other assets of wealth. The higher the desire for an asset, the higher its value will be. If its value rises for whatever reason — illusory, fictitious or deserved — by the standards of today's financial world, it means that wealth has increased. Of course, real wealth may not have actually risen, just the vanities and idolatries of its prospective owners. Theoretically then, the value of all financial wealth in the world can increase merely because of greed or a rampant investment mania. That being the case, we see that human emotions make up the final capstone of the money tower.

A "Financialized" World Emerges With Its Own Altars

We have reviewed the six pistons of the money machine which capture the essence of the world's money tower and explain how it throws up an apparition of wealth — mostly false riches. It's a clever scheme. Once deceptively defined and accepted in this way, wealth can be expanded without limit. It becomes a very effective lure — a possible money trap of unlimited scope. Indeed, if the Lord doesn't come first, or if God doesn't mete out His displeasure with mankind's misplaced worship any time soon, these money pistons we examined will likely continue accelerating, though not necessarily all at the same time, or without temporary reversals.

Having surveyed the six pistons of the money machine, we can see that our generation has become thoroughly "financialized." Almost every aspect of our lives intersects with money, finance and monetary economics.

Does the false god of MOFI receive your worship if you live in one of the higher-income countries of the world? If so, you will have opened yourself up to an *Endtime Money Snare*. Most people actually worship at MOFI's altars — the mutual fund sales counters, the stock brokerages, and the E-trade terminal. They hanker after his high priests — the money managers, bankers, and investment dealers who arrogantly say they have the power of creating wealth; the financiers, bankers, investment dealers and the like.

The Hopes may not know that they are being enticed to worship at the same altars.

The Fuel That Energizes The Money Machine

Now that we understand how financial systems spew out unlimited wealth, what energizes it? What is its fuel? Largely, it is the human emotions of greed and fear. The love of money serves as the high-power octane. In one sense, we have already examined the role of the love of money. It was also represented in Money Piston #6. The love of money really plays two roles; both a motivational one as well as a perverted object of worship.

But fuel alone will not propel the money machine for very long. It needs lubrication in order to run smoothly. The money machine will soon seize up without the oil of justification. What are the lubricants that allow the end-time money machine to keep running and speeding up?

I believe that there are at least two mainstream doctrines that grease this beast. These are the theories of debt and the famous notion of the "invisible hand." Both are fundamentally corrupt ideas God finds repulsive. More than anything else, these two doctrines have served as the smoothing agents behind the whole architecture of the "free market" money system. I will briefly explain each of them.

The "Invisible Hand" Of Another God

Adam Smith, the venerated economist of the 1700s, set the famous cornerstone for modern-day economics in his book, *The Wealth of Nations*.[5] He wrote:

> ...the market participant intends only his own gain,

and he is in this, as in many other cases, led by an invisible hand to promote an end which was no part of
his intention. By pursuing his own interest he frequently promotes that of the society more effectually
than when he really intends to promote it.

Though his words may not have been exactly meant as
they are popularly interpreted today, they launched the
notion that markets — "the" Market — left to its devices,
will promote the best interest of society and humanity.
People acting narrowly in their own interest — selfishly
fulfilling their own wants and needs, upon their greed and
fears — work as an "invisible hand." Therefore, this market action of many people pursuing their own interest is
the benevolent "invisible hand." Radical interpretations of
this idea suggest that there should be no economic and financial controls of any kind upon people. According to
this thinking, the more that people are free to live their
lives as they wish, the better off society will be and the
higher the overall standard of living. In a way, it raises the
"free market" concept to the level of godhood and bless-
es greed and craving. Whether dealing with the sale and
manufacture of consumer goods or stock and bond prices,
the "market" now becomes an all-seeing creature, capable
of looking forward into the future and fairly tending to the
needs of society. If left to its own devices, the "market" can
then be counted on to more efficiently deliver prosperity
and wealth.

Human Markets Are Not Good

While it is good to have competitive markets, the concept of the benevolent "invisible hand" is fundamentally

an occultic one. The market is not a god; it is not inherently good. It simply represents the collective action of human buyers and sellers. Since a single human is not a god, massed humanity cannot be gods either. If the world is not godly, then how can this "invisible hand" be considered benevolent? It is worldly; therefore, it is controlled by Satan, the god of this age. Jesus Christ was clear about this when He said: *"If anyone loves the world, the love of the Father is not in him. For everything in the world — the cravings of sinful man, the lust of his eyes and the boasting of what he has and does — comes not from the Father but from the world."* [6]

A Corrupt Concept Underlying The World's Monetary System

Another doctrine that lubricates the pistons of our money machine concerns how debt is employed in underpinning the world's monetary system. Debt serves several important roles in the *Endtime Money Snare*. I only mention its role here in underpinning the world's banking functions. Virtually all banking systems (at least 99% of them) are based upon the idea of fractional-reserve banking. This is another technical term that serves as an elegant cover for a simple idea. Entire textbooks are dedicated to the explanation of this concept. I will attempt a brief one.

Fractional reserve banking is nothing more than the practice of lending out something that really isn't yours. Banks take deposits — perhaps a checking or savings account deposit. When we deposit money in this way, it remains our property. The bank typically promises to pay back this money to us on a moment's notice. That's why these deposits are also known as "demand deposits." In the course of its business, a bank will take in deposits from many people. The bank figures that it is very unlikely that all of its depositors will ask for their money back at the same time. They then decide to lend out a portion of these deposits to other people, for example, in the form of a car or home loan. Or, the bank may invest these deposits in the form of bonds or other types of savings instruments. However, the monetary process does not stop here. The person that may have borrowed the money will eventually spend it on a purchase or investment. This money then ends up in the bank account of the seller. It now has become a new deposit in the name of the account holder who received the money. In essence what has happened is that the original deposit taken in by the bank has become two deposits — the original one and that of the seller we identified. Money has appeared out of thin air. If this process wasn't regulated, the bank could theoretically continue lending out money as long as the loans returned as new deposits. The money supply could potentially increase without end, with no relationship to real earnings or savings. Almost all central banks — for example the Federal Reserve in the U.S. — control this practice of money creation by setting certain limits — fractions and reserves (therefore the origin of the term "fractional reserve").

There are two potential flaws in this system. One stems from the fact that money today can be manufactured in unlimited quantities at virtually zero cost. Almost all money is backed by government debt, paper bills and metal coins. The intrinsic value of these things are far less than what their denomination may indicate. One way or another, this leads to inflation. In short, inflation can be defined as theft. It depreciates the purchasing value of existing savings. In this sense, the "fractional reserve" system is corrupt.

The second vulnerability of this monetary system is that it really rests on a shaky promise. Remember that the bank promised to repay our deposit on demand at any time we choose. Suppose a large number of people wanted to do this all at the same time. If this happened, the bank would not be able to honor its promise. It wouldn't have enough money on hand since it invested our deposits in loans and other investments. The bank would not be able to recall these loans very quickly. As a result, this bank would go bankrupt instantaneously. Only the first few people at the teller's counter would get their money back; the rest would lose their money. If these banking concepts are new to you, you're probably shocked to learn that the whole edifice of most of the world's financial wealth rests on such a shaky edifice. It really is a confidence game in a sense; its very security is based upon the faith of financial service providers and consumers. No wonder Babylon the Great comes to a sudden end and its entire wealth disappears within one hour!

Can you imagine if salvation was based on a similar concept? Though offered to all human beings in the world, it would really only be available to the first few people at the conversion altar. True revivals wouldn't be possible because there would be a run on heaven. As a result, heaven would have to close its doors.

An Endtime Explosion Of Wealth Based On Godless Doctrines

The whole concept of central banking — giving rise to the fractional-reserve system we just reviewed — originated in the early 1600s. Only 18 central banks existed in the year 1900. Today there are more than 175. Most coordinate their activities with the policies of the Bank of International Settlements based in Basel, Switzerland. The franchise of manufacturing money carries an enormous amount of power over people, countries, and the world, as the supply of money can be easily manipulated as may be required to suit any purpose. Central bankers are positioned to control this process. It matters not that money today is largely of fictitious value. Not many people either know or care. They have come to trust in their currency.

We see that this endtime system of monetary economics has been founded on a few godless doctrines that slipped their way into the mainstream of public acceptance and confidence some time ago. They no longer receive any critical reappraisal in a world that is increasingly smitten with the love of money and its idolatry with financial wealth. These doctrines are lodged in our textbooks. Courses specializing in training students in the creation of monetary wealth are swamped with applicants. For example, the well-known Chartered Financial Analyst (CFA) designation has become one of the marks of discipleship in

165

this academy of wealth creation. To be a CFA is to wealth creation as ordainment is to the priesthood. The membership of its Association of Investment Management and Research (AIMR), its sponsoring organization, booms every year. Though the CFA designation was founded almost forty years ago, more people are writing the annual exams for this course in recent years than there are existing CFAs.

Money Reflects Morality

Most of our modern-day society is pretty happy in their morality, as long as financial markets continue to go up and economies continue to grow. "What's morality got to do with business and the pursuit of wealth and prosperity as long as the god of MOFI is smiling benevolently?" some may ask. If economic growth appears robust and healthy, that should be the over-riding test of good destiny. What goes up is good; what goes down is bad. The litmus test is the monetarily defined price. Apparently, there can be no wrong reason for an increase in wealth. Sadly, this is the test of much of our society's morality. More is better; the higher the monetary wealth, the more that is right. That makes wealth the arbiter of what is truth, a concept partially explored in a previous chapter.

Together, the six engine pistons of the monetary/financial system bring a greater part of our individual activities and affairs into the realm of money and wealth. We become subject to its control once we find ourselves in that domain. We open ourselves up to scrutiny. This would be fine if it was God who was doing the scrutinizing, but such is not the case. Worldly values — increasingly materialistic and idolatrous — are setting the benchmarks for evaluation. The money system acts as a very effective mechanism to quantify, count, monitor and tax our incomes and expenditures. It's very useful for governments. Today, almost two-fifths[6] of the Gross Domestic Product is accounted for by the governments of high-income countries. And the manufacture of financial wealth has become so large that it amounts to several times the size of the annual world economy[7] as we have already discussed. Its value — fluctuating daily on the financial exchanges — tantalizes us, drawing us to want to own it.

Albert and Alice Hope are apparently unaware of the insidious fallacies and spiritual pitfalls of the modern-day money system. On the other hand, the Bilfrie family of the 1850s would shudder to discover how invasive and controlling our money system has become. Their faith has not yet been polluted by MOFI. They have not yet complacently cozied up to a world financial system essentially based on a confidence game. Of course, they would be amazed at all of the technological advancements of our day as well. For example, they would be flabbergasted and probably even frightened at their first sight of a roaring helicopter suspended in mid-air. However, they'd soon understand that this was a man-made vehicle of transportation, not a new god made out of shiny metal. It certainly wouldn't be something they'd stake their faith in. It requires no gullibility to believe that a helicopter may slip the bounds of gravity and hang suspended in the air, yet, when it comes to understanding the ensnaring role that money and modern finance has upon mankind today, it helps to be gullible. Rooted in the hard realities of the 1850s, try as they might, the Bilfries would have difficulty believing that wealth can be created out of thin air, with invisible hands, no less.

Christ said that we cannot serve both God and money. There's no hidden meaning in that statement. To decide to serve money is one thing, but to even suggest that money can be used to even define truth, the truth is an even greater perversion.

Today, MOFI sits resplendent atop our society. The 12 members of the Federal Open Market Committee[8] inquire of him in the inner sanctum of their temple every six weeks. The 17-member policy committee of the European Center Bank does the same.

Just try and escape him.

He has already vanquished the richest nations of the earth. He is now busily promoting himself to the rest of the world on the coattails of the gospels of globalization and free market economics.

"There cannot be intrinsically a more insignificant thing, in the economy of society, than money; except in the character of a contrivance of sparing time and labor. It only exerts a distinctive and independent influence of its own when it gets out of order."
– John Stuart Mill, *Principles of Political Economy,*
1848, Book III, Chapter 7, p. 3.

ENDNOTES

1. Organization for Economic Cooperation and Development. It has 30-member countries, representing essentially the rich nations of the world.

2. World Bank estimates for world Gross National Product (GNP) for 2000 are used for this estimate. In that year, the average per capita GDP of the high income countries was $USD 27,510 and $USD 1,230 for the rest of the world. The population estimated for these two groups were 902 million and 5,151 million, respectively.

3. According to the *Emerging Markets Factbook* of 1999, compiled by the International Finance Corporation, both Taiwan and Spain had a turnover rate of its stock markets of greater than 200% in 1999.

4. See footnote 7 in Chapter 11 for a detailed estimate supporting part of this claim.

5. Adam Smith, *An Inquiry into the Nature and Causes of the Wealth of Nations,* 1776.

6. John 2:15-16.

7. Source: OECD. In 1997 the total tax receipts of the 29-member countries of the Organization for Economic Cooperation and Development amounted to an average of 37.4% of annual Gross Domestic Product.

8. Financial wealth for this statistic is defined as M1 (an economic acronym for short-term bank deposits) and all securities, both debt and stocks.

9. Federal Open Market Committee or FOMC is headed by the Chairman of the Board of Governors of the Federal Reserve. This group is responsible for setting monetary policy and administred interest rate levels for the U.S. economy. Its current chairman is Mr. Alan Greenspan.

CHAPTER 10

SCITE – God of Fortresses

All Things Are Possible With Man

A slogan for a prominent financial service firm offers the following advice, "Admire machines. Worship their inventors."[1] The jingle reflects the spirit of our times. We live during an age in which society believes in the power of technology. What human ailment or world condition cannot be solved by the wonders of science? Is there any barrier to human progress that will not someday fall captive to "high-tech?" Some even believe that science will ultimately transform us into gods, endowing us with physical bodies that will live forever.

Movie theaters are full of amusing films that propose wild and varied visions of future worlds. Given the rapidity of technological advances in recent decades, few would deny that many of these fictional worlds wouldn't someday be possible. We really are living in a time during which the impossible actually seems possible.

How fast has our western society conditioned itself to

the pace of technological advance? Only 200 years of scientific discovery has rocketed the world into a heavenly orbit from a plateau of thousands of years of sweat and glacial progress. Now, we barely even blink an eye when we learn of new scientific breakthroughs. There doesn't seem to be any end to progress. It is viewed as an unstoppable and inalienable force, almost as if physical creation itself had no borders. Progress is apparently destined for geometric growth forever. So we see that the power of the human mind is now venerated as the source of all creativity. Apparently with humans, all things are possible.

Such is the hubris of our day: The mind of the created inventor is glorified as the creator, while the Creator is reinvented as a figment of the mind. It has gone even one step further: The imperative for human existence itself has become progress. The god of SCITE — the *god of fortresses* as Daniel called him; the modern-day faith in science and technology as we have proposed — is worshipped as the giver of progress.

Science And Technology Are A Testimony To God's Greatness

Science and technology are wonderful things to the Christian mind. They do not intimidate our faith, nor do they diminish the God whom we worship. Rather, our increased understanding in these areas actually serve to illuminate and magnify His greatness. The more we learn about His creation, the more we discover that there is no end to Him. We see infinity no matter which end of the scope we peer into. Gazing heavenward, we see no limits.

Squinting into the molecular world another universe opens up just as large. The more that we dare to discover and probe the world around us, the exponentially greater our God becomes. We learn that the only thing that can experience infinite progress is knowledge of Him.

Yet, the world's view is otherwise, choosing to set itself up against God. Perversely, in its view, science and technology eclipse Him. With higher understanding there is no longer a need for God. Instead, the world is content to put its faith in the promises of science and technology. As such, humanity has erected a new god. In our study of Daniel's prophecies in earlier chapters we learned that this god very probably would be one of the three worshipped during the last days. We concluded that this was the god who represented the endtime worship of science and technology — SCITE.

He is a powerful god, though perhaps not as strong as GLOBO. Yet, Satan's endtime objective could not work if just one of the triumvirate of the false endtime gods were absent. Globalism (GLOBO) could not advance its unification of the world's affections and monetary finance and (MOFI) could not snare the world so completely without the aid of SCITE. SCITE's role in setting the money trap befalling mankind is absolutely essential.

The Spiritual Temptations Of SCITE

Christians of previous generations were quick to sense the spiritual dangers of SCITE — the challenges presented to our hearts. Today, we have been desensitized to his advance, becoming careless in guarding our hearts from his dangers. I remember the response of a friend's grand-mother 25 years ago when she first saw a video camera demonstrated. She was amazed when she saw her image replayed on the video cassette player. Immediately, she theorized that with technological wonders like videos in the world, Christ would surely return very soon.

Though her response was simplistic, she was correct in more ways than she could have known.

Anything written about the state of technology and science is, by definition, considered outdated from virtually the moment paper meets pen. In reviewing my files for this chapter, I discovered them to be the thickest. They were also the most obsolete. Almost everything I had clipped and copied in recent years ended up in the discard pile. Any information older than 18 months had been superseded by a new technological frontier.

Therefore, it is hardly worth documenting the current state of technological and scientific capability. Instead, it is more important to understand the pace of this change itself and to fathom the impact that technology is having upon faith, family and broader society.

The Advance Of Technology Never Reverses

Without a doubt, the pace of change has picked up from its already harried state in the twentieth century. Technology industries have been in a state of hyper-activity in recent years. This observation has little to do with the "high-tech" bubble that has inflated stock markets around the world. Technology manias have been a regular hallucinogenic of stock markets down through modern history. The Internet craze of the 1990s was just another example, as was the technological wave early in the last century following the invention of the telephone. A financial bust has always followed the boom. Yet, what never fails to advance to new and higher ground is the state of science and technology. Like a twig thrust upon a sandy seashore by a surging surf, it is pushed further with every successive and larger advance of the foaming wave. The water recedes, falling in upon itself, its force spent. The twig keeps its new ground. So it is with technology.

Technology's Role In The Endtimes

Not only has technology changed the world so rapidly, other factors have contributed to the swift rise of SCITE's reign. Global regulatory changes have been highly stimulative and have played a particularly major role in the telecommunications industries. Old-economy telephone businesses have been freed up to more aggressively compete and align themselves with other service providers. The World Trade Organization has done much to liberalize the world's telecommunication industries by promoting a "level playing ground" to spur competition. As a result, in recent years the entire global telecommunications industry has been virtually "sliced and diced" into globally-aligned business groups, voraciously demanding new and better equipment and technological edges over its competitors. Powerful global networks have literally emerged overnight in all of this industry's sectors — long distance, mobile, Internet, satellite and cable. The pace of change has been almost unimaginable. To quote one senior advisor to the World Bank, "Nowhere is the trauma of adjustment being felt more keenly than within the communications industry itself. After more than a century of stable development the structure of the telecom value chain is undergoing total transformation."

The applications of new technologies have revolutionized almost every industry. Yet, trends in the telecommunications and information industries hold more significance for the endtime world than any other. That is not to say that other trends are unimportant. Yet, developments in these two industries are crucial in order to facilitate the type of events and world conditions that the Bible indicates will strike very close to midnight on the "last-day" clock. For one, these trends enable Satan to spread his influence and deception as never before. At the same time, the Church harnesses technology as well. Now it can preach the Gospel to the four corners of the earth. Christ Himself said that the end will not come before the whole world is reached: *"And this gospel of the kingdom will be preached in the whole world as a testimony to all nations, and then the end will come"* (Matthew 24:14).

Here we see that science and technology is neither inherently good nor evil. The potential for good and evil is found in their masters — in the people and spiritual forces that are allowed to employ them.

Where Is The Inspiration For Technological Advance?

What inspires advances in technology? What impulses work to find applications for new discoveries and machines and to drive human progress and advancements in productivity? These questions are fodder for a long philosophical discussion that is beyond the scope of this book. Countless books attempt to deal with this set of questions. Most of them try to find answers without an appeal to the spiritual realm, seeking all causes and effects in natural, materialistic terms.

Of course, the Judeo-Christian perspective does not agree with the view that human history is pre-programmed into the physical order of the world. Something other than naturalistic forces shapes our choices and destiny. We make moral choices whether or not we believe in a morality of right and wrong. Our inspirations and choices are an intermediary to the spiritual and physical worlds. In that context, we must ask again what impulses drive the advances in science and technology? Are they malevolent or benevolent? What is the source of our inspirations that impact the material world? The answers will vary for different discoveries and inventions. For example, most major advances in medicine were arguably motivated out of a compassion to alleviate human suffering.[2] The impulses lying behind other inventions are surely more complex.

Today's "high tech" industry provides an illustrative case study for these questions. Its example directly pertains to our examination of SCITE. It is an industry that has been abuzz with excitement, centering its focus upon communications and information technology. The trade conventions of these industries are swamped with delegates. For example, in recent years the annual Telecom shows in Geneva, Switzerland have been swamped with more than 200,000 delegates, snarling up traffic and hotel bookings for miles around the city. During its heyday, COMDEX, the trade convention for the computer and software industry held annually in Las Vegas attracted more than 600,000 visitors. It is obvious that technology has the world aflutter, generating epochal enthusiasm. But what is the inspiration behind all this frenetic activity? We already know that technology is neither good nor evil, yet, which master — God or Mammon — demands such motivation? Could there be a lurking malevolence behind the world's high-tech push, or is most invention fathered by divine providence?

Forces For Good Not The Main Driver Of Technology

Which force is most interested in the advantages of new technology — good or evil? It is a debate that we will not be able to resolve within the constraints of this book. What we can say with some certainty is that the Great Commission God has set before the Church is not the prime mover behind technological advancements. Of course, the Church can hardly be expected to be a major financier of developmental research in the area of telecommunications and information technology. The profit-motive operating in the "free-market" world takes most of the credit for shepherding the world's advances in these areas. Yet, this profit motive can only be satisfied if there can be found marketable applications and sufficient customers for a new technology. With no potential customers, any application of science will be consigned to the "uneconomic" dust heap. But can the Church — charged with world evangelism — at least be counted as one of the major, cutting-edge consumers of any of the new technological advancements that are necessary to preach the Gospel into the four corners of the world?

Sadly, for the most part, the answer is largely no. Yes, there are many Christian organizations that have harnessed the power of radio and satellite and are effectively disseminating the Gospel to the world. While that is true, it has really been other impulses that have first pushed the frontiers of technology. "The two contents that drive technology are warfare and sex. And sex generates the revenues,"[3] says one enthusiastic industry participant. Perhaps unwittingly choosing these two words, this observer pointed to at least two of the lustful weaknesses of mankind — craving and the lust of the eyes.

Technology And Sin: Good Bed Partners

Examining the question of what demands are driving technological advancements, the *Economist* magazine opined, "The main early use of many kinds of electronic communications is to let men watch and talk to naked women. It may, in the end, lead to better things."[4] It is even a view shared by the telephone industry, according to comments from the International Telecommunications Union (ITU).[5] We learn that many of the main innovations in communications are first tried out — sometimes even developed — by the pornography industry. When videocassette players were first introduced in the late 70's, over 75% of all video tapes sold were placed in the category of adult entertainment.[6] In the case of each of the succeeding communications and entertainment formats, the pornography industry was always its earliest customer, thus providing the revenue base for its further development. This holds true for DVD (digital video disks) as well as the many technologies that have served to increase the speed and bandwidth of the Internet. The business of sex is so profitable that it is able to pay the high service costs of new technologies in their early stages of development.

Other cravings have augmented the appetite for faster Internet services as well. In recent years, greed has added its stimulus. On-line gambling and e-trading of financial securities has boomed. Industries catering to sex and greed are still among the most profitable money-makers on the Web.

What can we conclude from these examples without making unjustified generalizations? It is safe to say that the development of world-wide communication systems and the condition of global connectedness has had an inordinate push by playing on human weaknesses of lust, greed and "couch potato" leisure. Was this accidental? Do we see the imprint of a sinister architect working behind the scenes? The answer to this last question must be yes. Satan's endtime agenda is much too serious that he would allow any human weaknesses to go without advantage as already pointed out. And we seem to be much too unaware of his agenda and the truths of eternal salvation, thereby forfeiting our advantage.

Warfare: Another Primary Driver Of Technological Advance

Seen through the long-term lens of human history, there can be no doubt that defense and warfare have been primary incubators of technology. The superiority of a nation's armies has always been determined by the state of its technology. It is this connection that allowed us to deduce that the god of fortresses (SCITE) could represent the modern-day faith in science and technology in the first place.

In recent decades, America reigns supreme in the technologies of warfare and defense. Just as the iron broadsword won over bronze rapiers, smart missiles and superior surveillance systems set the balance of power today. The constant press for world superiority — the quest to satiate the lust of the eyes and boasting — has focused the human mind to push the frontier of science. One illustration of these motives at work is the American Space Program, funded through the National Aeronautical and Space Agency (NASA). Born out of an arms race with the Soviet Union, this agency has contributed to the development of countless thousands of inventions that have found application in virtually every industry and household.

Dangerous Technology In The Hands Of The Enemy

Having briefly surveyed the major drivers of modern technology — sex, greed and warfare — we can identify Satan as both an opportunist and a motivator. He has much to gain from the advancement of technology and science. Not only do they empower SCITE, enticing the world to worship him, the many applications of new technology serve as useful tools. For one, it has helped achieve the construction of a global telecommunications network that affords him simultaneous access to the entire world. It's the next best thing to omnipresence. Information technologies — database management, electronic storage, surveillance systems and the like — are the closest things to omniscience. Furthermore, communications technology also provides Satan with the means to jam our minds with useless information and a surfeit of worldly entertainment, robbing much of humanity of its thinking skills and abilities to discern. It is definitely part of his masterful strategy to prey on the lusts of humans to advance his endtime telecommunications and information capabilities as well as to magnify SCITE.

Many Other Endtime Applications Of Technology

Many other applications of modern technology serve the cause of the great endtime trap that we must not overlook. Importantly, technology has allowed mankind to bridge the language barrier. Not since the Tower of Babel have all the different races, nations and people of the world been able to so effortlessly converse. Video images have partly replaced the roles of the spoken and written word. Even more convergence lies ahead. The International Telecommunications Union (ITU) has sponsored a voice-activated language translation technology. Soon, we will all be able to speak through our telephones in our own language, to be heard almost instantaneously in the language of the person on the other end.

As well, the role of money and its businesses has been greatly transformed. New forms of currency have emerged in recent history. Paper and metal money have long ago been consigned to the role of petty cash. Most money is now held in the form of book entries and electronic memories. Global payment systems now exist that can send money streaming around the world in a matter of seconds. As we discovered in a previous chapter, the majority of the world's wealth is now represented by financial claims of debt and ownership. In the process, the wealth of the world and the labors of its people have become much more transferable and tradable. The prices of financial wealth are continuously quoted. The value of other types of wealth such as real estate, art, antiques and baseball cards are regularly surveyed and catalogued. The rise and fall in the value of wealth in all of its forms are constantly before us. Every up and down in the price of every significant storehouse of wealth is knowable in real time or just a keystroke away. Our hearts are involved every time a stock market index records a major up or down move. Either we experience palpitations of fear on the downside, or skipped beats of joy on the upside. All of these developments would not have been possible without advances in technology. All of them are integral to the successful execution of an *Endtime Money Snare*.

The Three Gods: All For One And One For All

Having understood the important role of technology in creating the prophesied conditions of the endtime, is it not coincidental that MOFI, the god of monetary finance, has had a hand in promoting the same agenda in more ways than one. Every one of the great new technological advancements the world has experienced has been celebrated and financed with huge stock market gains. At the outset of each new major invention — from the railroad, telephones, the automobile, the microchip and now the Internet — the related stock market boom has infected virtually the entire world with giddiness and euphoria. This boom has in turn triggered a further explosion of competitors and further technological developments. Yet, in the end, these booms always collapse. Most investors lose most of their investment; sometimes they lose everything. What remains are a few strong companies that survive, and an elevated state of technological know how — a twig pushed up higher on the shore line. The vast financial wealth that initially erupted has mostly disappeared; however, the technological capability of the world does not reverse.

Seeing this ratchet-like process of advance at work, the role of greed can hardly be as happenstance. The love of money is readily invoked whenever it is required to push along the necessary developments for the final and great endtime trap that Satan seeks to orchestrate. As we already learned, the love of money inspires and serves to the advantage of all three of the endtime false gods.

The Spiritual Seductions Of SCITE

The successful advance of technology has opened mankind up to tremendous spiritual seduction, both subtle and direct, even though science is not evil in and of itself. Hardly anyone reading this book will not have succumbed to its comfortable inventions in one way or another. Some will have swallowed the whole hook, line and sinker, flatly rejecting the existence of God. Instead, these people would rather place their full faith in the present and future promises of technology and the intelligence of the human brain. Though this group is rapidly increasing in size over past decades, they are still small in number. Most of us would reject their conclusion as being much too extreme and stark. It's too obviously wrong. For that reason, SCITE's subtle seductions are much more dangerous. We are not aware of them, as these seductions do not confront us in terms of black and white trade-offs. They stake their advance in tiny steps of convenience and novelty. Though consciously we still believe in God's existence, He has become very small subconsciously. We have allowed our faith in technology to whittle Him down. Now God is only the weatherman or the God of random chance. We need to better understand how the advances of technology impact our faith.

Personal Application: Guidelines On How Christians And Technology Can Co-Exist

Is high-tech really the answer to the world's deep ills? No doubt, new conveniences and improvements in human living conditions that are attributable to our mastery of the sciences are obviously welcome. Few would disagree that advances, particularly in the field of medical science, have done much good for humanity. But not every new invention is applied to improve mankind's condition.

Looked at simplistically, the advance of science and technology touches each of us in at least five different areas:

1. Health: Improving physical living conditions and longevity, reducing suffering and disability.

2. Material: Raising the potential for material wealth. Lessening physical labor.

3. Mind: Occupying a wider bandwidth of our minds with more information and entertainment options.

4. Network: Increase the connection of our personal lives with the values of the world, pulling us into the global vortex of convergence, centralization and mass distribution.

5. Spiritual: Influencing the affections of our souls and faith.

Though representing different channels, they pose the same proposal to our souls: To trade a higher vulnerability to worldliness for new convenience; to opt for increased exposure to a godless world in return for higher material comfort. All that is fine and good if we commit to a higher discipline of spiritual separation from the world or an elevated watchfulness over the affections of our heart.

We must see that all the pleasures and conveniences offered by new technology come attached with a price tag. In some ways, high-tech is no exception to the adage, "There's no free lunch." Every improvement comes with a new vulnerability in spiritual terms.

As I've explained, an endtime trap would not be possible without SCITE. He is the "god of fortresses" which Daniel warned us about. He is definitely a member of the unholy triad.

The Bible says that God is our only true Fortress. There can be no other fortress we can safely depend upon. In this endtime world, where the forces of evil are rapidly trapping humanity through the lure of the false gods of MOFI, SCITE and GLOBO, we need to rely upon Him more than ever. These false gods are tyrants that have little tolerance for those of us who will not worship them. Though they campaign in the name of "freedom," "choice," and "personal empowerment," they are really slave masters, captors and dictators.

Of course we can benefit from science and technology, but we don't have to transform them into a SCITE that demands our worship. In order to do so, we must constantly fend off subtle inroads into our minds. We must be resolute, living disciplined and Spirit-led lives, willing to sacrifice anything in order to ensure that our affections remain upon the true Fortress, the God of the Bible.

ENDNOTES

1.   Merrill Lynch ad, *Forbes* magazine, 1999.

2.   Today, the profit motive cannot be underestimated in the world's pharmaceuticals industry. Almost all drug research today caters to wants of the developed countries—weight loss, and mood control drugs perhaps being among the more frivolous examples. The pharmaceutical needs of a majority of the world's population living in the developing world are largely overlooked. There

aren't enough well-heeled consumers in these countries to make this a lucrative business prospect. The World Health Organization reports that less than 5% of all research of the world's pharmaceuticals business is directed to tropical diseases. Not a single new drug has been developed in this category since the 1950s, though the needs are enormous.

3.   Mr. Dan Guess, head of Virtual Dreams, a video-conferencing service provider, quoted in the *Economist* magazine.

4.   The *Economist*, January 4, 1997, An adult affair.

5.   Ibid. The *Economist* quotes the ITU as saying, "Telephone sex may be good for development."

6.   Even today, video cassettes of this type still account for approximately 25% of the dollar value of total sales and rentals in America. Source: Adult Video News, the *Economist*.

CHAPTER 11

GLOBO: The Foreign God

Security in Global Oneness

Listen to what the New Age prophets say about the present and future power of GLOBO. There is no shortage of fawning words for him. To recall, according to Daniel, GLOBO, the "foreign god," would be the most powerful of the three endtime gods. In the view of modern-day seers, he is a great and munificent force that will bring much blessing to the endtime world. But a little warning when reading the following tributes: These seers speak with words of high learning and many syllables. The buzz word factor is high. As a quick deciphering aid, make the following word substitutions: GLOBO for the words "globalization" and "global"; MOFI for "capitalism," "finance," or "economics"; GREED for "market forces," "free-market," and "self-interest"; and TRUTH for the words "good" or "prosperity." In doing so, the spirit behind these quotes will become much clearer.

"By interweaving owners, producers, consumers, and

savers of nations all around the globe into a single fabric, the globalization of finance [GLOBO and MOFI], has a shot at achieving what dreamers have long ago envisioned: peace based on mutual economic self-interest [GREED]."[1]

"Global capitalism [GLOBO and MOFI], is being unleashed with an intensity and scale we have not witnessed before in economic history, in a world where national governments are becoming progressively less able to protect businesses, investors, and individuals from rapidly evolving market forces [GREED]. We are moving toward a world where the capital markets [GLOBO and MOFI], constrain what governments can do — not the other way around. In this environment, government policy is influenced [...] by whether or not it makes economic sense [favoring GREED]. Bad policies will carry real penalties, and good policies [TRUTH], will be quickly rewarded."[2]

"The driving idea behind globalization [GLOBO], is free-market capitalism [GREED]. The more you let market forces [GREED], rule and the more you open your economy to free trade and competition [GLOBO], the more efficient and flourishing your economy will be. Globalization [GLOBO], means the spread of free-market capitalism [GREED and MOFI], to virtually every country in the world."[3]

"The spread of free markets [GREED], and democracy around the world is permitting more people everywhere to turn their aspirations into achievements. And technology [SCITE], properly harnessed and liberally distributed, has the power to erase not just geographical borders but also human ones."[4]

"A 'New Global Age' [GLOBO, SCITE and MOFI], is now taking shape, where all countries can be active players, where people currently trapped in poverty can aspire to much better levels of material well-being."[5]

There is no end to the supporting praises and promises of the world's new global god. I could cite many more of GLOBO's apostles, but by now you will have already gained a sense of their frame of reference.

Globalism Has A Huge Fan Club

The terms "globalization" or "globalism" are used often in today's vernacular. They urgently require our examination. Why? The pace of globalization has picked up these past few decades as never before in human history. The wave of changes that globalization has fostered has had enormous implications for each and every one of us — our families, incomes, investments, jobs and values. Yet, not many understand the nature of this world-changing power—the great emerging clout of GLOBO. We will see just how fast both North America and the world are being engulfed by this endtime phenomenon. In fact, while we are asking these very questions, the world is being relentlessly reordered and proselytized by this endtime god more quickly and completely than ever before.

The Foreign God — GLOBO: Who Cares?

One of the reasons the workings of globalization are largely invisible to most individuals is that remarkably few people read the international news. Fewer still are exposed to the ideas and philosophies promulgated by large transnational organizations such as the World Bank, the World Trade Organization and the interests of large multinational corporations and their major investors. Who has time to examine such things when you consider the harried lifestyles most of us live in order to support our households and Western-style comforts? Not many. Admittedly, it is even difficult for those of us who have dedicated a bulk of our time to keep track of all the developments that impinge upon globalization. After all, our era is an age of great deception and much misinformation. Powers and agendas are not always as they seem, and the information highway is jammed with enormous clogs of trivial information.

Even so, there exists a disturbing paradox. On one hand we see that we live in an era marked by more change and prophetic fulfillment than ever before in human history yet, the interest of the mass audience (in America and other countries) in events beyond their borders is declining. While we see more global change underway with the power to dramatically affect each of our lives and households, at the same time there is less interest in knowing. According to the Tyndall Report, foreign news coverage in nightly newscasts declined by as much as one half to two-thirds at the major US networks between 1989 and 1996. This is alarming. Not surprisingly, globalism has made remarkable advances precisely during the very same period that the North American public began tuning out.

Where Does The Strength Of Globalism Lie?

It is important to recognize the objective behind globalism. In one sense, the process of globalization is a pervasive multi-headed juggernaut enveloping the world by leaps and bounds, affecting virtually every area of human endeavor (for both good and bad). It is so broad that it would literally take volumes to document. Yet, at its very essence, it can be reduced to a single impulse...a simple end-point objective: A world system in which all individual and collective actions are governed through the incentive of wealth and prosperity.

Globalization...a race to a state of world affairs in which as much human activity as possible comes under the thumb screws of a unified monetary/economic system. Boiled down to its very core, the driving motivation is nothing other than materialism and humanism on a global scale...both of which preclude any role for God. Simply put, it's a world-wide religious convergence to materialism.

The Real Conspiracy Theory

Some aspects of globalization have been popularized by names such as "One World Order," "New World Order" (NWO), "New Wave Economics," etc. Some writers even suggest that a group of people in high places is conspiring together to bring the world under its control down through time.[6] Generally, I don't ascribe to the view of a grand human conspiracy that has been handed down through the ranks of successive generations over many centuries. Yes, I do believe that many people have been conscripted into Satan's grand endtime agenda, both willingly and unwittingly. Since he has an earthly presence that spans thousands of years, he is able to weave his plan through these many human generations under the cover of time. Like a continental drift, the natural eye of just one human lifetime is not long enough to document this slow-moving phenomenon. Only in our generation has the pace of Satan's agenda quickened. The stealthy, careful stalking of this roaring lion has finally given way to a brazen, final pounce.

Globalism Becomes A World Bully

I don't believe its too harsh to say that globalization is a tyrannical force. It truly is rapacious and brutal in nature, and there are several reasons why. First, GLOBO is in the service of money. To serve money one must first accept the notion that wealth and material prosperity is the ultimate goal of human existence. The Bible says: *"People who want to get rich fall into temptation and a trap and into many foolish and harmful desires that plunge men into ruin and destruction"* (1st Timothy 6:9). It follows then that globalization will ultimately prove to be "destructive."

Second, global financial markets now command the ability to either bless with prosperity, or punish with economic hardship. This holds true for both individuals and nation states. Daniel 11:39 says that the ruler of the last days *"...will attack the mightiest fortresses with the help of a foreign god."* We learned that even the ramparts of the mightiest countries would be broken down by this foreign god. Countries not conforming to the policies prescribed by various transnational organizations, governments or think-tanks that speak for the world's New Economic Order will get pummeled into submission very quickly (I will explain how this happens). Even the United States' sovereignty, the largest nation and economy in the world, can be easily threatened. In fact, I believer it has already happened. The truth be known, America and its Anglo-Saxon siblings — Britain, Canada and Australia — also serve as a harbor for much of GLOBO's assault machinery and its many promoters.

The Battery Machinery Of Globalism At Work

Do the claimed powers of GLOBO sound intimidating? They should. Globalization running free can be brutal. But where does its awesome disciplinarian power come from? Let me illustrate with a few examples:

To begin, it is helpful to understand another aspect of how powerful money has become in recent decades as far as ruling world affairs is concerned. We live in the age of global capital. The flow of money around the world — across borders, within countries, and circulating outside any country's jurisdiction — has virtually exploded in the space of several decades. An earlier chapter on the god of MOFI already described how the machinery of money and financial economics works. Total financial capital in the world — the kind of wealth that can be traded and moved quickly — may currently approach the $100 trillion mark. As a rough estimate, that's 6–7 times greater than in 1980.[7] Money does grow on trees in the age of global capital. This financial wealth towers above the world of commerce, now almost three times as large as the entire size of the world's annual economy. Not only has the volume of financial capital increased substantially, so has its movement and activity. For example, the value of foreign currency exchange — the trading of one currency for another country's money — has risen by more than 50 times — yes, 50 times! — over the past twenty years.[8] The buying and selling of common stocks of other countries by foreign investors has boomed by a factor of 30 times over the same period.[9] I can cite many more statistics. It all amounts to a tidal wave of frenetic money rolling around the world looking for gain and fortune.

All of these transactions involve the profit motive in some way or another. A wolf pack of carnivorous money is on the global hunt for profit and increase. You can be sure that none of this mobile money is seeking loss or financial collapse. Viewed as a whole, you can sense how enormous the role of global money has become in the world today.

Testimony Of GLOBO's Recent Sovereign Casualties

Suppose that a certain country is not following the prescriptions of the global policy-making bodies. Let's assume further that this country continues to pursue some activity that doesn't meet the prosperity doctrines of the various transnational organizations — what has come to be called the "Washington consensus"[10] — or the captains of money. It may be that this country continues to limit foreign investment in some of its domestic industries such as banking or communications. Or, it suggests that it might tax or limit the flow of investor's money into its financial markets. It could be any number of policies that go against the grain of financial and economic liberalization — free market economics. Liberalization in this sense means permissiveness in consorting with GLOBO and MOFI. Woe to this country if it ever allows itself to become vulnerable. If it does, it won't be too long before its currency and securities markets get smashed. The United States will be no exception. Ultimately, when it is convenient, the three false gods will be mobilized against this country as well.

The collapse of many Asian markets in the late 1990s is a good case in point. A number of Asian countries became vulnerable to foreign financiers and investors. All of them were fairly dependent upon exports to the US and other industrial countries. The most vulnerable among these were Thailand, Indonesia, Malaysia and South Korea. These countries allowed their foreign debts and trade deficits to become too large. When investors sensed that the situation was becoming unsustainable, though these very same investors and financiers contributed to some of these problems in the first place, they began running for the exits. A global panic ensued before long.

Once a decline begins, global portfolio investors quickly head for the escape doors. Most of this footloose investment capital is managed by professional portfolio managers who commandeer billions of dollars of other people's money — primarily mutual and pension funds. Since these managers compete with each other to achieve the best investment returns, they cannot afford to be the last investor out the door. Victory in their business usually goes to the quickest. When the exodus begins, it rapidly builds momentum as investors race to avoid further declines. A massive destruction of wealth strikes the country. Its currency collapses, as do its stock and bond markets. As a result, the central bank of such a country must sharply raise interest rates in order to discourage investors from selling its currency. In turn, these higher interest rates begin to cripple the economy. The damage that ensues from these economic and financial declines quickly cascade into the banking system, undermining credit quality and locking up the credit system by destroying the value of the loans owned by lenders. The destruction is enormous. Millions of unsuspecting people lose their jobs, face bankruptcy, or perhaps lose their homes. Food shortages were the result in Indonesia's case. Some of these countries experienced collapses in their stock markets on the order of almost 90% in US dollar terms—virtually overnight. What to do?

Do what transnational organizations and the "Washington consensus" prescribe. These organizations are called to bail these countries out by offering to extend credit and support. As soon as they do, investors begin to regain their confidence. The collapse of financial markets is then stopped.

Help Does Not Come Without Strings Attached

Assistance from the International Monetary Fund and other organizations do not come without conditions. The countries borrowing the money must agree to certain "reforms." The changes forced upon countries in this way almost always lead in the direction of further globalization and financial and economic liberalization. This means that the country must open up its financial system and economy to the rest of the world even more. Some of the prescribed changes are good; some are not. For example, measures to curb corruption are good. But by far, most changes promote the free reign of GLOBO and his cohorts — MOFI and SCITE. In the end, foreigners are usually allowed greater participation and are freed from some of the previous restrictions that might have existed. Big multinational corporations (MNCs) and other astute investors then swoop in and buy up strategic companies and industry positions at bargain basement prices in these crisis countries. The MNCs become bigger and more global. The effect upon a country is a loss of control of its financial policies and its monetary systems. In today's world, that means a loss of sovereignty. What then becomes sovereign? The collective greed represented by nameless global capital. So we see that tidal waves of international money, governed by a small band of players, can quickly bludgeon countries into subservience to the demands of the reigning commercial colossus spanning the globe.

Globalism Has Invoked Greed And Fear To Further Its Advance

Once a country has totally given itself over to the world's emerging money system as an open participant, its own political affairs eventually come under global dominance. Don't believe it? The election results of most countries in recent years closely follow this theory. If any political party appears to favor policies seen as potentially harmful to the value of its financial markets, stock and bond markets sell off sharply and quickly. Voters with savings and retirement nest eggs invested in financial markets — stocks and bonds — quickly get the message to "vote their pocket." Here we have a glimpse of one aspect of the *Endtime Money Snare* at work.

Such forces of persuasion were evident when European countries decided their policies with respect to EMU (European Monetary Union). At the slightest indication that any of the participating countries were drifting away from this goal, its stock, bond and currency market would promptly react on the downside. Global capital — the big agent of globalism itself — was there in full force, pushing toward world unity and the ultimate goals of an *Endtime Money Snare.*

Invariably, the disciplinary actions of GLOBO tend to open access and control to certain strategic industries. They always include the financial services and telecommunications sectors, key industries in helping the advancement of globalism, a connection we made in the chapter discussing SCITE (science and technology). The success of this diabolical strategy ultimately depends on the control of these sectors for most, if not the entire world. An integrated, worldwide financial/economic system is essential to control the actions of humanity. A worldwide communications industry, devoid of censorship and local control is also necessary. It is useful to communicate with all the citizens of the world, to promote the values of humanism and materialism, and to amuse and senselessly preoccupy. The Spirit of God is omnipresent; Satan and his hordes are not. Therefore, a globally coordinated communications industry — whether by global regulation or common ownership — is a necessity as we concluded in the previous chapter.

An Awakening Required Of Christians

There is a dire need to alert Christians to understand this global age and be able to discern the direction of the changes hurtling the world to its prophetic destiny. Rather than be unknowing pawns of this global advancement of a new materialistic order — perhaps even instruments or unwitting victims — Christians should at least be knowledgeable and informed. Unfortunately, many are not.

Why are so many individuals not aware? Deception and distraction. Mainly it works like this: Two sets of scenes are playing out on the world stage, each involving different plots and groups of actors. One show is very visible. It is billed with a bright neon marquee and broadcasted for wide public consumption. Its players and audiences are the world of uninformed citizens, investors and newsreaders, mesmerized by the apparent disorder of financial markets and world affairs. The media seizes upon any potential news event, spinning them into sound bites and items of temporal entertainment. The acts of this play take place over shorter timeframes and are complicated by many side plots. Observed from a position close to the stage, the plot seems random and unpredictable. The audience responds with reflexive and mindless emotions. It all serves as a distraction to the real agendas behind history.

A very different show is playing on a much larger stage. It unfolds behind a smoke screen of chaos and dense confusion of the highly publicized "public" play. The plot of this second theatre is an epic one, advancing much more slowly and stealthily, spanning lifetimes. Fickle human emotions and the disinterest of the masses supply the dry ice for this stage's fog machines. National and world crisis serves as the inflection points for change. It is a great agenda orchestrated by the god of this age, the spirit of the Antichrist who seeks to misdirect the worship of humanity and ensnare them into complicity.

Financial markets have increasingly captured the attention of many people. Volatile stock and bond markets have preoccupied emotions and hopes, distracted and jammed discernment. In the meantime, incredible and crucial changes have been taking place in the world order.

Is A One-World Monetary System Necessary?

What about the advancement of a unified world monetary system? The many financial disasters of the past 10 years — more than 125 nations have suffered some kind of financial crisis during this period — have wreaked havoc with the currencies of many countries. The crashing waves of "hot money" capital have already had a notable impact in shifting opinion on this question. Michael Howell, an influential global strategist (Crossborder Capital) comments: "...national currencies have become a luxury that few countries can afford." As a result, he sees the world quickly moving into three main money blocs, the yen (most of Asia), the U.S. dollar, and the euro. Countries facing the brunt of GLOBO's attacks are thinking hard about quickly linking to one of the main currency blocs. Russia may think it needs to be freed from the shackle of its volatile currency (the ruble). Why not link to the euro? In Brazil's case of repeated suffering from sky-high interest rates, some argue in favor of "dollarizing" its economy. They may eventually choose to dump the "real" (the Brazilian currency), and adapt the dollar. Quoting the secular opinion of Michael Howell further: "National currencies are the antithesis of global capital markets [GLOBO and MOFI]. Governments should not try to slow down the inevitable globalization. Each emerging market [small country or economy] must choose one bloc to join." What is he saying? Give in to GLOBO's power; it's pointless to resist.

Will Globalization See A Reversal In The Future?

Surely all trends must face a reversal at some point. Will the dramatic market events of past years trigger a backlash against globalization, the brutal tyrant that enforces compliance to the New World Economic and Financial Order? Yes, it's possible that financial events could careen out of control, providing fuel for a reversal of the globalization trends ... at least for a time. Many knowledgeable observers are worrying that this might happen in various forms — a return to trade protectionism, independent capital controls, a breakdown in global financial cooperation, etc. Demonstrations against globalization have become much more violent and organized in recent years.

Then again, when a major world financial crisis occurs, it could be used as an argument for even greater global institutions with even more power. Many committees and task forces have been formed in recent years to consider solutions of this type should another big crisis occur. Whatever the case, sooner or later the longer-running trend will likely continue toward more centralization and financial control of the world. Why? Because that is what the world will choose. The world loves money and wealth whether it is fabricated or real. That's the bait — the very essence of the *Endtime Money Snare*. The love of money is at its root. It is a trend that caters to, and is a symptom of, a world increasingly focused on a material heaven here on earth.

William Greider eloquently sums up the emotional pulls of globalization on the human spirit in the closing comments of his book, *One World, Ready or Not:*

> "The utopian vision of the marketplace offers, after all, an enthralling religion, a self-satisfied belief system that attracts fervent and influential adherents. The wondrous machine of free-running enterprise has fantastic capabilities and people defer to its powers, persuaded it will carry them forward to millennial outcomes. Abstracted from human reality, the market's intricate mechanisms convey an entrancing sense of perfection, logical and self-correcting. Many intelligent people have come to worship these market principles, like a spiritu-

al code that will resolve all the larger questions for us, social and moral and otherwise, so long as no one interferes with its authority. In this modern secular age, many who think of themselves as rational and urbane have put their faith in this idea of the self regulating market as piously as others put their trust in God."[11]

A great economic/monetary colossus — very probably represented by Babylon the Great of Revelation 18 that captures and lures the kings and people of the world — is presently enveloping the world. MOFI, SCITE and GLOBO are its three patron saints. People worship them as the givers of prosperity and perpetual security. In this sense a new religion is sweeping the world, gaining billions of converts. Globalization is the supposed benevolent process that brings unity to the world in its perverse quest for prosperity and wealth.

A Challenge To Christians — Come Out And Be Separate

A world given over to the worship of three false gods — MOFI, SCITE and GLOBO — will become increasingly inhospitable to those who trust in God. As a global commercial/monetary colossus increases its grip on the world, overcoming Christians stand to become marginalized. How can we find an escape from this endtime money machine in heart and spirit? I believe it is possible. However, it will require some sacrifices. But be warned: Spiritual escape may possible, but not without physical consequences.

The good news is this: No sacrifice for Christ will ever go unrewarded. Those who choose to put their faith and hope in God stand to become even richer if they perseverate. They will be rewarded with great heavenly riches that will last for an eternity for their troubles: *"These have come so that your faith — of greater worth than gold, which perishes even though refined by fire — may be proved genuine and may result in praise, glory and honor when Jesus Christ is revealed"* (1st Peter 1:7).

ENDNOTES

1.   Guthrie McTigue Ellen Leander and Iain Jenkins in a *Global Finance* magazine article entitled, "The Globalization of Finance, Why You Need to be Plugged in," November 1995.

2.   *Market Unbound,* Lowell Bryan & Diana Farrell, John Wiley & Sons Inc., 1996, Pg.3.

3.   Thomas L. Friedman, "A Manifesto for a Fast World," *The New York Times Magazine*, March 28, 1999.

4.   Merrill Lynch advertisement, *Foreign Review*, 1998.

5.   Organization for Economic Cooperation and Development, *Towards a New Global Age,* 1998.

6.   Some writers make the case that certain groups have conspired to bring the world under their dominion, some of them apparently existing from several centuries. The Illuminati, The Group, Bilderbergers, and the "International Bankers" are some of the terms used to name these groups. While groups of people indeed can, and do, form conspiracies from time to time, the idea that a malevolent group of human beings have been able to consistently control world events down through the ages seems unlikely. The Bible supports the view that a conspiracy is indeed underway — one coordinated and promoted by the spirit of the Antichrist. It is this spirit that provides the common motivational thread to all actions — whether by groups or individuals — that deny the sovereignty and worship of the one and only God.

7.   I have compiled this estimate from various sources including the World Bank, the Bank of International Settlements, Morgan Stanley Dean Witter, In-

ternational Finance Corporation, The Bond Market Association.

8. Bank of International Settlements, various publications.

9. The International Finance Corporation, a subsidiary of the World Bank.

10. The "Washington Consensus" represents a group of organizations and economists that prescribe similar economic liberalization policies. It was a term coined by British economist John Williamson in 1989 to describe the similar policy reforms of these organizations. Chief among these are the World Bank and the International Monetary Fund. The headquarters of both are located in Washington, D.C.

11. Greider, William, *One World, Ready or Not: The Manic Logic of Global Capitalism,* Simon & Shuster, 1997.

CHAPTER 12

A Global Press Release

Pipers of Self-Interest

We have now gained a perspective on the main forces leading to an emerging *Endtime Money Snare*. We hopefully better understand the role of numbers and how human existence has become so intensely "financialized." The advances in technology, globalism and monetary finance are all venerated and worshipped because they give life to an enormous world trade and monetary system which in turn underpins a booming pile of wealth. However, to this point we have not focused very much on people. Albert and Alice Hope are drawn to the stock and bond markets because they have been led to believe that these might bless them with a comfortable retirement. The Hopes have really not done any critical analysis of Mr. Guinn's promises and claims. Actually, they want to believe. They want to enjoy the same lifestyle as their friends, the Gowiths. But in reality, the Hopes are really not well equipped to test Mr. Guinn's claims. Besides perhaps being carried away with a little fanciful coveting, they cannot be faulted very much. After all, they are not among the key players who have access to the frontiers of the world financial and economic developments. And, in any case, where would they get the reliable information and perspectives? From the newspapers or the evening news? The din of world events is so loud, so confusing, even deliberately misleading. It is reminiscent of the condition portrayed in Psalm 82:4–5: *"Rescue the weak and needy; deliver them from the hand of the wicked. They know nothing, they understand nothing. They walk about in darkness; all the foundations of the earth are shaken."*

It is confusing for a reason.

Scanning The World News And Developments: A Daunting Exercise

Let's log-in for a news break. Listen to the jungle drums of the modern-day world for a moment. The summary captions of our news service scrolls down the page below:

New Global Order Requested. Developing countries of the world, arguing that they risk being excluded from the benefits of an increasingly globalized world economy, have called for a "new global human order" to close the gap between rich and poor. Leaders and delegates of the 133-member states of the group of 77 in the "south summit meeting" here in Havana agreed to a declaration demanding a fairer deal of developing countries in world trade, and greater participation in international economic decision-making.

–*Financial Times,* Havana, 15 April 2000

New Rival Net Exchange. Eleven of the world's

leading retailers yesterday banded together to set up a business-to-business on-line exchange in direct competition to the electronic marketplace formed by rivals Carrefour and Sears. The retailers said they would form an open network available to all retailers. The exchange will enable members to buy, sell, trade or auction all types of goods and services over the Internet in a $5 trillion world market.

–Financial Times, 12 April 2000

Pensions for the Poor. Four billion people — 90% of the world's workers — have no pension for their old age, the International Labour Organization said yesterday. Its report on this issue recommended that institutions such as savings clubs, co-operatives and other voluntary bodies should be offered assistance by governments to develop anti-poverty retirement protection schemes.

–Financial Times, 28 April 2000

Battle for World Accounting Turf. A furious political debate — a euphemism for who gets control — rages over international accounting standards between the US Financial Accounting Standards Board (FASB) and the International Accounting Standards Committee (IASC). The World Bank or the International Monetary Fund may yet seek to broker a compromise. An inability to drop vested interests could be disastrous for the accounting profession.

–Financial Times, 8 February 2000

Europe Versus America. At a recent summit meeting of European Union leaders in Lisbon, governments

211

dedicated themselves to transforming the region. Their goal, they said, was nothing less than to make Europe the most "dynamic" place in the world by 2010.

—*The Economist,* 8 April 2000

Asian Nations in Currency Pact. Hoping to decrease their reliance on financial bailouts from Western countries and the International Monetary Fund, Asia's 13 largest economies are forming a unified front to protect each other's currencies from speculators who sparked the 1997 Asian financial meltdown. The 13 nations reached a landmark agreement over the weekend at a meeting of finance officials in Chiang Mai, Thailand.

—*The Globe and Mail,* Hong Kong 8 May 2000

Gold Here to Stay. The World Gold Council, an industry organization of the world's gold producers, is protesting the gold reserve sales of several world banks. The group claims that currency stability of various countries will be undermined.

— www.gold.org — Various press releases

The above news items may read little different from those found in our local newspapers, yet what ties them together is a fast-breaking development that is a mark of the last days.

We see all types of new coalitions and interest groups emerging on the world stage, eager to promote their common self-interests. A confusing maelstrom of organizations, entities, forums, unions, associations, and blocs clamor for the world's attention through its increasingly

internationalized media and telecommunications channels. The silver tongues of public relations consultants,
the spokesmen of political parties and the loaded commercial "sound bite" hurls incessantly upon the consciousness of humanity in a torrential downpour.

Diversity And Randomness Not With Purpose And Design

The prophet Daniel foretold that the endtime kingdom
— the world system of rule during the last days — would
be very different from any that had gone before. It would
be a kingdom like no other. It was to be diverse. Though
its pieces form a whole, they are divisible, not mixing
well. It would be a confusing world. Its form would be a
loose amalgam of clay and iron. Brittle in nature, it would
not bind together very well. It seemed that its people and
organization of power would be a strange hodge-podge of
associations. The sovereign nation, traditionally the main
rule of power and rule down through history, would lose
much of its influence. We learned that the "foreign god"
would be instrumental in breaking down the power of
sovereign nations.

Daniel was confused by his visions of this last day kingdom. Superficially, it didn't represent a recognizable form of
organization to him. The vision appeared to represent one
regime, yet, its elements remained separate. It spoke of turmoil and randomness. But apparent behind it all was order,
the invisible hand of a common motivating power. Can we
who are living today make sense of this world that Daniel
saw? It may be remarkably close to the global order of our day.

213

A World Of Marketers And Pitchmen

As the earlier newscast brought to our attention, the world is full of different groups of people and various kinds of agendas, seemingly acting together yet independent, random yet focused. Christ's comment about the world of His day seems appropriate: *"To what can I compare this generation? They are like children sitting in the marketplaces and calling out to others: We played the flute for you, and you did not dance; we sang a dirge, and you did not mourn"* (Matthew 11: 16-17).

These words provide an accurate picture of our day. Countless entities and groups are calling out to us. We drown in the cacophony of competing interest — mostly self-interest.

Consider All The Groups Playing Flutes And Singing Dirges:

• **Labor unions, domestic and international:** They number in the hundreds of thousands around the world. A key umbrella organization is the International Labor Organization (ILO) based in Geneva, Switzerland. Labor unions are becoming interlinked around the world, often coordinating their union organizing efforts and contract negotiations with multi-national companies.

• **Non-governmental organizations (NGOs):** There are millions of them, both domestic and international, representing thousands of causes and interests from aid, to the environment to human rights. Greenpeace, OXFAM, the Red Cross and Amnesty International are among the larger and better known of these types of organizations.

214

• **Religious non-government organizations (or RIN-GOs)**: These are NGOs with either a religious mission or are affiliated with a certain faith. World Vision and Samaritan's Purse are well-known examples of this type.

• **Intergovernmental agencies:** Among these are included such large international organizations as the World Bank, the International Monetary Fund, the Association of South East Asian Nations (ASEAN). There are literally hundreds of organizations of this type around the world with various objectives, many of them concerned with economic development in low-income countries and funded by governments of the high-income countries.

• **Banking and monetary organizations:** Though they may not be owned by governments, these organizations and institutions are given their power by statute or government decree. Examples of these include most central banks and the Bank of International Settlements (BIS) based in Basel, Switzerland. These organizations concern themselves with the control of money and credit. They also work very closely with many industry associations in the financial services industry. These groups number into the many hundreds.

• **Industry Associations:** These are mostly the lobby groups and self-regulatory organizations of various industries whether domestic or global. Some examples are the World Gold Council (which promotes the uses of gold), the Association of Investment Management Research (AIMR, the umbrella association governing the field of investment research), the Commercial Bankers Association (CBA) and so on. Again, these types of groups number into the tens of thousands around the globe.

• **Multinational companies:** Or MNCs, also known as transnational companies or TNCs. These companies warrant a special category of their own as they have become such a large influence upon the world and probably now represent the biggest power base on the planet. MNCs are companies that have operations in more than one country. It is estimated that there are more than 60,000 MNCs in the world today accounting for as much as 45% of world economic output.

• **World industry cartels and associations:** These are not much different than industry associations except that their aim is to control the prices and production of the product, service or commodity for which they are organized. Examples of these might include the Organization of Petroleum Exporting Countries (OPEC) and the De-Beer's Diamond Exchange.

• **Clandestine terrorists groups and other political extremist organizations that seek to impose their views through violence and coercion:** The Palestinian Liberation Organization or al-Queda are two high-profile examples of these.

We have only scratched the surface of the many types of groups and associations that have been formed to pursue their interest or promote their views. We could include criminal groups such as the Mafia or the Japanese Yakuza, or ideological groups such as the famous Council on Foreign Relations (CFR), the Club of Rome, or just plain political parties and social clubs. The more we list, the more blurred the categories will become. All the same, viewing the many different associations of humankind, one quickly realizes how partisan and full of vested interest the world has become. Our world has become a raucous, competitive arena of self-interest. Of course, many associations are truly altruistic, wanting only to do good for the sake of world improvement. However, such groups as these are in the minority. Without a doubt, the overriding goals and aims of most all of these, the many organizations densely dotting the globe, is the pursuit of economic interest-gaining or preserving money, material gain and prosperity.

A Deep Preoccupation With The Material Emerges

Guilds and associations have probably always existed. In this sense, organized human activities are nothing new. What is interesting is the rapidity with which vested interest and tribalism have erupted upon the world stage in recent decades. It is a fascinating phenomenon of our time. Just reconsider the explosive growth of non-governmental organizations (NGOs). Their number has boomed in recent years as never before. During the past decade, international NGOs have quintupled in number to nearly 30,000 according to the Union of International Associations.[1] That's an amazingly fast trend. These may include associations of a few individuals or large, powerful institutions with hundreds of thousand of members or more and annual budgets of several hundred million dollars. Domestic NGOs have grown even faster. One estimate suggests that there are more than two million in the United

States alone.[2] About 70% of these were formed in the last 30 years. More than 100,000 NGOs have sprung up in Eastern Europe between 1988 and 1995. In Russia, there are now reported to be as many as 65,000 of these groups, whereas there were virtually none before the fall of communism. Many more statistics could be cited in documenting this explosion of human organization. In some countries today both the NGO and non-profit sector is so large that it accounts for as much as 10% or more of total employment.[3]

What's going on? Why this frenetic pace of activity? Ours is a world full of forces and interests competing with each other for influence and power. An MNC may gain an advantage from the government of a country, an international labor union may win a larger pay raise, or a collection of 150 NGOs may disrupt the meetings of the World Trade Organization. Can there be any sense in it all?

For one, this worldwide development of organized interest we have reviewed is very much in character with the world that the prophet Daniel described. The intensity of this condition has developed only recently in human history. Given the theme of this book, the heavy preoccupation with material and money that we discover is more than just of passing interest. It rings in character with the endtime world that the Bible foretells.

The apparent chaos at the surface of world affairs is misleading. There is an unseen hand at work in the background. The confusion at the surface serves as an effective camouflage. Just what force — disciplinary or motivational — serves to hold the competing interests of all the world's organized groups in balance? What is the unseen power of coordination behind this ordered chaos of the endtimes? It may be the common idolatry with money and gain — Mammonism — the very stronghold under the direction of Satan himself.

Tribalism And One-World Order Co-Exist

We have already established that the world is being unified with a set of common values and standards more rapidly than ever before. Yet, having just reviewed all of the potential centrifugal forces of different interests in the world today, we see that mankind remains as tribal and cliquish as ever. How can these two trends exist simultaneously? Isn't there a paradox here?

Actually, tribalism and globalism are very compatible. Both developments are rapidly advancing at the same time. The bargaining arena for modern material man has simply enlarged to a new global stage. The local town crier in the village square has been superseded by the global megaphone and the international cybersquare. New tribes of people have emerged. Color and race have blurred. Though race, ethnicity and religion remain a strong focus of tribal distinctions, now the cause of common economic interest has become just as important if not more so. As familial blood is thicker than water, related monetary interest is now at least as thick. As we concluded earlier, much of the world's explosive growth in tribalism is related to the pursuit of material prosperity.

But isn't globalization all about global world convergence and oneness? Yes, but only in one important sense.

It is the collection of trends and developments that invest greater power and authority in Mammon to control and dictate the course of our lives. Therefore it has do with a convergence in beliefs and values that apply to wealth creation and the pursuit of world prosperity.

Tribalism and globalization work together. Globalization is all about the widening agreement on materialism and the maximization of wealth. Tribalism is all about maximizing one's own share. The former has to do with the size of the world pie; the latter is focused on the size of the slice.

In that regard, globalization is just another unprecedented development of our time. Its pace of advance has been incredible as it seeks to convert and harness the world into a one-world faith of materialism and the veneration of money and wealth. However, globalization is not about merging all of the people of the world into one group, or one world-spanning country, or necessarily under a one-world currency. While these things may happen, it isn't actually necessary. Even though globalization has dramatically accelerated in the past two decades, it is clear that it will not unify the world into one tribe. After all, there are more countries today than ever before, not less. Even though the European Union has taken form in recent years, many other countries have split into two or more entities. Revealingly, world immigration levels remain low. Though financial markets may be globalizing and converging, labor markets are not. Critically, foreign populations remain less than 6% of the domestic population in virtually every major country of the world, its share hardly having risen at all in recent decades. Therefore a global culture of common material values is beginning to exist — one that is made up of local parts and identities.

Who Are The Ten Kings Seen By Daniel?

The ten-horned beast of Daniel 11 and the beast of Revelation 12 with seven heads and ten horns may already exist. Given how different the kingdom of the last days is supposed to be, we may be wrong in assuming that the ten kings[4] of the world represent countries or world regions. They may very well be kings, political leaders or countries. They could just as well be the powerful heads of ten world-spanning multinational corporations (MNCs), non-governmental-organizations (NGOs), industry cartels or any other powerful group. Or, they could be the heads of ten financial regions, much as the world banking system is already organized. Today, we can still only guess at the exact identity of these kings.

Back to our news report. One more press release is scheduled to be sent out shortly:

Today World News Colossus Inc. reports this announcement from the NGO of the kingdom of God. A radiant figure, as bright as molten metal, reportedly to have descended out of the clouds and alighted on Mount Zion said:

Today we announce: *"Turn to me and be saved, all*

you ends of the earth; for I am God, and there is no other. By myself I have sworn, my mouth has uttered in all integrity a word that will not be revoked: Before me every knee will bow; by me every tongue will swear. They will say of me, 'In the LORD alone are righteousness and strength.' " All who have raged against him will come to him and be put to shame. But in the LORD all the descendants of Israel will be found righteous and will exult." [5]

ENDNOTES

1.   A United Nations report on global governance in 1995 suggested that there are nearly 29,000 international NGOs This is a larger number than is estimated by the Union of International Associations.

2.   World Watch Institute An article in *World Watch* magazine, 1999.

3.   According to the Organization for Economic Cooperation and Development (OECD) in 1995, non-profit groups (including NGOs) provided over 12% of all employment in the Netherlands, 8% in the U.S. and 6% in Britain.

4.   *"The ten horns you saw are ten kings who have not yet received a kingdom, but who for one hour will receive authority as kings along with the beast. They have one purpose and will give their power and authority to the beast. They will make war against the Lamb, but the Lamb will overcome them because he is Lord of lords and King of kings—and with him will be his called, chosen and faithful followers"* (Revelation 17:12–14).

5.   Isaiah 45:22-25

CHAPTER 13

Endtime Markets

The Bible on Bubbles

As we saw in the previous chapter, the whole world has mobilized itself into special interest groups. Most of these are concerned with protecting or establishing a claim in a world of booming wealth and commerce. In this context, numbers have a very important function in the satanic endtime conquest of the affections and worship of mankind as we discovered in Chapter 8. They present a common global language and launch point for deception and a global religion of Mammonism. The spirits of human idolatry that give life to MOFI, GLOBO and SCITE play integral and mutually supportive roles in setting the hooks for an *Endtime Money Snare*. Prophetic Scriptures point to the conclusion that the worship of three false gods — the monetary/financial god of prosperity, the foreign god of globalism and the science/technology god — spur mankind toward its destined endtime saga.

But why should money and the financial and commercial systems that it enervates play such a central role in this endtime trap for humanity? Isn't there anything else that might be better suited to serving Satan's intentions? After all, money is an invention. Couldn't something else do the job better?

John Stuart Mill, author of *Principles of Political Economy,* a classic from 1848 wrote, "There cannot be intrinsically a more insignificant thing, in the economy of society, than money [...]. It only exerts a distinctive and independent influence of its own when it gets out of order." He hits on an important point. Money that's out of order has the capability of exerting a great influence on the world. The biblical perspective on this insight is that money "out of order" is the "love of money" allowed to run rampant. Modern-day financial systems in the service of the "love of money" are the only things capable of invading and ensnaring the motives and actions of the entire world. To the globalized earth of the new millennium, an integrated, interconnected financial/ commercial web has become the intermediary of the new common religion of humanity — numbers denominated in currencies. Mammon is its supreme god.

The Vast Domain And Rule Of Money

Consider the reach and power of financial and monetary systems. Today, they represent the interests of virtually every person on earth. Every single monetary unit of value harbored within world financial systems is ultimately underpinned by an owner or debtor of some kind.

The same applies to virtually all real assets and human obligations. In some form, they find a monetary expression. Almost all of this wealth can be traced down to the ownership of people like you and me. My point? To recall, all of us are being increasingly embraced by the financial system in one way or another. Money intersects more than four-fifths of our livelihoods. It no longer serves as a utility. Rather, mankind serves money. All of our labors and activities are encouraged so as to support a mountain of global financial wealth.

Money has even become entertainment. The daily gyrations of stocks and bonds — and anything else that is quotable and tradable — are noted slavishly as a scorecard of worth or as the barometer of truth and human progress. We are even asked to consume things as a patriotic duty. To do so is to buttress and support an over-inflated edifice of shaky financial wealth, the very thing that has become the central altar of mankind's idolatrous faith in Mammonism. More and more people are employed to manage the tangled webs and many layers of financial relationships embedded in our numbered, monetary world. Bit by bit our actions and very lives are being captured in a numerical or financial form of one kind or another. There is hardly any way of escaping its invasive advance.

In a sense, we are all boarded on ships sailing the same financial sea. Storms and tempests will affect the course of all of these vessels to varying degrees. We are increasingly held hostage—trapped by human lusts for gain and wealth with little course of escape.

The Role Of Fear And Greed Sets The Hook

In recent decades, fear and greed have become powerful motivators of economic moods and consumer behavior. This has mainly happened for two reasons. For one, financial market participation by the general public in the western world is now at an all-time high. To recall, it's an integral part of the financialization of humanity that we reviewed in Chapter 9. This is true for the US, Canada, Britain, Australia, Europe and the whole world. Today, the public puts more faith in its mutual and pension funds than it does its banks. Mutual fund assets are near all-time high levels — both in absolute terms and as a proportion of total personal financial assets. The value of pension funds continues to climb to new heights. This whole mass of commingled investment funds — money that is professionally managed on behalf of its ultimate owners in large pools such as pensions and mutual funds — continues to grow rapidly. These assets represent the largest financial sector in the world today, far surpassing the influence of any other group of financial institutions—even the mightiest central banks. The crucial point to realize is that the vast majority of these fund assets are invested in securities markets of one type or another. Total financial instruments in the world are now fifty times larger than just several decades ago. The result of this monetary explosion is that the well-being of North American consumers, as well as of consumers in most countries, depends more upon financial market trends today than ever before. The fortunes of markets have set their hooks ever deeper into the jaws of mankind.

Financial Markets Become A Powerful Influence On People

Just what or who holds the fishing line to all these hooks? The false god of MOFI? But he is only powerful through our worship of gain and money. However, these affections can be played like a fiddle. Securities markets — stocks and bonds, for example — are highly sensitive to swings in economic conditions and human emotions. Since the ownership of financial assets can be transferred almost instantaneously, their prices are continuously open to the fickle expressions of human faith or doubt. Now, with the advent of global financial markets, interlinked exchanges and trading desks around the globe, the prices of securities are open to the voting machine of a large number of potential buyers and sellers 24 hours a day.

Securities markets are also highly prone to manipulation through various means. For example, tiny adjustments in the level of interest rates that are controlled by central banks can work to erase or add many trillions of dollars to people's investment portfolios. Rising and falling financial markets in turn can have a very direct impact upon the spending patterns of consumers and the overall tone of the economy. Interest rates, the little rudder on the boat, can steer a mighty ship of human actions. This is especially true when many of our actions have been schooled and conditioned by greed and a penchant for the easy life. In that regard, our expectations for economies and financial markets trends play a guiding and stimulative role. As such, securities markets are a powerful determinant of human moods and actions. Put another way, they are a highly sensitive barometer and magnifier of human emotions of fear, greed, or their absence.

Nowadays, the sudden report of a news item that is perceived as negative for the value of a financial asset usually triggers a quick decline in its price. Obviously, the opposite is true as well. The anticipation of good news, or the surprise announcement of something that is considered beneficial to the price of a bond, stock or other investments will quickly drive up their value. But the two reactions are not exactly the same. A drop in price has a very different emotional response than does an increase. A price decline implies a potential loss of money. Losses are crushing, a powerful catalyst of fear and anxiety. These trigger adrenaline rushes, setting in motion a self-reinforcing process of fear and price erosion. Therefore, price declines usually occur at twice the speed of increases. Seen this way, fear is the more powerful emotion. On the other hand, greed is more of an intoxicant. Though it's not as raw an emotion as fear, it can still drive people to incredible extremes of irrationality and fantasy.

The Modern Monkey Trap: Our Own Greed

Greed is now firmly institutionalized in our society. It is widely accepted in our society's morality and in its institutions as a common good. To illustrate this point consider the rise of the "star" investment portfolio managers. As a group, these managers are a small, elite band of professionals who control an amazingly large amount of capital in the world today. As one futurist says, they are the new "high priests"[1] of the modern age. They are worshipped as shamans of wealth creation. The fact that a larger amount of capital in the world is being controlled by smaller groups is partially attributable to the rapid growth of the portfolio management industry which employs them. Portfolio managers are paid to be greedy. In fact, they can make enormous amounts of money for themselves finding expert and sophisticated ways of extracting gain from all types of financial markets. Their mission is shaped by a single dimension of raw, brutal greed. They must make the portfolios under their care grow in value at a competitive rate. If they don't, they may lose their job. Therefore, portfolio managers are a very active group of investors, selling and buying multi-millions in securities on the slightest provocation. Their harried and pressured actions can produce wide, exaggerated swings in financial markets because the whole profession basically operates in a "herd" mentality. Though portfolio managers enjoy above-average compensation, they can hardly be credited with independent thinking. Of course there are exceptions. The point is, that as a group they can have an over-sized impact on financial market trends and have the potential of destabilizing the foundations of financial and economic systems.

All of us in the larger society are increasingly vulnerable to their financial influence with little prospect of escape. Yet, it's our own appetite for gain that is really holding us hostage. After all, it's the average saver and investor who is placing the performance pressure on these fund managers. For example, if one mutual fund doesn't perform as well as another, we may be quick to sell it in favor of purchasing another fund with a better investment return record. Usually, not much thought is given to the fact that it is all part of a process to lure mankind into the tentacles of the *Endtime Money Snare*.

Greed has enormously extended its enticement in another significant way. Incentives pervade almost the entire corporate business world. A greater proportion of worker's pay is now variable — in other words, it is dependent upon performance and overall corporate results (bonuses and commissions are some of the forms of variable pay). A fixed-salary or wage may often represent less than half the value of total compensation for many professions. But the most effective device transforming corporate incentive systems is the employee stock option.[2] These confer rights to its holder (the employee or executive) to purchase a company's stock at a fixed price in the future. If the company's share price soars above this level, employees can exercise these options — buying the stock at a favorable price — then pocketing the difference as they sell them in the open marketplace. More than ever before, employees of all kinds are incentivized through their use. Whereas a little more than a decade ago only 12% of the top 500 companies in the US provided these options to their entire workforce, today more than half do so. According to the Internal Revenue Agency, hundreds of billions are earned by employees in this way every year. Virtually all senior executive are incented and muzzled with these compensation carrots—sometimes heavily so. Hundred million dollar plus pay-offs are hardly uncommon. As such, executives will be loathe to do anything — whether right or wrong — to lower the value of these options. Such heavy incentives make falsehood and manipulation very lucrative. Any action that can boost a share price has the potential of a large reward. With such a wide distribution of employee stock options, again we see that emotions of greed and fear are inextricably tied into the financial system for a greater portion of society than ever before.

A Possible Endtime Role Of Securities Markets

Securities markets serve some very important roles in the *Endtime Money Snare*. As already shown, they will (and already do) serve as an enormous motivational net that ensnares humanity to the endtime trinity of false gods by the hooks of the gain and love of money. As such, financial markets act as a high-profile testimony to the effectiveness and pervasiveness of rampant endtime materialism. The more expensive financial assets, the greater the implied faith in their promise of future security. For example, if the stock of a company pays a dividend yield of less than 1%, the investor is obviously staking a great amount of hope and confidence in this company's future prospects. With such little real income in prospect, there then must be great hope that this company will pay much higher income in years to come. That's a logical view. In fact, this type of thinking is actually very sophisticated by the standards of greed evident in the financial world today. These days, not many investors stake their faith on such foundations as the real business prospects of a company such as its earnings outlook, or dividend paying potential. The faith of an investor is more reliant upon the apparent promise of MOFI himself — in the mistaken belief that markets always go up over time no matter what. The implied belief is that MOFI will always deliver prosperity.

But, if financial markets overall display a condition of expensiveness, then it must be true that the greater majority of investors are convinced about the usefulness of these investments as a store of value for their savings. After all, no one would deliberately pay an expensive price for an investment if he didn't think that it would return at least the same value or more at some point in the future. Otherwise, why invest? For that reason, the price of financial markets is an extremely sensitive barometer of the faith put in Mammon.

Since financial market prices remain extremely high in most of the world, the gods of MOFI, GLOBO and SCITE must be held in high repute. It is no accident that the root word of securities is "security." Our level of "security" with securities determines their value. Does that mean that wealth is simply the figment of our values and feelings of security? No.

Real Vs. Fictitious Wealth

In the world's chase after financial wealth, few really understand its true essence. It is a term used very loosely these days. Even wealth masquerades in a deceitful form in our day. It can mean anything from jewels and natural resources to over-valued baseball card collections and high-flying financial investments stocks.

As we learned in our brief visit with the Bilfrie family earlier, wealth was perceived much differently **centuries ago**. Then, wealth tended to be considered as the direct ownership of material things such as gold, land, flocks, stores of food, slaves, etc. Wealth represented in the ownership of a flock of goats did not have a primary expression in the form of money. Today, wealth is more likely to be defined in financial terms. Yet, whatever the changes in perception and forms of riches down through the ages, real wealth really hasn't changed at all.

At its core, wealth is nothing more than the totality of the physical creation and collective productive capacity of mankind's labor — both present and future. We can define these types of wealth as either created or of human origin. Both of these forms of wealth are finite at any given point of time. The earth already exists with its minerals, oceans and landmasses. As well, the labor supply is static at any one time. After all, there are only so many people of potential working age on earth at any given moment. And all of us are bound by the same 24 hours each day.

We see that the world's wealth has a maximal physical or productive potential. It is fixed at any one moment. Yet, the volume of real wealth can change over time. It can do so mainly in two ways. The most important and sustainable means is through an increase in the earth's population. The more people there are, the greater the capacity for labor, the more hours of human labor that are available in the world. The greater the potential amount of labor, the greater the opportunity to create or hoard wealth. After all, without labor, there can be no prospect of human income; and without savings there can be no human wealth. This is an important concept to understand and is a foundation that is absolutely necessary in understanding the deceptions behind modern-day financial and wealth trends.

A Simple Example Of How Real Wealth Takes Form

Let's briefly examine this notion of wealth with a basic illustration. Let's suppose that we are wandering nomads roaming the Judean desert. In our random travels, we happen to come upon some wild vines. It is late summer and these vines are loaded with grapes. We're hungry, so we reach for one cluster and eat them. In doing so, what have we done? We have expended our labor and then consumed it. We worked — admittedly not very hard — by picking the naturally created grapes from the vine and eating them. The created wealth — the naturally growing grapes that were preserved on the vine — no longer exists. We saved nothing. What if we picked all of the grapes on the vine, ate only a portion, and then brought the rest back to our camp? We would have worked harder, having picked all the grapes and transported them home. Wealth has been created since we've picked more grapes than we have eaten. Why? Simply because our labor has been saved in some form — in this case, grapes in a bag. We are now in a position to exchange our harvest for some other product or service. Or, we might choose to consume these savings (eat the remaining grapes) ourselves at some other time. Whatever the case, wealth was created by translating our labor into something that has potential value in excess of our present consumption requirements.

But what is the "potential" value of what we have saved? Value is a nebulous concept. Prices can fluctuate independently of real wealth. Like beauty, value exists in the "eye of the beholder." Since we've picked these grapes, we will keep them for our own use unless we find someone else who offers to buy them in exchange for something that we might want more. If we decide to do so, we will have chosen to receive something of value to us that the other party will have saved or promised. Perhaps the buyer of our grapes will offer us an exchange for a chicken he has raised. But what if our buyer has nothing saved — whether they be chickens or silver coins — with which to buy our product? He could instead offer us a promise for a service he will perform in the future. Let's say that a buyer makes us an offer that he will repair our tent the next time it is damaged in a sandstorm in return for our grapes. If we accept his offer, we have chosen to allow our buyer to take ownership of our grapes in return for his promise to perform a service for us in the future. He is now indebted to us. We still have our savings, only now it is transformed into a claim upon our buyer. We have chosen to buy an income — the output of someone's labor — in the future. Having made the deal, our buyer eats the grapes. The real wealth — fresh grapes picked and delivered to the village — now no longer exists. Yet, wealth hasn't vanished. It now takes the form of a promise of future labor.

Of course the above example is simplistic. I have used

a consumable item as the product. Had we sold something like a machine, quite a number of other wealth-creating concepts would need to be explored as well. However, these will not add anything to the truths about real wealth and hoarding.

Three Important Truths About Wealth

Our grape-picking exercise highlights three important truths about human wealth. First, it is inextricably tied to human labor. Ultimately the value of all wealth rests on the foundation of income — someone's labors somewhere on earth. Second, wealth can only be accumulated when we consume less than our labor produces. Third, if we exchange our savings for a promise of payment in the future, the underlying support for that liability ultimately depends on the labors of another human sometime in the future. The inviolable fact of God's creation is this: There can be no human wealth without human labor whether present, past or future — either accumulated as savings in the past or an exchange for the promise of savings in the future.

The accumulation of real wealth is a slow-moving process. Viewed very simply, human wealth in the world expands as the working population grows, and our incomes and labor exceed our consumption. Many financial institutions — mutual fund management companies, for example — like to convince their clients that financial markets create limitless wealth. They would have us believe that stock and bond markets supposedly build wealth all on their own, independent of incomes, savings and human labors. And of course, each mutual fund company likes to claim that it can extract more of this wealth out of the markets for its clients and its own profit than any other mutual fund company. While these may be attractive concepts that sell billions in mutual funds, it is a total fallacy that financial markets create wealth. Neither do the financial industries. The truth is that they do not. By and large, their business is more concerned with the transfer of wealth. That's not to say that financial services do not have value or are unimportant. But to the extent that these industries promote the perception of "value" as wealth, or their ability to create wealth apart from human labor, they are mostly bamboozling us.

Real Wealth Really Growing Slowly

In recent years, the value of financial assets has risen by leaps and bounds. In fact, rates of increase of 15% to 25% per annum and more have not been uncommon. There's no denying that some people have accumulated an incredible amount of financial wealth during this period. But how do these gains compare to the growth of real wealth? Just how fast has real wealth expanded these days? We can calculate this fairly easily.

To begin, the world's population is growing at a rate slightly above 1.1%. Though that is less than half the rate of the mid-1960s, it's still growing much faster than the average growth rate of the world's population since the dawn of time. The higher the population growth rate, eventually the greater will be the working age population. As a result, the available pool of income-producing labor hours is higher. By this measure, potential human wealth must also be growing 1.1% per annum. However, there are other factors at work that we have overlooked thus far. For example, we have not considered productivity that captures the idea that by working harder or smarter, the efficiency of human labor is increased. Higher productivity means that we are producing more potential wealth for each hour that we work. For instance, had we used an automatic grape-picking machine in our earlier example, we could have picked 20 times more grapes than we did by picking them manually. We would have greatly improved the productivity of one hour of labor by using a machine.

World productivity growth can be estimated, though its measures are not precise. Presently, economists believe that it is expanding at a rate of approximately 2%-3% per year. In other words, for a given amount of labor hours, 3% more output is being produced than the year before, every year. Knowing this, we can now determine how fast real wealth is expanding. By combining both population and productivity growth we know that real wealth can grow no faster than 3.1% – 4.1% per year on a sustainable basis. That's a fast pace in the context of human history. For centuries and millennia, wealth increases crawled along at a rate of little above zero. All the same, a 4.1% growth rate in real wealth pales in comparison to the pie-eyed expectations of gain in financial markets these days.

Foundations Of Modern Financial Wealth Are False

As already documented in earlier chapters, financial

wealth has been booming during our generation. How can this be when real wealth is creeping along at a fraction of that rate? Here again we see that the main driver behind this apparently huge rise in wealth has been nothing more than a boom in the perception of value.[3] The value of any financial asset — stock or bond — depends on the willingness of someone else to buy it. If no one wants to buy it, then theoretically, it has no value. The highest priced stock would be worth nothing if no one was willing to buy it — a truth that has recently again been discovered. But what does financial value have to do with real wealth in any case? They are not one and the same. Even if there were no value, there can still be wealth.

Perceptions of wealth cannot feed the world any more than the world can buy its groceries on love. The point is that at the end of the day, in order to live, the world as a whole can only buy its food and necessary amenities out of income. Only the output of labor and the accumulation of real wealth can provide sustenance. If apparent wealth (perceived financial wealth and otherwise) is rising much faster than underlying income growth and savings, then something potentially very dangerous is occurring. It gives rise to a very deceitful environment, one in which claims on true wealth — the ownership of human labor; past, present and future — are being misrepresented. It allows the world to fall into an enormous bondage to fictitious financial wealth and as true wealth is being hoarded by a select few as never before.

No matter what happens to financial market wealth, what matters in the end is who owns claims to income -

in other words, who owns the fruit of other people's labor.

Giving Away Labor For A Mess Of Pottage

Misunderstanding the nature of true wealth, many people have been selling their birthright — their God-given years on earth and capacity for labor — for a mess of pottage. To help explain this point, consider US stock market prices relative to wage trends. At year-end of the century (1999), the S&P 500 (Standard and Poor) stock market index was at a level of 1,469—or $1,469 for the sake of illustration. At that time, the average weekly wage per employed private worker as calculated by the US Bureau of Labor was $463.68. Taking these two figures, we could say that one index unit of the S&P 500 would cost 3.2 weeks of wages. When an investor chooses to buy one unit of the S&P, he has chosen to store 3.2 weeks of labor in the stock market. Is that a good trade? Ten years earlier at the end of 1989, a unit of the S&P 500 index would have cost considerably less — only a little more than one week's labor of the average worker. Ten years earlier again (year-end 1979) a unit of the S&P would have cost even less — only 0.48 weeks labor income or approximately a half of a week's work.

What we see is that over a period of two decades, US stock markets have become more expensive relative to labor by a factor of six times. Put another way, investors at the end of the last decade saw the stock market as a storehouse for their labor as six times better than 20 years earlier. Did investors actually believe that they were trading their labors for something that would return their 3.2

weeks of labor income (the equivalent amount paid for an investment in one unit of the S&P) or more in the future? Does one unit of the stock market yield better earnings and dividends than 20 years before? Hardly. While the stock market had risen 13.6 times over the two decades reviewed, earnings rose only 3.3 times, dividend income only 3 times. While it is true that the reported earnings represented by the S&P 500 stock index rose faster than labor income — 62% more — stewards still chose to store their labor in stocks for only a fraction of the value 20 years earlier. Valuation swings of this magnitude are irrational. Knowledgeable investors wouldn't trade their valuable labors — a resource that each of us have only been given by God in a finite, unknowable quantity — so cheaply.

The False Gospel Of Increase And Gain

Despite the financial deceptions of wealth, faith in securities markets and world economies has generally been richly rewarded in the past seven decades. In fact, a record of ever-rising economies and stock prices over this period, even though there were some very steep dips and prolonged declines in between, has led to a new belief: Over the long-term, financial markets at large provide positive and superior investment returns. For example, the mantra that stocks always go up now has the same credibility as the slogan "you can bank on it." It has become a new rule on par with the physical laws of the universe that have held since creation.

The truth be known, the gospel that stock prices always

go up is really an Anglo-Saxon marketing campaign of the twentieth century to the rest of the world. Though it is a gospel that's eagerly gobbled up, it's really a hoax. In fact, it could be one of the sinister hoaxes that plays a role in an ultimate endtime deception. No one seems to notice the obvious and spurious underpinnings to this claim. For one, this new law that says stock prices always go up has only applied to less than 5% of the world's population and only for a very short period of time at that. The experiences of the other 95% of humanity have been conveniently forgotten. This claim is based upon evidence taken from a very brief period of history, an era that's really much too brief to qualify as reliable proof for a new universal theory for the world. In fact, only two countries in the world have experienced uninterrupted stock markets over the past century or so — the United States and Britain. Investors in the securities markets of any other country have had their expectations and fortunes dashed at least once over this same time. Wars, political upheavals and disasters have intervened in these cases. A prominent example is Continental Europe. Every one of its stock markets has been forced to close at some point this past century or their economies may have succumbed to a hyperinflation. Their securities markets were far from secure. Therefore, they were a much less credible springboard for the emergence of a new god. For that, the Anglo-Saxon markets are more useful.

Academics even argue whether the claim of the superiority of stock market returns over that of other types of investments is really true. Recent studies have debunked this notion as well.[4] Yet, as far as most financial marketers are concerned, the facts can't be allowed to stand in the way of a mad chase for paper wealth. Therefore, high-flying stock markets have persisted in recent decades.

Differing Outlooks For Prosperity And Consumerism

What is the outlook in light of the encroaching Luciferic snare of booming financial wealth?

That question meets a wide range of answers. Some view the developments cited as the new "promised land" for humanity — limitless consumption and wealth for all and a human heaven on earth. A small number sees it as a precursor to a coming economic collapse and financial crashes for the US and world stock markets. Even fewer see it as signs of a prophesied end.

The latter predictions prompt two extreme reactions: morbid fear or searing ridicule — hardly anything in between. Both responses have their reasons. After all, there have been so many false predictions of final doom over past decades — "crying wolf" so to speak — that few will listen to any "Chicken Little." At the same time, there have been many serious financial crises over this period around the globe and yet the financial markets have continued to climb in value. Therefore, either of these responses may be right. It all depends on the facts. And, of course, there have always been seers predicting that the end is nigh, that Christ's return and Judgment Day is at the very door. So far it hasn't happened.

If the doomsters are correct, then our financial situations could turn grim at some point. Our mutual fund holdings and the vested portion of each of our pension plans would face significant declines in value if there were any serious calamity on the financial high seas. As such, the wisdom and security of all the hopes and emotions that have been placed in the hulls of any financial vessel could be disappointed. On the other hand, if the doomsters are wrong, the great monetary/commercial colossus could still shower trillions and trillions of dollars in new wealth upon its participants. The lure of this wealth, ease and materialistic nirvana, will convert and hold millions more captive. Then there is the third possibility: The very demise of the monetary colossus — the very Babylon the Great of Revelation 18 — may be at hand. Who to believe — the doomsters, the optimists, the prophecy teachers?

But given the great and successful domains of GLOBO, MOFI and SCITE this past century, surely the doomsters must be wrong. How could the vast economic/financial system of the world ever stumble seriously, let alone fall? Surely the leading nations are secure.

These are questions we must attempt to answer in the remaining chapters.

ENDNOTES

1. Faith Popcorn
2. Employee stock options are essentially a contract that allows employees to buy the common shares of the company that they work for at a predeter-

mined price They can elect to buy these shares without risk at some future date. Employees almost always elect to do so after the share prices have risen, then selling them to pocket the gain. The phenomena of their use is further explained in Chapter 17. There is no research that conclusively proves that employee stock options appropriately reward employees, much less many corporate executives. Rather, there is strong evidence that their use is being heavily abused. As such, I conclude that the unbridled use of employee stock options as it is practiced today, really serves as a corrupt means of transferring wealth (stealing) from shareholders.

3. An increase in general debt levels has played a major role in the explosion of financial market values. Though net wealth does not increase, the amount of claims upon wealth still increase as do many other distortions upon in the world economy.

4. A study by Stephen Brown of New York University and William Goetzman and Stephen Ross of Yale School of Management in 1995 roundly debunks the fast-held view that equity investment yields a significant premium return over types of investments Their report shows that by removing "survivor bias" — the practice of only considering the performance record of those companies and stocks that have survived for the period reviewed — equities have hardly outperformed other types of investments. The implication is that stock market investments are bound to be much less reliable than the general public has been led to believe.

CHAPTER 14

America: Where Does it Figure?

A Look in the Mirror

Is it conceivable that a country of such world influence as the United States will not also have complicity in an idolatrous world economic order? In considering this question, we must not overlook the influence of the rest of the Anglo world: the countries of Canada, the United Kingdom, Australia and New Zealand, not to mention a host of lesser satellites states and protectorates.

The US is the world economic leader, the largest financial and economic power on earth. Today, this country accounts for approximately 30% of world economic activity, an eighth of all world trade, approximately half of the entire value of world stock markets and a third of world bond markets. Combining all of the Anglo-Saxon countries, they account for greater than two-fifths of world economic output, two-thirds of world stock market value, and more than 40% of the value of the world bond market. These countries together are also home to the vast majority of the world's financial centers. Given this massive domination of the world economic conditions, the US is the logical starting point in our investigation. Is it really likely that the US is headed for a judgment — perhaps a great financial and economic bust — as some predict? Before drawing any firm conclusions I first want to tell you a story.

It is a nation admired around the world. We are told that it can do no wrong. This sovereign realm believes in the superiority of its policies and ways, openly celebrating and trumpeting it. Its political and business leaders are not afraid to preach its commercial gospel from the global speaker's podiums. Its business people scour the world for investment opportunities, and not surprisingly, most of the globe's commercial and financial community stands in awe and wants to emulate everything this nation does. Others are jealous and annoyed with this country's seeming arrogance. Its apparent prosperity and ease of created wealth are the object of envy. The nation's stock markets soar far beyond any reasonable expectation — the largest equity market in the world. Its people tour abroad, choking up many tourist locations in camera-flashing hordes. The world's vacation resorts and luxury goods exporters are grateful for this country's consumers. The nation's factories spew out products that flood the export markets of the world with well-known brand names. Competitors tremble in fear. Foreign industries are concerned that they will be annihilated by this country's extremely efficient manufacturing practices. They send trade missions to study the successful techniques of its companies and the progressive policies of its government. Management consultants publish volumes of books that claim to unlock the secret of this country's economic prowess. Commentators speculate that the country is unstoppable. This nation will surely take over the world of commerce. And, the truth be known, some of this nation's leaders become a touch arrogant, and openly derisory of the practices of other countries. Do you recognize this nation?

You will have easily identified the country in the story. No, it is not the United States. Surprised? The story is actually about Japan. The time is the late 1980s. If you did answer the United States, please do not feel betrayed. The similarities between the two countries and their times are more than a few. In fact, there are so many similarities it is very unsettling.

The Forewarnings And Similarities Of Japan

It's worth recalling those days when Japan was in its prime. Just a few years ago it was a country admired for its progressive and enlightened ways. Its economy grew at rates over 4% per year. It was praised for the paternalistic commitment of its companies to its employees. Unemployment was extremely low — less than 2% — and workers could expect to have a job with one company for a lifetime. Its manufacturing concepts[1] were studied and adopted in the US and elsewhere. The country filed torrents of patents and continues to do so today. Japan's government[2] was lauded for its wise industrial and financial policies. Rather than rely on market forces, the country tightly controlled economic activity and dictated which industries were to flourish and grow. The country was seen as a monument to the wisdom of centralized industrial planning. Japan's success was attributed to the fact that companies and major industries were able to concentrate on long-term plans because they were insulated from the short-termism of investors and fickle financial markets evident in other countries.

Japan looked like an unstoppable juggernaut, gobbling up competitors and commercial opportunities without end. On the strength of its good reputation, Japan was able to borrow money around the world at virtually no cost, sometimes at effective interest rates that were even below zero. And, as always, the capstone: Its leaders and industrial scions showed plenty of arrogance. Leading Japanese businessmen were openly derisive of the United States, even calling Americans "fat and stupid." But obviously, underneath all of this bravado, the seeds of Japan's downfall must have already been sown. Somewhere in Japan's armor, not evident to the blinded masses of adorers and emulators, were the beginning fissures of its following collapse. Could Japan's success have been just a flash in the pan? Perhaps Japan's prosperity was founded upon nothing more than corruption, deception and illusion. There are some who believe that today.

How The Mighty Fall

Look how far Japan has fallen. Today the world views it as the economic and financial runt of the globe, having tumbled from paragon to pariah in less than ten years, with an equity market that slipped from 45% of the world stock market value to as low as 10%. During that same ten-year period, the US stock market more than quintupled. Newspaper editorials and academic studies from around the world now all seem to have discovered what Japan did wrong and how it should redeem itself, though they were blind to these supposed weaknesses ten and fifteen years ago. Now, the virtues of Japan's people are long forgotten. According to the popular media, all that remains is the country's collective ineptitude. Of course, such opinions are highly unfair. This view of Japan is as underestimated as it was over-exaggerated in the late 1980s. After all, many countries and senior business leaders were terrified of Japan in its former glory days.

The New Proven Success Story

Today, the United States and its Anglo-Saxon sister countries triumphantly reign across the world's economic and financial stage. Now, the world's leaders and its academics are studying its successful ways. Japan's example is no longer relevant. But is it? Should we be so hasty to forget about Japan?

Actually, Japan's shocking story poses many questions. The answers hold many humbling lessons. How could what was believed to be so right by most of the leading brains of the world just a decade ago be so wrong today? Was Japan's downfall foreseeable? Could such a wild swing in fortune happen again? If not, why not?

Before addressing America's future, let's take a moment to learn if there are any lessons from Japan's example. Reflecting upon Japan's fall from blessed prosperity, it is amazing to

251

witness how quickly and radically the wisdom of its heyday has changed. After all, the popular prescriptions for wealth and prosperity have been completely reversed in less than ten years! Today, Japan is ridiculed for its past policies which are the exact opposite of which is reckoned to be the cause of America's success. Yet, these policies were accepted as the received wisdom of the world of commerce in Japan's day. Now, a willingness to trash employees is seen to be much more enlightened than the policy of lifetime employment. The direction and wisdom of all-seeing and unfettered financial markets — allowing the free reign of private ambition and greed, in other words — is now supposedly more infallible than central industrial planning. There are a whole host of reversals in beliefs. Clearly, it is evident that the chase for wealth seems to be very fickle indeed. If there are no fixed and eternal maxims, could America's brilliant success amount to so much puffery that it evaporates into another disappointment?

The Lessons of Japan

I see three main lessons in the Japanese saga of the past two decades. First, Japan's economic and financial bubble of the 1980s — when its stock and real estate markets soared year after year to incredible highs — is another example of how easily humans allow themselves to be deceived when it comes to matters of money and wealth. Financial history is marked with such examples. As soon as a trend or belief emerges that promises effortless wealth, markets and people are quick to follow suit in fawning worship. Greed succumbs to the lure of easy wealth, so much so in fact, that otherwise rational people willingly and knowingly embrace delusion. In this there is a second lesson: In the scramble to travel the sure road to riches, blindness is purposefully promoted and willingly accepted. Facts and truths are sacrificed. Who wants to find fault with something that feels so good, showering participants in easy increase?

There were solid reasons for Japan's relative economic and productive successes in the early years — in the late 1970s and early 1980s. The Japanese diligently labored working long hours with little vacation. Many of their children attended school seven days a week. They were prodigious savers who heavily invested for the future. These efforts reaped rewards as Japan's economy grew rapidly and its standard of living increased substantially. Yet, eventually a financial bubble took hold. Runaway credit and debt were allowed to work their dangerous havoc. No one wanted to take responsibility for stopping an unsustainable trend, one that was destined for certain disaster. Yet, it was allowed to continue. Eventually falsehoods were believed and deceptions were allowed to replace reality. And, as these were accepted as truth and common wisdom, they were difficult to combat. As I remember at the time, it was extremely hard to see Japan's feet of clay under the radiant halo of its exuberant market mania. Though more than a few observers thought that Japan's stock market must ultimately crash, few could point to any potential weaknesses in Japan's economy. Today, in retrospect of course, Japan's flaws seem perfectly clear to everyone, both on Main and Wall Streets.

A third lesson from Japan's ordeal is this: Successful financial trends often have less to do with wise and correct policies than they do with the spirit and motivations behind them. Motivation is the engine of human activity and progress. The means is less important than the end. More often than not, the motivational impulse that drives financial trends — both up and down — are nothing more than the human emotions of greed and fear. The more that these emotions are allowed to exist unchecked, transcending reality and truth, the harder and deeper the fall will be later. Look at Japan. More than a decade after its fall, the country's economy and financial system continues to swirl down the drain. America's Great Depression of the 1930s is another example of how painful the aftermath of rampant greed, materialism and idolatry can be.

Lessons Already Forgotten

Even while Japan still suffers for its recent excesses, another great financial bubble is underway. In my view, it is the biggest in modern financial history. Many of its features are so similar to Japan ten years ago, that Japan's leaders worry about the US today.

As it was in Japan, the triumphalism of North America and its sibling countries isn't what it may have cracked up to be. In fact, America's great boom is likely headed for a big bust as well. America's era of prosperity may have even less substance than that of Japan's in the previous decade. Its prosperity in time has come to be built primarily upon deception and greed. This is not to deny that there have been some significant changes in the structures of the US economy or the competitiveness of its businesses and workers. These trends have definitely played a role, yet seen in the overall, their impact has been rather modest. Today, massive deceptions are being fostered as corruption runs deep. The scale of the theft, conspiracy and corruption is massive, if not unprecedented. The huge financial bubble that has resulted is the physical reflection of these immoralities.

Searching For The Feet Of Clay

My statements must seem very harsh, maybe even crazily out of line. How can these allegations be true when all the evidence says that America is indeed at the top of the world with its business and culture engulfing the rest of the world? Just where is the evidence supporting my view?

Permit me to search for any feet of clay, difficult as it may be. There is some clay, though few people realize it. When God's judgment comes, these aspects will become clearly and painfully evident. Yet, even so, these clay foundations are more ignored than hidden. An honest examination will show this to be true.

I could shed light on dozens of examples of deception, fallacy and corruption that have given rise to America's massive orgy of greed and materialism. I could present a painstaking case that logically explains why America's trends are unsustainable and must face a certain disappointment. But, to do so, my explanations would read like an economic text. Therefore I will only touch upon a few simple examples. I will argue with the economists elsewhere.

Of course, many observers claim that the US has now entered a "new era" of permanently high economic growth and strength and that many more years of prosperity are ahead of us. Therefore, wealth will boom by leaps and bounds for many more decades. Some boldly claim that the next 100 years will belong to the US.[3] Maybe so. But, such is the hubris and arrogance of our day that 100-year forecasts are not only common, but are believed to be convincingly solid.

Why should stocks continue booming? Marketers of wealth management services and politicians have a ready answer. They have continued to come up with convincing stories these past years of a new world of opportunity made possible by advanced technology and knowledge. America excels in these areas. So far, this story is true, but that isn't sufficient to launch such a large financial boom as is being witnessed in the world. To do so, the story has been spun into an inventive tale of effortless and endless wealth creation due to booming corporate profits, low inflation and surging productivity, apparently a new age of human enlightenment and empowerment. It's an appealing argument. People have become intoxicated by this story desiring its promise of wealth and ease, even choosing to ignore threatening recessions and financial tremors. Leading thinkers call this great vision of endless wealth the "new paradigm."

In a sense, there is a new paradigm. Who can doubt that a great deal has changed in recent years? New technologies have revolutionized world commerce and its business cycles in irreversible ways. Financial transaction and communication costs have dropped like a stone. Efficiency seems to have soared. And no doubt that some people have made incredible amounts of money. There have been massive changes with many more expected in the future.

But, there's much more to the new paradigm than meets the eye. Not only are its basic premises false or exaggerated, other influences are at work, ones that are conveniently ignored which falsely make it appear as though a new paradigm of endless wealth and ease is occurring.

The Wobbly Pillars Of The New Economy

Let's briefly look at each of the main pillars that are said to underpin the "new paradigm"—booming corporate profits, low inflation, and high labor productivity. They are all exaggerated or complete lies.

Today, corporate profits are not what they seem. The whole story about extraordinary productivity and profit growth in today's economy is mostly a fable. The record of this past decade on these counts is hardly notable when compared to the entire post-war economic period — certainly nothing worth today's soaring stock market prices.

Corporate profits are vastly overstated — fabricated, in other words. There are countless ways that this is done. The "granddaddy" of them all stems from the popular rush to issue employee stock options. In the past ten years there has been a virtual revolution in their use. Outstanding stock options have more than doubled since the start of the 1990s. Today, most senior executive officers of public companies are awarded stock options as part of their compensation packages. On average, more than 40% of their income can be derived from this source. Further, employee option plans, or other programs that make company shares widely available to non-executive employees through favorable terms, have also boomed. More than half of the employees of the largest companies in the United States today have stock options as compared to less than 10% fifteen to twenty years ago. That's a massive change. Is this a bad thing? Not in and of itself, of course. Only when it gives rise to deceptive practices, greed and theft. And that is precisely what is happening.

The use of options has led to a gross overstatement of company earnings. The first and most important reason why this is so is that the cost of stock options is not expensed.[4] How prevalent is this practice? It's out of control. Estimates by some reputable analysts suggest that as much as 25% to 50% of the reported earnings of the S&P 500 group of companies may be overstated in recent years.

Obviously, with so many executives and employees laden with stock options, they will have focused their attention to the discovery of any and all techniques that might boost corporate earnings and stock prices. An article in *Forbes* magazine reviewing corporate accounting techniques quipped, "The bull market has put a premium upon deception because it pays so well." Some of these accounting tactics are downright misleading. I would need to add several chapters to this book if I were to explain just some of these inventive techniques.[5] I don't believe it an exaggeration to conclude that corporate profits of companies listed on public markets today are overstated by as much as one half and more in many cases. As such, this destroys the first pillar of the "new paradigm." Just imagine it: In recent years, America experienced a stock market which was the most over-valued in its history relative to the underlying earnings of its companies. On top of this, we discover that these earnings have been drastically overstated. Based on these facts, it is not unreasonable to expect that stock market prices are not well supported.

A Clearer Understanding Of Inflation's Dangers

What about low inflation? This argument for the new paradigm is repeated so often that it qualifies as the mantra of the "new paradigm" religion. Here again, the truth is contrary to the perception. In reality, inflation is running rampant. Inflation is not low, as many financial economists would want us to believe. The problem lies in the fact that few people understand the nature of inflation. Just what is it? In reality, it's a chameleon that masquerades under a number of guises. Its most popular definition is the common Consumer Price Index (CPI) that gets the intensive attention of consumers, pensioners, contract negotiators, and almost everyone else. What's crucial to realize is that the CPI measures only one kind of inflation — the kind that reduces the purchasing power of consumers when they are buying goods and services. But this is not inflation itself; it is only one of its many faces.

Where can we find the true wellspring of inflation? It's a simple and logical answer. Inflation results when more money is created than is earned and saved. Economists say this in a more technical way. Inflation results when the supply of money and credit expands faster than savings. It makes logical sense. Money can only be borrowed from someone who has saved it. If, by some means, more money is being borrowed than is being saved, inflation arises. In today's fractional-reserve banking system, this happens when money is created by increasing credit faster than savings. This can occur in a number of ways. However, they are too technical to examine here. But it follows that if more money is being borrowed than is saved, excess money is being created somewhere. This excess money is the inflation of money — the root of all types of inflation. The channel this excess money takes will determine the type of inflationary symptom.

So we see that there can be many kinds of inflation other than price inflation — the type we experience in the grocery store. Another type is even more dangerous and deceptive. It is called "asset inflation." This variety only impacts the price of assets — real estate, other real assets, and financial securities. Therein lies the deception in the present new paradigm. While economists dwell on the fact that consumer price inflation is low, they ignore or fail to mention that asset inflation and other manifestations of inflation are running uncontrolled. How can we know for sure that inflation is roaring? We only need to compare a nation's savings levels to the amount being borrowed. On this score, America is experiencing one of its biggest inflations in history. Debt is expanding in America at a rate many multiples higher than savings.[6] The same is also true in Canada, Britain, Australia and many other countries.

We have just demolished the second pillar of the new paradigm.

Other Productive Lies

Surely, the third pillar — high productivity — must be true. The high valuations of the US and other stock markets are often justified with the argument that the US economy is enjoying a new era of high productivity growth and capital efficiency. Many prominent voices support this view, even arguing that "there are no more limits to growth and employment."[7] In this camp's view, "due to a combination of positive developments, including the far-reaching impact of the Internet, the long bull market cycle of prosperity is alive and well, regardless of what the Fed does." With so many voices of learning expressing this same view, surely productivity must be as healthy and high as they claim.

Unfortunately, the high productivity argument is mostly a fable as well. Significant studies prove this to be so.[8] It is normal for productivity statistics to experience periodic and cyclical spurts and ebbs. In any case, US productivity in the past decade has been hardly notable or extraordinary when compared to the entire post-war period. Productivity growth in the staid Continental Europe — which, interestingly, does not have a large technology industry — has far outpaced the US on this count over the past ten years. Yet, no one talks of a new paradigm there.

The new paradigm is a fraud. All of its pillars are hollow or exaggerated. No doubt, our world is witnessing incredible and irreversible changes. But these assuredly do not lead to the promised land of eternal profits and booming prosperity. They are the lies of Mammon. Because the perversions of the new paradigm have been believed and trusted upon by vast legions of investors and citizens, a painful disappointment could yet be in the works much more than has already been experienced. Clearly, it is not an impossibility.

Stimulated Through A Rush Into Debt

As mentioned before, there is more to the new paradigm than meets the eye. One of its conveniently overlooked engines is actually some old-time financial magic — the stimulant of debt. It has continued to increase at a rate many times that of underlying savings and income in recent years. It's no secret: A borrowing binge will eventually stimulate the most stagnant of economies to fast growth. We all know from personal experience that borrowing only has a temporary effect. Ultimately it has to be repaid. Therefore, consuming today what we will need to pay for tomorrow does not represent a sustainable source of prosperity. In that sense, much of America's prosperity of the past few years has been borrowed from the future. It is astounding how fast debt has continued to rise. During the past half-decade, total debt rose by over $9.5 trillion—yes, nine and one half trillion dollars. That amounts to approximately $4.50 in increased debt for every $1 dollar of new growth in the US economy. That is a steep price for false prosperity. Yet, observers from around the world marvel at how strong the US economy has been in recent years. Little wonder. Surely, such increases in debt are not a sign of economic might and prowess. Just what kind of society puts such burdens upon future society—our children today?

To boot, all the classical signs of a financial bubble are clearly evident — not a sustainable new paradigm — though some still maintain that it is a beast of myth. Unfortunately, its footprints are most obvious in the US. I see at least four. To summarize, debt continues to soar far beyond underlying income and savings growth (the source of all inflation, whatever the manifestation); household savings rates remain near the lowest since the 1930s; a chronic and large reliance on foreign borrowing[9] has emerged; and lastly, the wealth skew continues to widen as never before. The rich become ever more wealthy while the prospects for our poor do not improve.

Quoting Thomas L. Friedman, "We Americans are the apostles of the fast world, the prophets of the free market and the high priests of high tech. We want enlargement of both our values and our Pizza Huts. We want the world to follow our lead and become democratic and capitalistic, with a Web site in every pot, a Pepsi on every lip, Microsoft Windows in every computer and with everyone everywhere, pumping their own gas."[10]

This comment applies to virtually all of the Anglo cultures of the world. In this sense, the answer to the question of where America figures really applies to these countries as well.

Even The Mighty Fall

In recent years the deceptions behind the story of the "new paradigm" have intoxicated most of the world, extending its influence far beyond the shores of the United States. When it is finally revealed as a sham, the consequences will reverberate around the world. As we have seen, most of the world — particularly the Anglo countries — has given itself over to a culture of greed. Facts and truth aren't allowed to get in the way. Deceptions are being devised, illusions are promoted and corruption overlooked. Complicity is found at all levels of society, even to the highest places.

Returning to our main question — where does America figure in the questions we are seeking to answer? Are the doomsters correct in predicting serious economic troubles ahead? Or, could the world be speeding towards the soon wrath of the Great Tribulation? Our brief story about Japan reveals an example of how pride precedes a fall. What God hates above all is a proud look and nations that profess themselves to be self-sufficient, staking their trust in their riches and might. The mightiest can be brought low very quickly.

Even reviewing the economic facts leads us to similar conclusions. America — indeed the world — is very vulnerable to judgment and a painful disciplining.

Should we expect God to respond soon?

☙

"What we are witnessing are indescribable financial excesses, an unprecedented increase in debt, the monstrous use of leverage upon leverage, a collapse in private savings and an exploding current-account deficit. This is history's greatest financial bubble."

–Dr. Kurt Richebächer

☙

"In the US many conclude [...] that their economic model is the only one worthy of imitation. But never mistake a bubble for enduring economic triumph. The great bull market cannot last forever; what cannot last will not do so; and the higher the climb the bigger the fall."

–Martin Wolf, *Financial Times of London*

ENDNOTES

1.   Just-in-time inventorying (JIT) is the concept that concludes that rather than have large inventories, it is better to have components shipped just hours before they are required for assembly.

2.   Specifically its Ministry of Industry and Trade (MITI) and the Ministry of Finance (MOF).

3.   Foreign Affairs that like the 20th century, the entire 21st century will belong to the US as well.

4.   Let us carefully explain how earning overstatement happens. Company A issues an option to buy its shares at $10. At this point the share does not exist, as it has not yet been issued. How have stock options been employed to overstate earnings? Let's then presume that these shares rise in value to $50.00 on the stock market. We now decide to exercise our option to buy these shares from the company. We do so at $10 and immediately sell them at $50. We have made a profit of $40. Wonderful. But see what happens next. Company A now has one more share outstanding than before. That means its Earnings Per Share (EPS) that it must report will now be less (nearly the same amount of earnings are now divided by more shares). What does Company A do next? It turns around and buys a share in the open market for $50 so that its earnings will not be diluted as a result of having issued the new share to the employee. Stock option-holders don't want this to happen because if earnings appear to be dropping, then the shares might decline in value (and so also the unexercised options). But what really has happened? In our view, theft and deception. Why? For one, when corporate share buy-backs are structured in such a deliberate way, the $40 the employee made really came out of the company's pocket. Remember, the company's pocket really belongs to the existing shareholders. After all, they are the ones who own the company. But even worse is the fact that the company does not expense this extra $40 as being a cost of business or employee remuneration. As such, the company is running down its balance sheet by using its cash to buy its high-priced shares, yet continues to report high profits. Present accounting conventions allow companies to get away with this ruse (although perhaps for not much longer).

5.   Reducing depreciation future costs by constantly reporting extraordinary losses, corporate spin-offs, optimistically reducing pension costs, aggressive earnings recognition policies, rationalization, to name a few...and the game goes on.

6.   Overall debt boomed in the US during the 1990s. In the last five years of the decade alone, total debt soared by over $8 trillion. In fact, debt increased by $3.73 for every dollar increase in Gross Domestic Product. Looked at another way, total debt increase by over $3.50 for every dollar of savings — personal savings and undistributed corporate profits. Source: Federal Reserve Board Flow of Funds

Statistics, and Eternal Value Review calculations.

7.   Lawrence Kudlow (Chief Economist at Schroders)

8.   Importantly, a comprehensive and thorough study recently published by Gordon Brown of Northwestern University and the NBER virtually demolishes the "high productivity" argument as a legitimate support to the superior performance of US investment markets. A review of the full text of this paper cites disturbing and incontrovertible facts: For example, the US "high tech" sector has accounted for virtually all of US productivity growth between 1998 and 1992. He states "there has been no productivity growth acceleration in 99 percent of the economy located outside the sector which manufactures computer hardware [...]. Indeed, far from exhibiting a productivity acceleration, the productivity slowdown in manufacturing has gotten worse; when computers are stripped out of durable manufacturing sector, there has been a further productivity slowdown in durable manufacturing in 1995-99 as compared to 1972-95." As such, the apparent productivity record for the US this decade has not been attributable to the application of technology (namely to the other sectors of the US economy), but rather to the development of technology itself.

9.   America's current account has a chronic deficit. The implicaiton of this is that the US must borrow heavily from the rest of the world in order to maintain its high growth and excess consumption and spending habits.

10. Thomas L. Friedman, "A Manifesto for the Fast World," *The New York Times Magazine,* 28 March 1999.

CHAPTER 15

Were Jeremiah Here Now

A Modern-day Forecaster?

Ever wonder what an Old Testament prophet like Jeremiah would be doing these days if he was living during our times? Would he be feeling complacent, comfortable and spiritually at ease? Or, would he be warning our society of an impending judgment and calling us to full obedience to God?

What were conditions like during Jeremiah's time? Are there any similarities to our day? Since God is fair and just, the standards He would use to measure His people then could hardly be any different today. If they were, it wouldn't be justice. Jeremiah's warning that Judah was judged and would soon be vanquished by the Babylonians serves as a useful example to those living more than 2,000 years later. We could even use Judah's history during Jeremiah's days as a type of timepiece. The more similar the conditions to our day, the more we may gain a sense of the season of our times and the imminence of Christ's return.

Well, what if Jeremiah was a prophet today? It's not an unimaginable situation. After all, the world is flooded with so-called "prophets" these days. Jeremiah's calling would hardly be out of place. He jousted with legions of financial forecasters in his day, too. Of course, in those days different techniques were employed to forecast prosperity. Today's modern forecasters may sound enlightened and academically rooted, talking about arcane economic developmental theories, technological advancements, future earnings growth, world geo-political alliances. Such talk makes them appear so knowledgeable, credible and definitely relevant to our times. Though the jargon and forecasting techniques may be different from 2,500 years ago, the fact remains that they are still making predictions about the future — sometimes far, far into the future. And since time memorial, that realm remains as mysterious, dark and surprising as ever.

The Danger Of Biased Forecasting

Whether by means of astrology, modern quantitative models, or spirit-led advisors, there's absolutely no evidence that the reliability and accuracy of forecasts concerning the future affairs of mankind have improved. In fact, if anything, the accuracy of seers may have even worsened. Swings in public consensus beliefs seem to be more rapid and fickle than ever. After all, society is very quick to discard its financial prophets and gurus for new ones with more favorable predictions. Moreover, forecasting inaccuracies are widely evident to anyone who cares to read a month-old newspaper, not to mention any forecasts of a decade earlier. No doubt, all predictions must be considered highly suspect, especially those that make claims about the distant future, two, five or more years ahead. Yet, the forecasting business is booming as never before. It must be, because there are more economists, brokers and financial planners than ever before.

Predictions have always been highly prone to certain forecaster biases such as the itching ears of a willing audience, a heavy bent toward optimism, tireless quests to find security in a volatile world, demagoguery contests, and of course, a love for financial prosperity. With all these imperfections, forecasting nevertheless remains big business — always has been. There was and will always be a large audience and clientele willing to pay for and listen to viewpoints that want to be heard. We all identify with this innate tendency, preferring good news to bad, and see this tendency at work all around us. We all know people that continue to seek advice from others until they hear the view that they want. "Give us no more visions of what is right! Tell us pleasant things, prophesy illusions. Leave this way, get off this path, and stop confronting us with the Holy One of Israel," is what the people told Isaiah.[1]

As it is, all forecasters — Christian or otherwise — seem to suffer from the same timing problems that beset all mortals. That's little wonder. The challenges of short-term forecasting are common to both the wicked and the righteous. Predicting the short-term timing of events is virtually impossible. It's always hit or miss. The same applies to God's plan. We cannot know His ways over the near term with any degree of precision. In fact, the Bible repeatedly warns about the futility of being able to predict events over the short-term. While we can know the trends and the "season" of the times, we cannot be sure about the exact timing of events. It couldn't be any other way. If we did know the exact timing of events in advance, the world would be a radically different place. A world with less risk and uncertainty would be much more sinful than it already is. As most everyone likes a sure bet, financial bubbles, manias and busts would become even bigger. Their destructive power upon humanity would ultimately be even more disastrous. Here we see that some uncertainty in our lives is actually a blessing.

Virtually all of the prophecies recorded in the Bible were longer-term, given years ahead, even thousands of years ahead of their actual fulfillment. But, even here there is opportunity for great abuse. There are no shortages of "pillow prophets"[2] these days claiming visions of an era of great prosperity as far as the eye can see. They always have been present throughout the course of history. On the other hand, not one of the prophets recorded in the Bible brought a message solely of peace and prosperity. Repentance, correction, and warning tended to be the main emphasis of their messages. Perhaps that is why God needed to call His own prophets. No one else could be counted upon to tell the truth when the forecast envisioned dark clouds or judgment.

Similarities With Old Testament Times

The parallels of our day with Jeremiah's age are many — in fact, alarmingly so. Israel and Judah were living in heady economic times, in a fraternizing frenzy on the international political stage. They had taken up with strange and morally perverse ideologies, and were totally preoccupied with prosperity and gain in the material world. Godliness and eternity were far from the popular focus of the public arena. The two sister countries were overrun with self-anointed prophets who were mostly politicians and priests trying to advance their views of the future. What was their popular message in that day? In short, peace and prosperity for as far as the eye could see. Similar conditions exist today, particularly for much of the Western world.

The similarities do not stop there. Jeremiah was very critical of the practices and conditions of that day; his forecasts were in direct opposition to the popular entertainers. God was very displeased with Israel and Judah, so much so that His wrath followed in the form of a Babylonian conquest. The result was near total economic destruction. The books of the prophets tell us of the conditions that angered God in that age. Reading through these books, I was struck by two realizations: First, how much of Israel and Judah's sins had to do with commerce, trade and economics; and second, how similar are conditions in our society today. Actually, conditions today may be even worse.

A good start on this road of personal discovery is to consider some of the statements made by Jeremiah, Hosea, and other prophets and to compare them to prevailing conditions today. In the economic arena we discover that God was displeased with the extent of greed, complacency, arrogance of the rich, deceit, widespread corruption, financial oppression, pronounced wealth skew (a few super rich and many poor), conspiracy and high intrigue.

The following verses perfectly capture the mood of the times: *"When will be the New Moon over that we may sell grain, and the Sabbath be ended that we may market wheat?...skimming the measure boosting the price and cheating with dishonest scales, buying the poor with silver and the needy for a pair of sandals, selling even the sweepings with the wheat"* (Amos 8:5–6). We see that commerce and making money were foremost in the people's minds. "How to get rich quick!" was a pervasive motive. No doubt, a presentation in the middle of the desert on the topic of how to double your money in two weeks would have pulled in big crowds in those days.

In the trample for wealth and gain, noble principles were crushed. Cheating and economic oppression were commonplace. The attitudes of business people were downright carnivorous. *"You have increased the number of your merchants till they are more than the stars of the sky, but like locusts they strip the land and then fly away"* (Nahum 3:16). They would constantly and incessantly push for productivity increases, whether through new technology or deceit. Every scrap was utilized and nothing was left for the poor. Laborers were scrimped of their fair wages, weigh scales were tampered with and labeled consumer products were sold with filler. Of course, all of these practices are evident in today's commerce. For example, hams are artificially impregnated with water to boost their weight; purchasing agents extort the sellers for lower prices. Beef is considered pure as long as it doesn't have more than a certain percentage of filler and chocolate containing 5% vegetable fat can still be called chocolate. Labor is treated as an inanimate commodity. The point of life is to make a profit, to boost the stock prices, to hoard wealth and to stake a secure claim in the material world.

The Impact Of Greed Upon Society

A materialistic society by necessity must be a greedy one. *"From the least to the greatest, all are greedy for gain; prophets and priests alike, all practice deceit"* (Jeremiah 6:13). We see that all of society was infected with burning greed. Gain had become the motive and incentive for all human action. And in the competitive sweepstakes to accrete wealth, gold diggers needed to resort to deceit. After all, if everyone was seeking gain, an advantage was necessary to succeed. One needed to be deceitful in order to win a bigger share of the pie. After a while, deceit became an accepted practice and society was "blessing the greedy." Truth was sacrificed for one shekel more.

Greed was not only limited to the heathen. Instead, the deceitful practices driven by greed found a home in the highest institutions of the land including its priesthood. *"With their mouths they express devotion, but their hearts are greedy for unjust gain"* (Ezekiel 33:31). That doesn't sound very different from today. A significant part of the Church is teaching so-called godly principles for no other reason than to achieve greater success in gaining increase and prosperity. Scripture is studied so as to be able to apply biblical principals to get rich as opposed to the purpose of worshipping and honoring God for who He is. Christians who aren't prosperous (wealthy, both in a relative and materialistic sense) apparently don't have enough faith. We are to believe that if Christians have been perfected in righteousness, we will accumulate above average wealth in a world that is governed by an ungodly financial system. Of course, that's not to say that Christians can't be wealthy (not withstanding the fact that it's harder to get into heaven that way). It's just impossible that all can be rich. And, it's even less likely that charitable Christians would be among the majority of that number. In my experience, businessmen that identify themselves as Christians are often no less treacherous in their dealings than unscrupulous operators who make no pretense of being ethical. The shark-like conduct systemized into our society's commercial activities is so pervasive and accepted that it's often difficult for us to see our weekday hypocrisy against our holy conduct on the Sabbath.

The pursuit of gain, aided with a good measure of deceit, ultimately leads to the hoarding of wealth. This presents a new challenge: arrogance and complacency.

• *"Ephraim boasts, 'I am very rich; I have become wealthy. With all my wealth they will not find in me any iniquity or sin"* (Hosea 12:8).

• *"They are all shepherds who lack understanding; they all turn to their own way, each seeks his own gain. "Come," each one cries, "let me get wine! Let us drink our fill of beer! And tomorrow will be like today, or even far better'"* (Isaiah 56:12).

• *"O unfaithful daughter, you trust in your riches and say, 'Who will attack me?'"* (Jeremiah 49:4).

Adulation Of The Wealthy

When looking at the magazines displayed on the newsstand, it becomes very obvious that wealth and arrogance are idolized. Business magazines such as *Forbes, Fortune, Money,* and many others tend to dote on the rich and powerful *ad nauseum.* Those who have accumulated great wealth are profiled for us to envy. They are scrutinized so as to discover their secrets of success. Most of them love to see themselves quoted, and arrogantly ascribe their success to their acumen, wisdom, and possibly a bit of luck. The implied message is this: Since they're rich, they must be intelligent, noble people.

The pervasive materialism of the prophet's day resulted in complacency. With the great accumulation of wealth, surely tomorrow won't be any different. Prosperity will continue. Why would anyone tamper with such a successful system of beliefs? Today, this same arrogance is expressed in many forms. Quantitative modeling is used to predict the future. These techniques, though they sound esoteric and sophisticated, are all based on a simple assumption that the future will be like the past. As mentioned in Chapter 8, some even openly claim that the superior mathematics of today has actually superseded the need for a belief in God. Like that society of old, what we see today is that society has put its trust in wealth, either real or its mathematical derivations.

When Desire For Wealth Supersedes Truth

The price of this headlong pursuit of wealth is that society agrees to sacrifice truth.

- *"From the least to the greatest, all are greedy for gain; prophets and priests alike, all practice deceit"* (Jeremiah 8:10).
- *"They strengthen the hands of evildoers, so that no one turns from his wickedness"* (Jeremiah 23:14).
- *"Truth is nowhere to be found, and whoever shuns evil becomes a prey"* (Isaiah 59:15).
- *"Truth has perished; it has vanished from their lips"* (Jeremiah 7:28).
- *"They make ready their tongue like a bow, to shoot lies; it is not by truth that they triumph in the land"* (Jeremiah 9:3).
- *"Their tongue is a deadly arrow; it speaks with deceit. With his mouth each speaks cordially to his neighbor, but in his heart he sets a trap for him"* (Jeremiah 9:8).

There are too many similar verses to quote them all. The message is clear: Today, great success in worldly terms is likely to come with a heavy price: the loss of truth, faithfulness and uprightness. In fact, it's gone far past this condition. We are told that only the strong survive. If you don't play the game, you will be the victim. The message? Join in. Play the game vigorously.

Our entire society winks. When a toothpaste company says that if we use their product our teeth will be whiter than white, we wink. Of course, nothing can be whiter than white, but that's OK. We know that they're only trying to sell their product. Salesmen pitch their products based upon what they believe clients will want to hear, not what the product will actually deliver. Marketers openly agree that their practices are really a form of gamesmanship. Therefore, a little artistic license is necessary with the concept of truth.

We also learn that economic oppression was a condition of society during the time of the prophets. *"Among my people are wicked men who lie in wait like men who snare birds and like those who set traps to catch men. Like cages full of birds, their houses are full of deceit; they have become rich and powerful and have grown fat and sleek. Their evil deeds have no limit; they do not plead the case of the fatherless to win it, they do not defend the rights of the poor"* (Jeremiah 5:26–28). By and large, in a deceitful society driven by greed, it is generally (though not always) true that for every winner, there's a loser. The wealthy can only become super rich if there are many others who are less than rich, or actually poor. To a degree, wealth is a relative concept. *"You have not obeyed me; you have not proclaimed freedom for your fellow countrymen"* (Jeremiah 34:17). It is obvious that many people became enslaved by the economic system of that day.

Rising Debt And Financial Inequality

One reliable sign of increasing oppression is the trend of indebtedness. High debt levels indicate two conditions, one the mirror image of the other. The higher that debts soar, the greater the oppression. This is true both for individual and sovereign nations. The handmaiden of high indebtedness is an increasing gap between the "haves" and the "have-nots." After all, debt is borrowed money. It must be borrowed from someone or some entity that has money to begin with. Therefore, the more borrowed money, the wealthier must be those who are lending it.

The more skewed the distribution of wealth in society or the world, the greater the oppression. Not only are debts higher today than ever before, wealth is more unevenly distributed than ever before in modern financial history.

The World Bank's research indicates that the gap between rich and poor countries continues to widen. In 1993, the richest country had 72 times the wealth of the poorest on a per capita basis. This difference was only a factor of 3 in 1920. No doubt, there is extreme financial enslavement in the world today: *"They trample on the heads of the poor as upon the dust of the ground and deny justice to the oppressed"* (Amos 2:7a). *"You trample on the poor and force him to give you grain"* (Amos 5: 11). All of the conditions referred to in this verse apply to today as never before. For example, today's poorest nation tends to be the commodity producing countries. It's not surprising then to discover that many commodity prices are no higher today in real terms than they were one hundred years ago.

Evidence Of Collusion

Are there conspiracies at work today? Of course. They were evident 2500 years ago: *"Woe to those who go to great depths to hide their plans from the LORD, who do their work in darkness and think "Who sees us? Who will know?"* (Isaiah 29:15). The dilemma of the commodity-producing countries alone raises the question. Conspiracies are seen everywhere despite rafts of laws that seek to counter such behavior. For example, an enormous amount of money is being plundered from today's shareholders through the unprecedented use of employee stock options for senior corporate executives. Few are trying to stop it. Securities regulators, accounting standards organizations, investment analysts and portfolio managers all have complicity. It's been a lucrative game for those who are part of this conspiracy. Why stop it? Corporations use aggressive and creative accounting practices to pump up their earnings in order to boost their share prices as we have already learned. The most heinous of these of many is the raiding of pension funds. It is currently being done by some of the most recognizable companies in North America. Conspiracies abound in today's global financial environment.

We may have become inured to this fact: No other cause or objective is nobler these days than the pursuit of money. It's true, isn't it? Reading all of the indictments of the prophets of several millennia ago casts this reality into stark relief.

God's Judgments Similar To The Past?

An important question to ponder is this: If God, who is slow to anger, did not tolerate the sins of Israel and Judah 2500 years ago, would He be more inclined to turn a blind eye to the practices of so-called "Christian" nations today? Furthermore, would Christ allow His Church to be part of such a system of conduct?

I don't dare answer, as I am hardly qualified to make such an assessment. Yet, looking at the facts, the answer must surely be no. Isn't it true that much of the Church is indistinguishable from broader society in terms of its heart and main focus? A good part of the Church is in the midst of the fray, trying to grab its share of financial prosperity. Saying this, I would be the first to admit that I carry personal culpability too. Through the study and research of these issues, I have come to realize how much I have yet to face up to my own idolatries. I've been born and raised in this society; therefore, my eyes are surely only partially opened to the moral reality of our day.

The Forecasts Of The Prophets Not Reliable

A crucial fact to realize is that only a handful of the prophets of 2500 hundred years ago actually spoke the truth, actually heard from God. *"They are prophesying to you false visions, divinations, idolatries and the delusions of their own minds"* (Jeremiah 14:14). The Old Testament prophets began their forecasting many years ahead of the calamities that eventually resulted. They weren't day-traders by any means. Their only interest was truth—the Truth. These prophets were more concerned about the road traveled, warning about where this path would ultimately lead. They had no interest in trying to predict the exact point that God's wrath would fall. They weren't making a living with timing services that tried to get their subscribers out of their real estate holdings not a moment too soon — near the point that the Babylonians were crashing the city gates. If they were managing real estate portfolios, I doubt they would have been concerned about short-term timing. Neither is it likely that the prophets would have been cashing in on their "predictions" (things revealed to them by God) and trying to build a reputation for themselves. Would they have tried to make themselves wealthy by setting up survival supply companies? I believe these types of thoughts were the furthest from their minds. They were singularly motivated to speak God's message. They were compelled. As unpopular as they were, it gave them relief to simply complete God's beckoning. To not prophesy would have filled them with even more anguish than did the rejection of society at large.

Jeremiah whined to God, *"I have neither lent nor borrowed, yet everyone curses me"* (Jeremiah 15:10). He was not participating in a financial system that operated to oppress the poor and transfer wealth to the "experts in greed" by way of a loose credit culture. Apparently, because he wasn't, people thought that Jeremiah was being judgmental. How dare he not endorse the "perpetual money machine" that was enriching a select few and oppressing the majority.

Lessons For Our Day

Having briefly examined the economic conditions during the times of some of the Old Testament prophets, we discover two lessons relevant to our current age. Those who don't want to endorse the prevailing system of greed will not have it easy; they will be seen as unwelcome misfits and labeled as "spoil sports."

The second message is that there is hope. Though conditions may seem difficult and insecurities may press in from every side, Jeremiah, with all his scare-mongering, provides a comforting promise: *"But blessed is the man who trusts in the LORD, whose confidence is in him. He will be like a tree planted by the water that sends out its roots by the stream. It does not fear when heat comes; its leaves are always green. It has no worries in a year of drought and never fails to bear fruit"* (Jeremiah 17:7– 8). It's a simple message: Trust not in gold or share portfolios; trust in the Lord and there will be no reason to worry about droughts.

⤚

Having reviewed some of the prophets and secular soothsayers of the Old Testament, how do our modern forecasters compare? What do they say about the prospects for North America and the rest of the world — even Babylon the Great, the sprawling commercial/ monetary colossus of our day?

ENDNOTES

1. Isaiah 30:10–11.
2. "Pillow prophets" is a phrase found in the King James Version of the Bible describing so-called "prophets" that constantly predicted peace and prosperity. See the book *Set the Trumpet to Thy Mouth* written by David Wilkerson.

CHAPTER 16

The Modern Prophets:
Doom Vs. Boom

Who Speaks the Truth?

W e have already learned from searching the Scriptures that the great idolatry evident in a satanic monetary/commercial system — Babylon the Great — will be judged. *"In one hour your doom has come,"* says Revelation 18:10, and again in verse 17, *"In one hour such great wealth has been brought to ruin!"* As well, the Old Testament prophets spoke similar things about the time of the end. The huge catastrophes and loss of human life mentioned in the book of Revelation that unfold as various disasters are inflicted upon the world are certain to obliterate economies and the value of financial investments. But are these warnings really relevant to our time — to North America and the rest of the world?

The prophets may have castigated Judah and Israel for their idolatries, immoral economic systems and oppression of the poor as reviewed in the previous chapter. But these warnings were not the precursor of the Great Tribulation of the world. Though this is true, these two nations individually did not escape the disciplines of their God. They experienced terrible, terrible hardships — utter decimation, slaughter and captivity. It surely felt like a great tribulation. But it did not usher in the Great Tribulation. Clearly, God deals with individual nations and states. The major prophets — Jeremiah, Ezekiel, and Isaiah — all spoke God's judgments against various nations and kings that had become too proud or immoral. These included Babylon, Tyre and many others. Eventually, these nations ended up as nothing more than rubble heaps. Is one of these types of downturns imminent? Having chronicled developments in Japan over the past few decades, we have seen a proud and arrogant nation brought low only recently. Are America and some of its sister countries next, perhaps even the entire world?

These are extremely important questions for more than a few reasons. Uppermost is this fact: The economic bust of the last days is not the only one that the prophets and men of the Bible either forewarned or foreknew. It just happens to be the only major bust foretold that has yet to happen. All the others — from the great famine during the time of Joseph, the Babylonian conquest of Israel, the destruction of Tyre, Assyria and Babylon and others — are the subjects of history books. All of these were prophesied. All of them happened. Only one remains unfulfilled.

How do the predictions of today's Bible teachers compare?

What Today's Prophets Are Saying

Many preachers and prophecy teachers these days are

also anticipating difficult and catastrophic times ahead for economies and financial markets. As a group, their predictions include huge drops in the S&P 500[1] Index, severe economic depressions, food shortages and the like. In fact, similar types of forecasts have been made for years. No, nothing is implausible about these forecasts. Indeed, economies have collapsed, currencies have swooned and financial markets have collapsed before.

United States' markets have not been excluded from these disasters. In fact, one of the largest one-day falls in stock markets this century occurred in the US during the 1980s. As well, the US dollar has experienced incredible swings during the past decade that almost rival the crashes witnessed by much smaller countries. At least once every decade since the advent of floating currencies (1970), the US currency has experienced a major decline. The US dollar swooned against the Japanese yen by over 40% in less than 3 months in the early months of 1994. This was the currency of the biggest economic power in the world. In that context, predictions of huge drops in the Dow Jones stock market index of thousands of points or more cannot be considered ridiculous. Such drops could happen at anytime.

But are the large financial and economic tremors of the type being forecasted really the disasters that they seem? These days, a large part of the financial community thrives on high risk and volatility — large, short-term swings in financial prices. More often than not, big swings in market prices benefit the movers and shakers in the financial world. High financial volatility provides an ideal smoke-screen to transfer huge amounts of wealth. This is nothing unusual. Therefore, predictions of future market declines within the range experienced in recent decades hardly rate sermons of fire, brimstone and judgment from the pulpits.

To suggest that past market swings, large as they were, might have represented a divine judgment — an intervention outside the normal physical laws that God has set in place — may overstate the case. Why? In the first instance, these types of crises have hardly caused any permanent change in people's attitudes. Despite the black days of October 1987 and the spectacular, gut-wrenching financial turmoil in Asia, Russia, Argentina and other countries in recent years, the world is still here, reason the secular world observers. Moreover, financial markets have continued to soar from one enriching high to the next and will do so again. With that being the case, why wouldn't investors ignore the doomsters? Who's afraid of God's judgment if financial markets can be counted on to march higher after another brief disciplining?

Endtime Or Short-Term Market Forecasts?

Given the great urgency of our times, financial and economic predictions by Christians today, whether pastors, prophecy teachers or stewardship counselors, must be about more than just the regular cyclical gyrations of the business world, as volatile as they may be these days. If not, their predictions of doom or boom would fall into the same category as all other forecasters, secular or otherwise. It would be difficult to draw any special differentiation between all these shorter-term forecasters, most of whom are intent on financial gain.

Then, what kinds of economic and financial disasters are being predicted by the preachers and prophecy scholars? There are different kinds, as already implied. Which one is it? Could it be the "big one" — the one prophesied in the books of Revelation and Daniel for Babylon the Great? Or, is it the more frequent type of bust that follows periods of excessive boom and arrogant humanism every 20 to 50 years or so? There's a big difference between these types of scenarios. Only one results from the direct intervention of God as a warning and punishment upon a morally wicked world. The others are a natural outcome of the physical laws that God originally set into motion when He created mankind and the earth. He does not need to directly intervene for these downturns to occur (though He may — God can do anything, of course.) Just as what goes up without foundation must come down, so an excessive rise in credit must be followed by a fall in financial markets. Built into the created order is a cyclic correctional phase. Busts follow booms both in the monetary affairs of mankind and in the ecosystem in which we live. Economic adjustments follow credit excesses; a boom in the lemming population is followed by a decline. We see that God's disciplinary boundaries are part of the physical creation. Just as our bodies are disciplined through exhaustion or disease if we abuse them, the same applies to all created order whether economic systems of mankind or nature.

It is true that in recent years, a good part of the business cycle has been smoothed out through the use of technology. Today, with computer-aided management systems and the practice of "just in time" inventorying[2] a major contributing factor to short-term business cycle swings has been greatly reduced. In itself, this is probably a good development in the sense that it makes it easier for producers and consumers to make decisions. On the other hand, in no way does this application of technology repeal God's natural laws. When a recession or depression takes hold, it will not be avoided through the help of technology. If anything, such declines will be accelerated.

Not all Christian forecasters have predicted doom. Not to be forgotten is Dave Hunt, who in his book *Peace, Prosperity and the Coming Holocaust,* published in 1983, went against the pessimistic grain of the times and suggested that a time of great economic prosperity was ahead. His main conclusion was certainly correct. A fallen world that is no longer in need of God will more likely be *"...eating and drinking, marrying, and giving in marriage"*[3] before Christ's return just as they were before the time of the great flood, than be chastened by a great economic tribulation. In his view, a period of great world prosperity was more likely before Christ's return than a great economic collapse. Although his view may have seemed iconoclastic at the time, I see Hunt's view as compatible to the predictions of other Christians who believe that great calamity is ahead — the calamities of the Great Tribulation and the fall of the commercial colossus, Babylon the Great. An *Endtime Money Snare* — one that is hugely deceptive, corrupt, unjust and that tests the very complicity of Christians as this book presents — is likely to take place before the Great Tribulation begins. Nothing could be so effective as a world-wide prosperity and boom in wealth to divert the attention of humanity from approaching judgment.

Does God really need modern-day prophets to make predictions about the normal, regular cyclic movements of financial markets? If anything, a modern-day prophet would warn about God's coming judgment of the entire fixation with materialism and money — the world financial system represented by Babylon the Great. Not only does it entail a financial and economic collapse like none ever before witnessed upon the face of the earth, it represents extreme and present dangers to Christians now for reasons we will yet examine.

False Prophets: Wolves In Sheep's Clothing

Many others are making forecasts about the future under the guise of Christianity and godliness. In recent years, there's been a flood of Christian financial planners and various other pulpit forecasters who promote the idea that if practiced correctly, Christian stewardship will lead to above-average wealth and riches. Some actually even delude themselves into believing that they have been anointed to forecast short-term investment markets for no other apparent purpose than gain and increase. They present themselves as God's diviners — Spirit-led apostles of prosperity. The fruit by which we are asked to test them is by the harvest of material riches. Many Christian radio stations carry their advertisements. I believe that for the most part these people are either well-meaning but deluded or outright false prophets. Either way, they serve the pocketbook, not Christ.

Are the financial and economic forecasts of these Christian forecasters intended to edify the Body of Christ either through reproof or preparation? Or, do they seek to promote a brand of successful Christian living that's evidenced through wealth and prosperity? The answers to these important questions reveal the true spirit behind their forecasts. It is hardly a call to repentance and purity.

A school of thought exists that believes that the Church will reform the world and its systems before Christ's return. Generally, this view is promoted by "preterists." *Reconstructionism* and *Dominion Theory* are some of its schools of thought. A general belief common to them all is that the world has already passed the Great Tribulation (generally thought to have occurred in 70 AD at the time of the Roman destruction of Jerusalem and the Temple) and is now in the period before the final return of Christ. They believe that Christian influence and world rule will succeed in introducing a godly society and a reformed economic system before Christ returns. The implication here is that financial idolatries will all be cleaned up on earth under Christian rule. This perspective contrasts sharply with the viewpoints expressed in this book. I do not intend to review the points of theological difference. Christians seem to be just as deceived and fallen these days with respect to the enticing prosperity of "market economics" as are non-Christians.

Idolatry More Dangerous Than A Great Depression

We are told of a great falling away in the last days that even affects the Church. There is an idolatry so deep and complete that sweeps the world to the point that it no longer needs God, though the foundations of the earth may shake. Consider the depth of the idolatry during those days. In Revelation 9:20-21 we read: *"The rest of mankind that were not killed by these plagues still did not repent of the work of their hands; they did not stop worshipping demons, and idols of gold, silver, bronze, stone and wood — idols that cannot see or hear or walk. Nor did they repent of their murders, their magic arts, their sexual immorality or their thefts."*

This passage illustrates the intensity of the challenge posed to believers. Just imagine! Catastrophes and calamities have raked the earth; stars have fallen; the sun has been obscured; more than a third of mankind has been killed. Six of the seven angels have carried out their tasks, the wrath of each having been unleashed upon the world. Yet, the idolatries remain. Still the world refuses to recognize and worship God and remains intoxicated with the memories of its past idols. Every knee has still not bowed. Talk of deep-seated idolatries!

Many of the idolatries mentioned in the above passage have to do with material things — the idols of gold, silver, bronze, stone and wood. Reading the books of the prophets in the Old Testament and the historical books of the *Apocrypha*, countless references are made to these same idols made out of gold, stone and wood. There are more than 200 references to material idols of this type in the Bible. Indeed, the pagans of the Old Testament surely worshipped images of gods made out of such materials. In the New Testament we learn of the silversmiths of Corinth who made a lucrative trade selling silver figurines and trinkets related to the god of Artemis (one of the many pagan gods of fertility). They were quite upset with the apostle Paul because he was depressing their sales volumes with his talk of the risen Christ.

To believe in the powers of gods that could be modeled and captured in three-dimensional form by human hands must surely seem ludicrous. The massive foolishness of this belief must surely seem obvious to those living at the start of the third millennium. Yet, the quote regarding idols found in Revelation refers to the people of the endtimes, our modern society. This verse uses the exact same wording as many other Scripture passages in the Old Testament which castigated societies for similar practices in that day. Are these endtime idols some kind of figurines or even statues made out of these materials? I don't believe so. The object of all the references associated with the idols of gold, stone and wood in the Old Testament was to point out that they were the work of their hands. As such, it's clear that the idolatry mentioned in Revelation was an idolatry of materialism and the works of mankind. These things have to do with the material aspects of the world today, namely; money, economics and commerce.

Based on the evidence this book has presented so far, we are not shocked to learn that the world today has fallen into worshipping new gods made by the work of their hands. Already, the *Endtime Money Snare* is in full swing.

Most of the world — certainly the Western world, North America and many Christians — are under the deep spell of MOFI, GLOBO and SCITE as well as the love of money.

The Outlook For Believers

We know that a great judgment will fall upon this present endtime system. A great collapse of the world's economy then ensues; the enormous false effigy of wealth and prosperity will be revealed, its promises of security shown to be hollow against the incomparable promises and grace of God that extends into eternity. Yet, we can't be certain when this will happen. To be sure, it will most certainly occur no later than during the first half of the Great Tribulation. Daniel numbers this time to extend to a full seven years. That means Babylon the Great — representing our present-day world financial and commercial system — will come to naught sometime before its mid-point.

Whether one believes in the pre-tribulation, post-tribulation or other views (these having to do with the timing of the Rapture or bodily resurrection of Christians), I believe that Christians will at least witness many, if not all of the prophesied conditions that lead to this event.

What's much more important for living Christians are the issues of complicity and moral impurity of such idolistic conditions that exist in the lead up to this time. We must live during at least part of these times where the processes that come to fruition in the Tribulation are already underway no matter what our beliefs about endtime events. Yet, all the same, we are also charged to be good stewards of the fruits of our labor and businesses. How do we steer between bad stewardship and idolatry and worldly complicity? It's no easy task. I lay out some guidelines to consider at the end of this book.

The fact is this: Whether we are savers, direct investors or not, our lives are tied up with the financial system and its markets in one way or another. All of our vessels are on the same financial sea. The only difference is that some of these boats aren't very seaworthy, while others are heavily overloaded with material goods; a precious few are securely anchored.

Comparing the life of Christian stewardship to a boat is appropriate. Quoting an anonymous writer, "A Christian is to the world as is a ship to the water. Woe to the ship if the water should get inside of it."

"In that day men will throw away
to the rodents and bats
their idols of silver and idols of gold,
which they made to worship.
They will flee to caverns in the rocks
and to the overhanging crags
from dread of the LORD
and the splendor of his majesty,
when he rises to shake the earth.
Stop trusting in man,
who has but a breath in his nostrils.
Of what account is he?"
Isaiah 2:20-22

ENDNOTES

1.   S&P 500 Index is a composite index of the price of 500 stocks. If the index level of the S&P 500 rises, it implies that the total value of the outstanding stocks of these 500 stocks has risen.

2.   JIT or "just-in-time" is an inventory technique that has gained popularity since the early 1980s. The Japanese were the originators of the concept. Briefly explained, it is the practice of tightly scheduling all suppliers to deliver their components and materials just days or hours before their use in assembly. This cuts down the amount of investment required by a manufacturer or assembly company for its inventories. More importantly, it tightly links production to demand, thereby reducing the possibility of huge swings in excess inventory. Inventory fluctuations have historically been a main cause of business cycles as well as sharp swings in short-term interest rates.

3.   Matthew 24:38.

CHAPTER 17

Epilogue: What's to Come?

Mere Survival

T o this point, we've searched and studied the Scriptures to discover what information God has provided us to be able to "tell the season" and to understand the nature of the spiritual trials and economic bondages the world is to face. Without a doubt, all of the conditions or processes of the endtimes are evident today. For the first time in human history all of the foretold financial, economic, social and moral conditions exist simultaneously. What urges our expectancy even more is our knowledge of how rapidly the steel jaws of an endtime snare are closing upon humanity. We discovered that a crafty trapper is masterminding its operation from behind the scenes, waiting for the precise moment to make his appearance.

Knowing all this, we ask, "What next?" Though we know that the time is short, we are still unable to make any reliable short-term predictions. How much longer will the Lord wait before He metes out His justice upon an ungodly world? Will He allow a great false prosperity to sweep the world even more completely, gaining many more converts to the promises of a materialistic realm? Or, will the Lord first allow one or more world economic depressions before the final one of the Great Tribulation? If so, God would only allow it out of a desire that none would be lost. His longsuffering nature would cause Him to graciously grant the world at least one more warning about the insecurity and temporality of the world.

Economic downturns — especially deep depressions — bring correction. Not only do they bring balance back to economies and financial markets; they also usually cause a revival in humility and faith. God often chooses to do His works of grace and discipline through adversity. No doubt about it, depressions bring pain and adversity. For many of us who have been pulled away from a full-faith and dependence upon God by the worldly lure of easy money and limitless earthly prosperity, an economic depression would not be a bad thing when measured across eternity. We might yet be corrected and purified — even saved.

Christ Will Likely Not Return During Hard Times

Though we can't predict the exact timing of Christ's return, the beginning of the Great Tribulation or the sudden onset of economic disaster, this one thing we know for sure: According to Christ Himself, He will not return during an economic depression.

"Just as it was in the days of Noah, so also will it be in the days of the Son of Man. People were eating, drinking, marrying and being given in marriage up to the day Noah entered the ark. Then the flood came and destroyed them all. It was the same in the days of Lot. People were eating and drinking, buying and selling, planting and building. But the day Lot left Sodom, fire and sulfur rained down from heaven and destroyed them all. It will be just like this on the day the Son of Man is revealed" (Luke 17:26–30). Matthew recorded Jesus' words that *"...they knew nothing about what would happen until the flood came and took them all away"* (Matthew 24:39).

These accounts of the day of the Son of Man (Christ's Second Coming) are hardly consistent with a time of great trouble. Things are going pretty satisfactorily for the world when He returns. People are eating and drinking. The world is not starving or preoccupied with economic collapse.

The Bible says nothing of a depression or destruction of wealth prior to the great deluge of Noah's time or the destruction of Sodom and Gomorrah. We could conclude that no such warning was given. Perhaps God had allowed minor famines and droughts to occur one or more times in previous decades in His loving, long-suffering attempts to reassert His sovereignty over mankind and creation. We cannot know, as such events are not recorded. Yet the appointed time came and God's wrath was unleashed. Only Noah's family survived the flood. In Israel's case — His chosen people — God provided repeated warnings through his prophets of coming destruction, even causing periods of droughts in his desire to awaken them to return to Him. All the same, Israel chose to ignore the prophets, preferring to live the high life as they wanted. From these parallel accounts and Scriptures we can safely assume that the world will not be in the depths of a great systemic financial collapse or depression at the time of Christ's return. We should expect just the opposite. The world will be caught up with a man-made prosperity, self-sufficiency, and certainly will not expect any intervention by a God who is supposedly obsolete in the modern technological age.

How Soon?

Scripture offers no statements allowing us to know the exact timing of Christ's Second Coming or of any great economic and financial collapse that might be associated with this great and expected event. Christ Himself said that only God Himself knew when He would return. Despite our perplexity about short-term events, we can still conclude without a doubt that the world is living in unprecedented times ... the endtimes. We can recognize the very season of Christ's return. By the measure of past world history, we must conclude that all the conditions are already in place for a massive economic depression at some point in the future; in fact, the very near future. Not only are all the economic and financial conditions primed for a great economic downturn, also present today are all of the necessary conditions prophesied for judgment.

Yet, we must be careful. I am not convinced that past events in human history — moral and economic — can serve as reliable benchmarks with which to predict the timing of the last great economic downturn of the Great Tribulation. Why? We must again remember that we are considering the great endtime agenda. It represents the last move, the grand finale of Satan's endtime agenda to woo a world into worshipping him, the false christ. The last economic upwards surge — a period of false prosperity — should be the greatest the world has ever experienced. Though it may largely be the product of massive deception, this prosperity must be extremely convincing, capable of even persuading the majority of the world of its continuing longevity. Because of this, knowledge of past human history and economic and financial precedent will only be of limited help to us in our quest to find any indications as to the timing of its end.

We know that the *Endtime Money Snare* is already at a state of high development, yet there is no telling how much further and longer its advance might continue. It's probably safe to assume that we should not be surprised at how far it might progress. In Ecclesiastes 7:25 we read about the "...*stupidity of wickedness and the madness of folly.*" Viewed from that perspective, much more stupidity and madness may be ahead. It presents a type of Catch-22 dilemma. Stupidity and madness by their nature are among the most difficult to predict—especially so for rational, thinking Christians. How mad is mad? What is the limit of irrationality?

Yet, to conclude that mankind's commercial systems promise inviolable prosperity forever and ever begs incredulity, too. That's exactly the belief that's implied by the optimistic bias of today's financial practitioners. It's really an attitude that demonstrates supreme arrogance, if not ignorance. For one, it entirely precludes a belief in a sovereign God, the source of all true wealth. Secondly, it represents a belief system, a faith that is really no different than the pagan worship of the *"...gods of wood and stone."* Financial markets are the works of man, not God. And, an arrogant dependence and faith in these works of man, rising up toward heaven itself as the Tower of Babel, surely invites the One and Only true God to make His displeasure and presence known.

The Likelihood Of An Economic Bust

Apart from what the Bible has to say, are there any indications that suggest difficult economic times are ahead? Yes, I believe there are. In my opinion, there can be little doubt that the next sustainable downturn in the US economy and its financial markets could be a humdinger. The US and the world are vulnerable to a financial bust that could make the economic and financial downturn of the 1930s pale in comparison.

Upon what facts — if any — do I base my opinions about future economic events? My answers with respect to near-term possibility of such events are based entirely upon secular economic theory and historical precedent. As already warned, short-term forecasts of any kind are notoriously unreliable. Any answers I provide are my personal opinions based upon my own limited understanding. Therefore, they could be flawed. You must draw your own conclusions.

I first appeal to a simple biblical principle: *"God cannot be mocked. A man reaps what he sows"* (Galatians 6:7).[1] By the measure of the depth and length of the excesses that have been allowed to occur beforehand, we can establish a pretty accurate idea of how severe the corrective downturn that must follow will be. The longer the duration of the excesses that have occurred during the preceding upward phase, the deeper and more severe the downward phase that follows. Actually, this is a doctrine of economic theory that has been forgotten long ago. Respected economist Gottfried Haberler stated, "The length and severity of depressions depend partly on the magnitude of the 'real' maladjustments, which developed during the preceding boom and partly on the aggravating monetary and credit conditions."[2] Few modern, mainstream financial economists practicing today make any appeal to this law.[3] It's much too restrictive in an age of unlimited gain, credit and money.

If an economic crash is just ahead, then we should be able to point to evidence of the excesses today that should precede this event. We should be able to identify a massive financial and economic bubble if my view is correct.

Undeniable Proof Of The Existence Of A Financial Bubble

Despite the high level of skepticism on the question of the existence of a financial bubble, some reliable diagnostic tests can identify such a dangerous financial condition. These come right out of the classic economic textbooks that no one seems to be reading anymore. Accordingly, the key signs to look for (please be patient with the technical jargon for the moment. I'll explain these symptoms in layman's terms) are chronic external account deficits; a collapse in savings levels; and debt and credit growth far in excess of underlying savings growth. Also, a significant widening in the wealth distribution skew is usually an attendant indicator.

We see that all of the classic signs of a financial bubble are evident today, though some still maintain that it is a beast of myth. Its footprints are most obvious in the US. It's worth reviewing some of these trends again in a little more detail. First, debt growth continues to soar far beyond underlying income and savings growth, as already reviewed in a previous chapter.[4] Credit excesses along with capital gains act like wine. In measured amounts they are not dangerous — even good. However, in excess, wine impairs judgment and in time even causes permanent detrimental effects upon its user. In the human body, a dependency known as alcoholism develops. In time, brain cells are destroyed and the liver malfunctions because it is overtaxed with poison. Death is the result. It is the same for an economy. Only here the addiction expresses itself in these other symptoms of a financial bubble.

These include a collapse in household savings levels. In the US they have fallen to the lowest levels since the 1930s, as we also reviewed in a prior chapter. Never before have savings fallen so deeply and for so long, certainly not during periods of supposed prosperity. Next, a chronic and large current account deficit has emerged in recent years. This means that the US has become an enormous borrower from the rest of the world, in effect, borrowing a good part of its current prosperity. And lastly, we must note that the wealth skew continues to widen as never before in America and around the globe. The rich become mega-rich; the rest more enslaved. Without a doubt, all of these tests indicate that an enormous financial bubble exists — in fact, the biggest ever in modern financial history. It has spread progressively to a large part of the world. The long-term effects are a damaged and distorted economy laden with debt and uneconomic investments that eventually succumb to a depression. These are all long-term effects. But, don't be fooled. They surely are underway.

We have only taken a brief, surface review of the various imbalances in the US and world economies. I could present volumes of evidence supported by arcane economic theory and reams of analysis, most of which would lead to a similar conclusion. The fact is that the excesses we see taking place in the US and around the world today are the worst and largest ever when compared with the annals of financial history. The many excesses reviewed all represent unsustainable trends and developments that are subject to the laws of a pendulum. In time, they must fall back in upon themselves once the energy of the upward momentum has been spent. A reverse movement then gains momentum. Economic growth then slows dramatically and even reverses. Financial markets fall steeply. The ultimate lows that financial markets will eventually plummet seem totally unfathomable to investors at the prior peaks. For example, many stocks will fall 90% or more — even 100% — in value. The prices of other assets could fall steeply as well.

I conclude that a serious financial and economic bust is not only possible but also probable before long.

There is one big problem with the view I have expressed. While it may be true, it cannot apply to America alone. Not in today's globalized world. Quite a few countries display similar conditions, primarily the Anglo-Saxon siblings, Britain, Canada, and Australia. As stated in Chapter 14, these countries together account for greater than two-fifths of world economic output, two-thirds of world stock market value, and more than 40% of the value of the world bond markets. It is simply not possible that these countries can face severe hardship without pulling down the entire world into similar calamity. Therefore we must conclude that the evidence we have considered points to a great vulnerability to an imminent collapse of the entire economic and financial system.

Could it be then that the next economic depression will be the final one of the Great Tribulation — possibly the one following Christ's return? This question is not intended to be sensationalist. Logic forces us to consider it further. Though we are still in the dark as to the exact timing of these possible events, it requires an urgent answer.

Finding No Safety In A Financial Ark

As readers now know, the world is busily building a financial/commercial ark of the endtime. It's the secular development of our times — an amazingly rapid one seen against human history. In any project as big as this, there are bound to be accidents and upsets on the way even if orchestrated by the mastermind Satan himself. Indeed, the promised new age of perpetual financial wealth and blessed self-interest and greed has been gaining millions of adherents. Yet, the physical forces of nature applying to economies and the weight of money and debt have not yet been entirely repealed. Any excesses still beg an adjustment eventually — a correction — even if only temporarily. While a certain measure of greed is praised, too much can still be a bad thing even in our modern-day monetary/commercial colossus. Even wolves have to take turns eating their prey. Everyone marching to the drumbeat of Mammon cannot be too greedy at the same time.

So we see that this great financial ark has begun facing a number of high waves. The swings in financial markets in recent times are simply unprecedented. Massive crashes are quickly followed by huge upward surges. Some experts say its part of the new era of financial wealth. Just get used to it, keep your eyes shut and your hope fixed on the inevitability of a long-term, upwards trend and you and everybody else will be rich, they counsel. Of course, this is nonsense. Yet it is readily believed.

But why is this happening? It's obvious that the accumulation of wealth has become a serious fixation for the average person. Otherwise, swings in financial values wouldn't so supercharged. Faced with the prospect of loss, near panic breaks out. Yet, at the same time raw greed prevails. Apparently, the biggest cardinal sin of our time is to not be fully invested and grab a piece of the booming pie of financial wealth. Few understand — or indeed, want to know — that much financial wealth is pure hot air. Wealth can never translate into income for society overall. Wealth exists in the mind. The lures of the *Endtime Money Snare* are enormous. With gushing gains in wealth, given the general lack of knowledge about the world and financial affairs, people can be excused if they think that financial markets are a source of real wealth.

The fact is that Western society is caught up in the biggest financial and materialistic idolatry ever recorded in the history of mankind. Indeed, an enormous infatuation with increase and gain is deluding and blinding the minds of many people. The lure of easy gain and wealth is a powerful lure that causes people to abandon rationality.

I see this happening around me virtually every day. Normally conservative, levelheaded people finally give in to the pull of easy gains and greed. Deep down in their hearts they may know that the boom in worldly wealth has little foundation. Yet, after missing out on fantastic financial market gains year after year and watching their friends and neighbors grow prosperous, they can't take it anymore. They throw caution to the wind. The newspapers are full of stories of instant mega-millionaires and mutual funds that have tripled and quadrupled in value. Their friends gloat about the gains they have made. They feel left out — even stupid. Many Christian financial planners strut around the church like they are modern-day prophets, seemingly legitimizing the *Endtime Money Snare*. Too few of them see any serious dangers even now. All together, it becomes like a powerful vortex that draws in many people. They feel forced to buy into the stock market and other financial investments even when they are expensive and the outlook for the world may be poor.

The Role Of Christians In The Financial World

I fail to see where Christian stewards fit into this picture. We are told not to be anxious for anything. Peace and contentment are to be a hallmark of our lives. We should not be pierced by many troubles because our priority is not the pursuit of earthly riches. We are to be good stewards with what has been entrusted us, yet our hearts are to be preoccupied with eternal things. Though we could become materially wealthy, it's far from the focus of our hearts.

But try as we might, it is getting very hard to live out eternal values in our financial world. To do so these days takes courage and perseverance. We must find a sure course — a tried and true approach with which to navigate through these treacherous shoals.

"If we panic about our personal finances or investment, we'll grieve our heavenly Father deeply. Our fretting betrays a fearful attitude that says we don't truly believe He can take care of us."
–God's Plan to Protest His People in the Coming Depression,
David Wilkerson 1998, p. 178

ENDNOTES

1. *"Do not be deceived: God cannot be mocked. A man reaps what he sows. The one who sows to please his sinful nature, from that nature will reap destruction; the one who sows to please the Spirit, from the Spirit will reap eternal life"* (Galatians 6:7-8).

2. Gottfried Haberler, *Prosperity and Depression*, published by George Allen & Unwin, London, 1937.

3. Although not considered mainstream, the last financial economist to continue in this tradition is Dr. Kurt Richebacher. Former chief economist and board member of the Dresdner Bank, this octogenarian still turns out incisive analysis in his monthly letter, *The Richebacher Letter*. His library of economic textbooks and world monetary history is spread into three rooms the last time I visited him. He counts among his friends many people in high places around the world. Though he does not claim that he is able to make short-term predictions through his insightful analysis, he is able to discern that the world is taking the wide road to a certain financial Armageddon.

4. The whole story about extraordinary productivity and profit growth in today's economy attributed to the "new paradigm" is mostly a fable. While a cyclical surge may be underway lately, the record of this past decade on these counts is hardly notable when compared to the entire post-war economic period — certainly nothing worth today's exorbitant P/E multiples. All the same, we are asked to believe that massive profit growth — and therefore mutual fund gains — will be racked up even as nominal economic growth rates run at the lowest pace since the 1930s. In the 1990s, economic growth in current dollars was only an average of 5.3% per annum, much less than the average of each of the prior six decades.

CHAPTER 18

How Shall We Live?

Free and Fearless

We have strong reason to escape the money snare of the last days. If we do not, we stand to suffer both in the world and in our relationship with Jesus Christ. As has been amply documented, the love of money definitely plays an important role in trapping the world and its Christians into serving a materialistic, anti-Christ order. Over and over we are warned about the deceiving attractions of money. We can use it, but we must not consort with it or have inordinate affections for it.

"People who want to get rich fall into temptation and a trap and into many foolish and harmful desires that plunge men into ruin and destruction. For the love of money is a root of all kinds of evil. Some people, eager for money, have wandered from the faith and pierced themselves with many griefs" (1st Timothy 6:9–10). We will experience grief, ruin and destruction if we allow the desire for money to master us, a point this verse makes in no uncertain terms.

We will not be spared these griefs just because we are Christians. Though our salvation may be sure, our travails on earth can still be of our own making. Even as God is with us and for us, we can still experience painful lives of defeat and slavery. It's our own choice. The apostle Paul made this clear by using the example of Moses and the Jews during their 40-year journey in the desert. In 1st Corinthians he said, *"For I do not want you to be ignorant of the fact, brothers, that our forefathers were all under the cloud and that they all passed through the sea. They were all baptized into Moses in the cloud and in the sea. They all ate the same spiritual food and drank the same spiritual drink; for they drank from the spiritual rock that accompanied them, and that rock was Christ. Nevertheless, God was not pleased with most of them; their bodies were scattered over the desert."*[1]

Although the Spirit of God went with them in the form of a cloud by day and fire by night, and though they passed through the parted sea, thousands of them still perished in the desert because God was not pleased with them. Their idolatries and unfaithfulness reaped unpleasant consequences while yet on earth. The lesson applies to us. Though we have passed through to salvation and the Holy Spirit indwells us, we are still open to ruin, destruction and anguish on earth if we make money and the accomplishments of modern technology and globalism our idols. If we give ourselves over to such idolatries, we become servants of a diabolical tyrant. *"There is no rest day or night for those who worship the beast and his image, or for anyone who receives the mark of his name"* (Revelation 14:11).

In addition, if we are not careful and allow the world's anxieties with money, finances and investments to weigh down our hearts we will open ourselves up to the ensnarements of the world. This is an offensive strategy of our enemy that requires a defense. If we are not careful, we won't escape some of the troubles that will afflict the world during the last days and will not even be able to stand before our Lord if we do not recognize this trap and remove ourselves to safety. Escape is possible, Christ tells us: *"Be always on the watch, and pray that you may be able to escape all that is about to happen, and that you may be able to stand before the Son of Man"* (Luke 21:36).

I believe the escape Christ is speaking of is mainly spiritual — one that ensures that our affections are not captured by an apostate world. Of course, He could also be referring to us escaping the Great Tribulation by way of the Rapture. Either one or both of these views lead to the same conclusion. We must strive to escape *"...all that is about to happen."* The possibility for our escape is linked to the condition of our hearts.

The ultimate test of our complicity with this endtime challenge to God's sovereignty is this: Who or what is the true object of our affections, the real object of our hope? Where do we claim our ultimate home? Whom do we worship: God or money? What or who do we love more?

Find Eternal Values In A Financial World

How can we stay spiritually pure and focused upon eternal values in a world that is so inescapably defined in financial terms? How can we continue to live out our faith despite increasing economic and monetary sanctions upon our freedoms now and in the future; how to remain untainted from the ungodly, worldly affections that pull at us like a raging vortex? In the meantime, we do need food and clothes. We must be responsible and prepare for our retirement and our children's education. We do need to use a bank account, debit cards and smart cards. How can we then not be part of this system? Isn't ensnarement in this worldly monetary and economic web of human action unavoidable? Surely, the answer is not to run into the hills; to set up survival camps; hoard food; stockpile gold and cords of wood; to buy guns; or to discover superior investment schemes.

I see the situation this way: Though we may be already physically trapped and ruled by an emergent world monetary/commercial colossus, our spirits and faith need not be. Though we live in a world where it is virtually impossible to escape the reach and dictates of its money system, our hearts do not need to be worldly. We can live godly lives even during times of monetary enslavement and be free people without complicity in the diabolical plot of the endtime kingdom. We can retain pure hearts, steadfastly fixed upon our eternal goal and certain hope, not worldly gain and temporal riches. In a spiritual sense, we can live free.

Physical escape may be another matter. While at this time I see no conflict using most kinds of money vehicles or financial intermediary services, someday this may not be possible. Today, we can still use all of these services as long as our affections remain centered upon God. However, the time may come when an anti-Christian government or world order may use the global financial system to restrict our testimony and religious freedoms. Due to our connectedness to a world monetary market system — an irreversible process of ensnarement explained in Chapter 9 — witnessing Christians can be very easily singled or screened out from participating in financial transactions. The technological capability already exists to control individual consumer privileges. What we buy or sell can be restricted. Surely this must sound overly sensational. If the Bible didn't say anything about this possibility, it surely would be. We do need to realize that such an entrapment is clearly foretold.

Look what the Antichrist is able to do: *"He also forced everyone, small and great, rich and poor, free and slave, to receive a mark on his right hand or on his forehead, so that no one could buy or sell unless he had the mark, which is the name of the beast or the number of his name. This calls for wisdom. If anyone has insight, let him calculate the number of the beast, for it is man's number. His number is 666"* (Revelation 13:16–18). We clearly see that the Antichrist is able to force the world to worship him through his power to control all economic activity.

In an integrated financial system such as we have today, it is virtually impossible for large numbers of people to live without the use of a bank account, a debit or a credit card. Today even the cash economy is under the monitoring eye of financial institutions and tax authorities. It would mean extreme hardship to be cut off from the world's financial system. To refuse to take the mark of the beast would mean almost certain starvation and death. As already argued in previous chapters, the beast that has a number for its name encompasses a worldwide system of numerical and quantitative control, administered through finance and technology.

This vision in Revelation doesn't appear very futuristic at all. These conditions exist this very day.

Will Christians Endure An Economic Collapse?

The Bible clearly says that a world system will come to complete devastation in the last days. A great collapse of the world's economy ensues; a false effigy of wealth and prosperity to be revealed, its promises of security shown to be hollow straws against the incomparable promises and grace of God that extends into eternity.

Will today's Christians witness this event? Will we live through the great economic and financial persecution of the Great Tribulation that is portrayed in Revelation 13? A wide range of views are held amongst respectable scholars and Bible teachers on this point. Will this time occur before or after the Rapture?

Though I cannot answer this question with any irrefutable proof, the view that I most identify with is that the Antichrist will carry out his worldwide campaign to persecute professing believers only after the Rapture.

No doubt, that view will be welcomed with great relief. It shouldn't.

This pretribulation view (believers being taken up to be with Christ at a time before the Great Tribulation) strikes me with great fear. Though saying this with trepidation, I'd rather face at least part of the Tribulation period. Why? Persecution of believers throughout history served to strengthen the faithful. The Church was always strengthened during such times. Real faith, purified by fire, flourished. The same will likely occur to professing Christians during the Great Tribulation. Think of it: If we were forced to recant our faith in Jesus Christ under the threat of economic or physical harm, what choice would we make? Would we worship the Beast? I doubt that any true Christian would. It is an easy decision to refuse to worship the beast when he is finally revealed, though the consequences may be grisly. Living at that time, the issues are cast so clearly in the stark contrasts of black and white, evil and good, that it would be impossible not to recognize the fulfillment of prophecy. How could one then betray Christ?

To conclude that Christians do not need to fear the outcome of this great and final collapse of financial markets and economies in the pretribulation view would be wrong. It doesn't absolve believers of any potential, involvement in the world condition that leads up to this period. It will be incredibly difficult for Christians to remain unaffected and pure in this prior age. I believe that time is today. James was prophesying about this time when he said the following: *"Now listen, you rich people, weep and wail because of the misery that is coming upon you. Your wealth has rotted, and moths have eaten your clothes. Your gold and silver are corroded. Their corrosion will testify against you and eat your flesh like fire. You have hoarded wealth in the last days. Look! The wages you failed to pay the workmen who mowed your fields are crying out against you. The cries of the harvesters have reached the ears of the Lord Almighty. You have lived on earth in luxury and self-indulgence. You have fattened yourselves in the day of slaughter. You have condemned and murdered innocent men, who were not opposing you"* (James 5:1–6).

No, living through all or part of the Great Tribulation is the easy "out" in my view. A pretribulation Rapture does not offer any easy escape. It presents much greater challenges. It places upon us the task of watchfulness, of living pure for Christ in a world that for the most part will be swallowed up by the deceptions, comforts and false gods of an endtime kingdom — one that seeks to challenge the very heavens. The challenges to our faith are subtle, cast in hues of gray. In the main, only the intensity of our love for Christ spurs us to be prepared for His coming, not the disciplines of hardship or persecution. Imagine the grief we would experience were He to appear only to catch us asleep, our lamps gone out. We would experience the same grief that Peter felt after he denied Christ three times. Think of the agony of having betrayed Christ — mired in the anxieties and lusts of an *Endtime Money Snare.*

It will take great courage and resolve in our day to live in a state of preparedness and anticipation of Christ's return.

The Rapture As A Catalyst Of Judgment

It may be the very Rapture itself that triggers the collapse of Babylon the Great. This makes sense for more than a few reasons. If even a few Christians were suddenly removed from the earth, it would represent immediate hardship for the shaky, financial systems that spans our globe today. A sudden drop in consumption and spending, even if minor, could not be easily sustained. Millions, perhaps even billions and trillions of dollars worth of transactions will be interrupted. Given the massive, multi-layered monetary system of owners, debtors and financial services that exists today, it will take some time to sort out all the various obligations that will have been broken so suddenly. Financial market confidence will therefore be seriously shaken. Economies will face gridlock. Without a doubt, a Rapture presents an effective catalyst for such a collapse.

The second reason I prefer this scenario is that it preserves the principle of "imminency." If it were believed that this great collapse must occur before Christ's Second Coming, the world would not be encouraged to live in the expectation that He can return at any time. This is directly contrary to Scripture. Christ will certainly not make his appearance during a time of great financial and economic distress. *"While people are saying, "Peace and safety," destruction will come on them suddenly, as labor pains on a pregnant woman, and they will not escape"* (1st Thessalonians 5:3).

The imagery of a pregnant woman presented by Paul's words is significant. A pregnancy is obvious and can hardly be kept secret for very long. It is soon apparent that a birth must follow. We can even know the approximate time of birth. Yet, we cannot know the exact onset. It is the same way with respect to an *Endtime Money Snare*. The world is already pregnant with the rise of a great monetary and financial colossus. We can see the processes at work. We can feel and see it moving, experiencing periodic tremors and shaking. Yet, its precise appointment with destiny cannot be known.

Staying Free And Fearless

Knowing that Christ can return at any time, let's then first examine our hearts. To begin, what role do we allow the cares of this world to play in our lives? Do we have any greed? Greed is the main doorway leading to a participation and entrapment with this endtime regime — the endtime trap. Immorality and greed are all connected. Just as we are to, "...*seek his kingdom* [before] *and these things will be given to you as well*" (Luke 12:31) we could say "seek ye first money, and all the other impurities and sins will be added unto us." Paul certainly held this view saying, "...*money is the root of all kinds of evil*" (1st Timothy 6:10). To be blunt, greed is idolatry. It places money and gain ahead of God. A greedy person worships at the altars of Mammon. It breaks the very first commandment, "*Thou shalt have no other gods before me.*" Therefore, the Bible is uncompromising in its judgment of greed: "*No immoral, impure or greedy person — such a man is an idolater — has any inheritance in the kingdom of Christ and of God*" (Ephesians 5:6). Greed seeks its inheritance upon earth.

God's command to us is clear. We are to come out of the world — out from the reach of the trap, the false promises and ensnarements of an all-encompassing monetary/

commercial colossus. *"Come out of her, my people, so that you will not share in her sins, so that you will not receive any of her plagues; for her sins are piled up to heaven, and God has remembered her crimes"* (Revelation 18:4–5). If we do not, we will be found to have had complicity with this system. In a sense, we will have been marked even as those who choose to worship the Antichrist during the Great Tribulation. *"If anyone worships the beast and his image and receives his mark on the forehead or on the hand, he, too, will drink of the wine of God's fury, which has been poured full strength into the cup of his wrath"* (Revelation 14:9–10). To come out of this endtime money trap — essentially represented by the world's worship of Babylon the Great — is to mean that we are not to worship it and place our trust in it. *"You cannot drink the cup of the Lord and the cup of demons too; you cannot have a part in both the Lord's table and the table of demons"* (1st Corinthians 10:21). We must sit at the Lord's table, dependent upon His provision as we honor and glorify Him.

A Sure Way Of Escape

I want to propose some guidelines that help deal with the monstrous spiritual challenges that Christians face living during the present time of an *Endtime Money Snare*. The suggestions and answers I lay out may not be popularly attractive. That may not be surprising just as true Christian faith is not welcomed by the world either. It goes against the grain. The Christian perspective will rub salt in the worldly advice of the prophets of our time — perhaps brokers, money managers, bankers, globalists, politicians and false-religion teachers. The advice in this book seeks to line up with Scripture. When put into practice, this counsel should offer a measure of peace, not anxiety about the cares of worldly, frenetic schemes.

All the same, godly stewardship requires sacrifice. Its biblical principles cannot simply be lived out aimlessly. They require a high level of awareness and discipline. Twice in Revelation we are called to endurance: *"This calls for patient endurance and faithfulness on the part of the saints"* (Revelation 13:10). Then again: *"This calls for patient endurance on the part of the saints who obey God's commandments and remain faithful to Jesus"* (Revelation 14:12). Contrary to the material appeals of the world to chase ease and financial security, we are called to endurance, not speculation and indulgence.

We do live in the world; therefore, some practical stewardship advice will be helpful as well. As the saying goes, there is no merit in being so heavenly that one serves no earthly good. For Christians who are saving up for their retirement years or those who are called to husband wealth, I suggest a simple stewardship approach suitable to our times in the remaining pages of this book. It offers a disentangled path through the treacheries of today's financial markets, not necessarily to high returns and riches, but to a standard of practical stewardship that has no complicity with worldly affections.

Is there a surefire way to escape the spiritual entrapment to the *Endtime Money Snare*? I believe there is. A plan of attack is laid out in 2nd Peter 1:5–7, *"For this very reason, make every effort to add to your faith goodness; and to goodness, knowledge; and to knowledge, self-control; and to self-control, perseverance; and to perseverance, godliness; and to godliness, brotherly kindness; and to brotherly kindness, love.*" All of these elements Peter outlines are essential in the exact order that he presents so that we might escape the spiritual lures of an endtime, materialistic world.

He begins with faith. Without it, salvation is not possible. We cannot be saved if we do not first have faith. And, if we have not first been saved, than no goodness can be found in us. God alone imparts His goodness to us through the atoning sacrifice of Jesus' crucifixion. Without these foundational elements there's little point in striving to be knowledgeable or self-controlled. Even if we were to meet the remaining requirements of Peter's list, we still wouldn't be saved. Only from this sure foundation is it worth striving for an escape that will reap true eternal rewards. Let's deal with the rest of Peter's outline, point by point.

Knowledge: First and foremost, we need information and insight. Through a study of the Bible we can know the season of the times we live in, the wiles of Satan, and everything else that we need to spiritually navigate our lives. We must not be unaware of his schemes. We should strive to stay informed about the factors and powers at play these days in world affairs and economies. Fewer and fewer North Americans have any notion of the times nor trends affecting the whole world.

I believe that an effective way of maintaining an awareness of the state of the world and its trends is to name the spirits that are in the service of Satan's agenda to depose God. As we now know, there are a least four. First is the love of money, the very spirit of Mammon. As we have discovered, it is the most powerful force for evil on earth. Coming against this powerful demonic force in our day will not be easy. The love of money shouts out to us from every quarter to consort with it, to run after it, to possess it. After all, the Bible says that a deep, perverted love of money will be a condition of the endtimes. *"But mark this: There will be terrible times in the last days. People will be lovers of themselves, lovers of money, boastful, proud..."* (2nd Timothy 3:1–2).

The other three evil spirits — MOFI, SCITE and GLOBO — should be named and watched as well. By doing so regularly we can discipline our daily lives, maintain our spiritual worship and place our hope upon God while yet living — and even benefiting — from the physical reality of their existence. We must also strive to stay informed about the factors and powers at play in our day in the field of commerce — financial markets and economies. These are the very ether of the great godless commercial colossus that arises in the last days, one that already exits.

Self-Control: We are called to guard our hearts and not allow our affections to fix on earthly possessions. Everything we own or seek upon earth must be under the ownership of our Lord Jesus Christ. Everything — small or large — must ultimately be in His service. This is where godly stewardship applies. Christ Himself implores us to guard against all kinds of greed. *"Watch out! Be on your guard against all kinds of greed; a man's life does not consist in the abundance of...possessions"* (Luke 12:15). We can use money and technology and enjoy God's global creation.

However, we do not need to be in their service, worship them or allow them to set up a kingdom in opposition to God.

In dealing with money we must guard against getting carried away by improper motivations. Why are we saving or investing? Is it a humble and balanced ethic of stewardship that is governing these activities? Or, is it purely the lure of high financial returns, the lure to engage the world in its competitive clamor to hoard wealth and comforts, to boastfully elevate ourselves over others? No eternal reward will accrue to our account in heaven if these impulses drive our lives. Disappointments could yet impact our lives upon earth if we chase such false gods of wood and stone.

Perseverance: The most difficult part of escaping the endtime money trap is perseverance. I believe this is the case for a number of reasons. Though we can live to honor God, the wicked will continue to prosper. While God tarries with His judgment, wishing that none might go lost, we watch many godless and evil people amass fortunes and kingdoms on earth. They flaunt it in our face, exulting in their ease and comfort. The world venerates them, giving them high profile in magazines, chronicling their lives as if they were gods. All this while we live quietly and humbly, enjoying our relationship with Jesus Christ.

If that weren't enough, we must contend with our close friends and Christian brothers and sisters. We meet them for coffee and they tell us of their conquests. Perhaps they boast about how much they have made staking their money in a risky, fast-growing mutual fund or a hedge fund. We nod in affirmation — possibly even congratulating them in an attempt to conceal our pangs of jealousy. Over dinner in our homes, or during conversation at a church social, we hear of the material indulgences and financial exploits of our fellow Christians. Even in this supposedly safe harbor of our churches we sometimes venerate rich people, treating affluence as the sure blessing of godly living and as evidence of wisdom. After experiences like these, the passions for the world and its temporal towers of wealth can be inflamed. It can require hours of being alone with God to again quiet these fires of lust for material gain.

Temptations to consort with a great endtime prosperity boom — deceitful as it may be — can come from within the Church, and not just from our Christian friends. Often, we are encouraged to strike out and make fortunes from the pulpits, from the supposed watchman of our faith, no less. Look what Isaiah had to say about the religious leaders of his day: *"Israel's watchmen are blind, they all lack knowledge; they are all mute dogs, they cannot bark; they lie around and dream, they love to sleep. They are dogs with mighty appetites; they never have enough. They are shepherds who lack understanding; they all turn to their own way, each seeks his own gain. "Come," each one cries "let me get wine! Let us drink our fill of beer! And tomorrow will be like today, or even far better"* (Isaiah 56:10–12). Prosperity theology is running rampant in the Western Church today. Eternal values are being preached for the sole purpose of earthly gain. Some well-known preachers even openly state that they don't want to wait for their eternal rewards but want materials blessings now.

In this environment of supposedly "blessed" materialism, many Christian financial counselors pass themselves off as virtual prophets. This may seem like a harsh thing to say, and of course this statement does not apply to everyone. Yet, as the prosperity gospel has invaded the Church, many financial planners are being venerated as wealth creators. Can these be the true disciples of Him who "...*has no place to lay His head*"?[2] In reality, most of these financial advisors have done nothing other than joining the world in its frenzied rush for financial wealth. In my view, they have pinned their clients to the tail of a false, deceptive endtime boom in world financial markets. This hardly qualifies as appropriate conduct for a true prophet. They have made no valiant predictions other than the fact that tomorrow will be as today.

Practicing biblical stewardship today in full truth and spirit will win few accolades and publicity. If you think the challenge of perseverance sounds tough to this point, it could get even worse. If the *Endtime Money Snare* continues to heighten, it'll get excruciatingly difficult. As it is now, few are able to withstand the temptations of consorting with a tower of hoarded financial wealth and are bowing to the three false endtime gods. Remember that the book of Revelation says that even great economic destruction and hardship will not turn people away from their idolatries. They will be so smitten by the successes of their idolatries and the massive scale of the wealth that has been created prior to the Great Tribulation that they will not let them go. The love of money, the greed for gain, the remembrance of the hearty times, ease and apparent wealth of the prior era will not break its hold.

How much further can an endtime boom in financial wealth continue? It has already progressed more than many thought possible. Yet, it is possible that GLOBO, MOFI and SCITE could yet shower trillions and quadrillions of dollars of financial wealth upon an idolatrous, endtime world. In Chapter 9, I speculated how the monetary value of financial wealth could still rise by a factor of five and more were the rest of the world to catch up to the stage of financial intensity existing in the high-income countries of the world. That is by no means a prediction. It only serves to illustrate that a world given over to its perversions can attain incredible heights of foolishness. And we do know that in the last days the world will do exactly that. How else could the people of the earth come to the point where it chooses to depose God and worship an Antichrist?

If Christians ever needed perseverance, the time is now.

Godliness: Just how can we remain godly in a financial world given over to greed and materialism? Of course, we are called to be good stewards; however, stewardship and investing is not necessarily one and the same. They are actually two entirely separate activities. Stewards may never be required to be investors. On the other hand, investors must always be good stewards. This view goes contrary to the message of many of today's Christian financial counselors: To be a good steward you must heavily invest, for example, buy purchasing mutual funds. If you do not, they claim that you are not stepping out in faith. Naturally, it's not that simple. In my opinion, stewardship is nine-tenths managing motivations and affections, one tenth actually managing money and possessions. True stewardship is not born out of the question, "How far can I run with the bulls of the world without getting gored? Or, "How can I grab onto the tail of an end-time money boom and still preserve my soul?" Why not carouse and frolic in the worldly financial markets — even though it is part of a complex system that seeks to ensnare the world of the last days — grab my share, and bail out just before the lights go out? According to the advice of many Christian financial planners, it is a greater sin to miss an uptrend in stock markets than to have complicity in a diabolically deceptive financial system. These attitudes do not reveal the spirit of a true steward who is fully serving Christ.

Paul suggests how we might live godly lives in an adulterous world: *"Make it your ambition to lead a quiet life, to mind your own business and to work with your hands, just as we told you, so that your daily life may win the respect of outsiders and so that you will not be dependent on anybody"* (1st Thessalonians 4:11). He recommended that the believers in Thessalonica should work in low profile professions and work with their hands. What did he mean by this directive? It flies straight into the face of today's push to boost the "knowledge economy." Most countries try to promote the growth of their "knowledge" businesses as opposed to the "old economy" smokestack industries.

I am inclined to believe that Paul was suggesting that

believers take jobs that do not lead them into complicity with a corrupt world. He chose to do so himself. He was a learned scholar, yet worked with his hands making tents. Supposedly, he could have been a consultant — a knowledge worker of some kind. Instead, he chose to work with his hands. However, I view Paul's writing as a suggestion only. Paul recommended to Timothy that it would also be better to not marry. If one wanted to serve the Lord without any diversions and unnecessary obligations, better to not marry was his view ... and better to not have a lofty elite job. Yes, one can be a knowledge worker, a lawyer or a financier, for example. God puts His people in all kinds of professions. However, Paul does make a point that is worth considering. Many professions today require that you become an accomplice (or at least harbor knowing complacency) in the corruption of the world or to enlist in an endtime conspiracy that sets itself up against God. I certainly believed that this had become the case in my career. I chose to leave voluntarily. You may choose to do the same if you feel that you are being subjected to unnecessary temptation or are forced to endorse corruption. Should you really do this? Only God can provide personal direction on this difficult question. In this regard, Paul provides us with a good benchmark to follow: *"You were bought at a price; do not become slaves of men. Brothers, each man, as responsible to God, should remain in the situation God called him to."*

⤳

We can enjoy the benefits of science and technology, monetary finance and knowledge of the created earth. We can invest and use most all financial services or employ any technical appliance provided that we can persevere in guarding our hearts. Yet, we are also free to not participate in financial markets or any other development if their function in the world has been given over to serve speculative greed or an endtime agenda as described in this book.

In these last days, Christians should not be found staking their hard-earned savings — the product of our labors — in storehouses that are subject to worldly whimsy. This will take courage, as it will open us up to ridicule. Remember how Jeremiah whined to God, *"I have neither lent nor borrowed, yet everyone curses me"* (Jeremiah 15:10). He was not participating in a financial system that operated to oppress the poor and transfer wealth to the "experts in greed" by way of a loose credit culture. And apparently because he wasn't, people thought that Jeremiah was just being judgmental. He was. He didn't want to have any part in the corruption and vain pursuits of the society of his day. I believe that that we should have the courage to separate ourselves from the idolatries of our day in the same way.

Summed up simply and succinctly, the highest and richest achievement of our earthly existence according to Scripture is nothing more than this: *"But godliness with contentment is great gain,"* (1st Timothy 6:6) for *"...godliness has value for all things, holding promise for both the present life and the life to come"* (1st Timothy 4:8)

But we must remember that this objective does not come without sacrifice. According to Peter, perseverance comes before godliness and contentment. None is required if we are traveling down the wide road in company with a vain-glorious and idolatrous world.

Just how can we be sure to pass through the test of perseverance in such an idolatrous and materialistic world as we live in today? More than that, how can we do so and yet stand at the end of the day before Christ? We need to focus fully upon Him and His promises of peace and salvation for eternity.

∽

"Provide purses for yourselves that will not wear out, a treasure in heaven that will not be exhausted, where no thief comes near and no moth destroys. For where your treasure is, there your heart will be also"
Luke 12:33–34.

ENDNOTES

1. (1st Corinthians 10:1–5).
2. Matthew 8:20.

CHAPTER 19

The Peace of Christ

A Portfolio of Securities

W e now can see how the Hopes, whom we met in the first chapter, are being lured. The siren call of easy financial gains, promising them a comfortable retirement, has coaxed them to accept a barrel of dubious assumptions about the world. As soon as Mr. Guinn has them fully invested in the stock and bond markets — something they know little about — their lives will be inextricably intertwined with an *Endtime Money Snare*. If markets continue to soar, bathing them in easy gains, they will grow even fonder and more reliant upon the world. They risk being held hostage by the sweet enticements of financial prosperity. On the other hand, every sharp downturn in financial markets may cause them disquiet — more than a few restless nights. Of course, as we've already learned, the economic enslavement of our age is much wider and more complex than through investments in financial markets.

Our journey to this point, from examining the words of God spoken by the Old Testament prophets through to a documentation of present world trends, certainly leaves little doubt that humanity is witnessing the last day rise of a materialistic snare. The unprecedented events of the time of the end have begun to unfold. Only the final scenes await. Already, we see that most of the Western world is clenched in the claws of a voracious beast-like money trap. Babylon the Great, likely representing the great monetary/commercial colossus of our day, is already sprawled across the earth.

Yet, for the most part, there is hardly any desire to escape. There is almost no resistance. Indeed, none should be expected. The world at large — even many Christians — is entirely unaware of the deception and treachery harbored in the seductive promises and prosperity of a great endtime agenda. Like the powerful rhythmic motions of a snake's gullet, each advance of ingestion by this world system — fostered by Satan and the three false gods: GLOBO, SCITE and MOFI — is virtually irreversible. The mandibles of the snake's jaws inch their way up the body of our resistance — entreating us to its promised delicacies of ease, comfort and prosperity — eventually to engulf us as its total captives. We struggle — sometimes valiantly — only to relent — eventually. The advance of this money trap is incessant, galvanized by a final determination never to give up its ground, to mount up its prophesied insurrection against the Holy One.

The serrated teeth of its death grip are really the entrenchment of our habits and affections — both real and imagined — for income and worldly sustenance. The main battle is really found at the level of our affections.

A safe conclusion is that we do not know exactly when the great collapse of mankind's systems will occur. In reality, however, this question is largely irrelevant. To debate the point of when a disaster such as this will take place only serves to take our focus away from the more subtle, spiritual lures that conspire at present. Are we already tangled in a spiritual endtime snare today? Have our affections already turned away from Jesus Christ? Are we running after GLOBO, MOFI and SCITE, venerating them instead of our glorious, omnipotent God? After all, it is here that the whole endtime entrapment of mankind begins.

My hope is as the apostle Paul said, *"...that* [we Christians] *will come to* [our] *senses and escape from the trap of the devil, who has taken them captive to do his will"* (2nd Timothy 2:26).

Viewed from this great cosmic perspective, the fate of our investment portfolios — our stakes of wealth in the material world — suddenly seems insignificant. The fear of losing everything in this final collapse is hardly the most important concern. We may be raptured before this great collapse in any case. Why then be concerned at all about managing our savings and possessions in a safe manner?

For one, we do not know exactly when the Lord will return. Moreover, we are charged to be good stewards of our talents and possessions. We are called to occupy until He comes. Therefore, we must be actively working out our faith and living out our godly values in the midst of immoral secular world systems through bubbles and busts. By implication, we must continually work out how we manage our savings and possessions without being ensnared by the enticements of greed and money.

The Outlook Ahead

What if the Lord's return is still some way off? We should still expect tough economic times ahead. Even if the final economic swoon associated with the Great Tribulation does not occur in this generation, North America and the world still faces the high probability of a depression in the not-too-distant future. This would not be unusual, as similar periods have occurred often over past centuries. Though economic depressions of this type present great hardship, they hardly compare to the destruction described in the book of Revelation.

An economic depression is already long overdue and could begin at any time. Economic and monetary history argues that such an outcome for North America and the world should not be a surprise. In that regard, the sad fate of Japan over the past decade serves as a warning message to America. A country given over to excess must eventually pay its bills. When that day comes, economic hardship will be multiplied. America, or any other country, is not exempt from this physical law of the universe that God Himself set in place. Given the evidence, we should live in the expectation of financial trouble.

Looking Ahead To The Securities Of God

We can only speculate as to the exact turn of events from this point forward — the exact timing, the extent and full depth of the delusion and deception. Though we may use our minds and work out the best ways to husband our savings and resources as good stewards here on earth, our ultimate hope is much greater. Provided we live as obedient stewards, we have a portfolio full of securities — the promises of Jesus Christ — that we can rely upon. Just look at these valuable securities and instructions that we find in the Bible:

1. Jesus Christ will never forsake us: *"Keep your lives free from the love of money and be content with what you have, because God has said, "Never will I leave you; never will I forsake you." So we say with confidence, The Lord is my helper; I will not be afraid. What can man do to me?"* (Hebrews 13:5–6).

Relying upon our money and seeking our security in the infinity of financial gains is fruitless. When God's disciplining — or judgment in the case of those who will live during the Great Tribulation — finally comes, our worldly investments will provide neither refuge nor eternal reward.

2. Do not worry about those things that are beyond our control: *"Therefore do not worry about tomorrow, for tomorrow will worry about itself. Each day has enough trouble of its own"* (Matthew 6:34).

We are not to preoccupy ourselves about the future. Spending our time and energies to overcome the boundaries of risk and the unknown will prove to be unsuccessful. God alone knows that which is unknowable to us. He alone knows the future perfectly. If we live in total service to Him, then we have absolutely nothing to worry about.

"Rejoice in the Lord always. I will say it again: Rejoice!

Let your gentleness be evident to all. The Lord is near. Do not be anxious about anything, but in everything, by prayer and petition, with thanksgiving, present your requests to God. And the peace of God, which transcends all understanding, will guard your hearts and your minds in Christ Jesus" (Philippians 4:4–7). Also, a similar security is found here: *"The LORD is the strength of his people, a fortress of salvation for his anointed one. Save your people and bless your inheritance; be their shepherd and carry them forever"* (Psalm 28:8–9).

3. Ignore the wicked who may become wealthy: The labors of the rich that the world idolizes will all go to waste with no eternal reward. Their pay-off is only for a very short season. And even for this short season, riches provide no peace. Seeking earthly wealth, they suffer much anguish and deceit. According to Isaiah's prophesies, there is little doubt what is in store for the wicked and their wealth.

"The LORD Almighty has a day in store for all the proud and lofty, for all that is exalted (and they will be humbled), for all the cedars of Lebanon, tall and lofty, and all the oaks of Bashan, for all the towering mountains and all the high hills, for every lofty tower and every fortified wall, for every trading ship and every stately vessel. The arrogance of man will be brought low and the pride of men humbled; the LORD alone will be exalted in that day, and the idols will totally disappear" (Isaiah 2:12–18).

Are we just getting by in this world, with little in our bank accounts? If we are serving the Lord faithfully it doesn't have any impact upon our eternal prospects for,

"Better the little that the righteous have than the wealth of many wicked; for the power of the wicked will be broken, but the LORD upholds the righteous" (Psalm 37:16).

4. Be gentle with others, seeking to save them from the consequences of complicity with the *Endtime Money Snare*: *"Be merciful to those who doubt; snatch others from the fire and save them; to others show mercy, mixed with fear — hating even the clothing stained by corrupted flesh"* (Jude 22–23).

5. Occupy and look up, for the Lord's return draws near: *"But you, dear friends, build yourselves up in your most holy faith and pray in the Holy Spirit. Keep yourselves in God's love as you wait for the mercy of our Lord Jesus Christ to bring you to eternal life"* (Jude 20–21).

6. Do not bow down to the "image of gold"— God will save us. We can glean hope from the experience of Daniel's companions; Shadrach, Meshach and Abednego. They refused to give into the idolatry forced upon them by King Nebuchadnezzar, no matter the price. If they had to die in the fire or live on the fringes of society as outcasts in order to stay faithful to their God so be it. *"If we are thrown into the blazing furnace, the God we serve is able to save us from it, and he will rescue us from your hand, O king. But even if he does not, we want you to know, O king, that we will not serve your gods or worship the image of gold you have set up"* (Daniel 3:17–18). Though the great financial/commercial colossus may entice us to worship it, even attempting to entrap us, it is better that we accept an existence on the fringes of society as outcasts, than have complicity in its sins.

7. Expect Persecution: *"...without being frightened in any*

way by those who oppose you. This is a sign to them that they will be destroyed, but that you will be saved—and that by God. For it has been granted to you on behalf of Christ not only to believe on him, but also to suffer for him, since you are going through the same struggle you saw I had, and now hear that I still have" (Philippians 1:28–39).

Here we are told that Christian persecution, whether subtle or direct, is to be expected. In fact, it is a sign that we are on the right path and that we are indeed living out our faith. If you are walking down the wide road of ease or surfing on the leading edge of society's values or world trends, you will not experience any persecution. Chances are that your understanding of true stewardship is also worldly. If so, you will find yourself caught deep in the net of Satan's endtime money agenda.

Finally, let's take a moment to do some securities analysis. To do so we don't need any financial degree, just common sense and spiritual eyes. Let's contrast the two portfolios of securities we have available to us — both the earthly and the eternal. The latter offers incredible returns and rewards. All of our investments placed there are safe from corruption, bankruptcy, inflation, devaluation, robbers and fiat decree. We don't necessarily need to pay money managers, advisors, financial planners, brokers and bankers to shield it against these dangers even if they could. Moreover, these eternal investments offer a guaranteed pay-off over eternity. We can know this for certain because we have the predictions of the most reliable forecaster and strategist of true riches ever known — Jesus Christ. His words are true, never wrong or wide of the mark. This heavenly investment portfolio that we are promised offers the most incredible investment return. Jesus Christ said, *"And everyone who has left houses or brothers or sisters or father or mother or children or fields for my sake will receive a hundred times as much and will inherit eternal life"* (Matthew 19: 29). Imagine! We will get a hundred-fold return — tax-free at that — for everything we give up to the total lordship of Jesus Christ. There isn't an investment anywhere that offers a risk-free rate of return like this. Contrast this investment proposition to that of an earthly investment. One is changeless and forever; the other is temporal and uncertain. Is there any comparison?

We can do even better. Although we will face persecution, we can come out far ahead. We can build immense eternal value out of this endtime financial world that we live in today. According to the Bible, the most valuable thing of all is our faith. *"In this you greatly rejoice, though now for a little while you may have had to suffer grief in all kinds of trials. These have come so that your faith — of greater worth than gold, which perishes even though refined by fire — may be proved genuine and may result in praise, glory and honor when Jesus Christ is revealed"* (1st Peter 1:6–7). Our faith, evidenced through the hearing and doing of the Word and the fear of the Lord is utterly precious for eternity.

Dear brothers and sisters, let's begin investing for eternity. Let's strive to avoid the *Endtime Money Snare*, giving no assistance or ground to Satan's diabolical plan to en-snare the world into worshipping him.

⊷

"But blessed is the man who trusts in the LORD, whose confidence is in him. He will be like a tree planted by the water that sends out its roots by the stream. It does not fear when heat comes; its leaves are always green. It has no worries in a year of drought and never fails to bear fruit" (Jeremiah 17:7–8).

Practical Stewardship Guidelines

How Christians Should Steward Their Possessions

We have already dealt with the spiritual dangers of our financial world in the previous chapters. Given what we now know about the *Endtime Money Snare,* its diabolic objectives and its many dangerous traps, is it likely that Christ's Church should be made up of complacent, contented stewards? Repeatedly we are called to be separate, we should be different — the salt of the world — and expect discomforts because the world will not like our perspectives because the world rejected Him first.

Christians are charged to avoid complicity and friendship with the world. James warns *"...that friendship with the world is hatred toward God"* (James 4:4). Christ Himself instructed believers to remain separate from the world and its fashionable cares ... to stay aloof of its standards, acceptance and praise: *"Do not love the world or anything in the world. If anyone loves the world, the love of the Father is not in him. For everything in the world — the cravings of sinful man, the lust of his eyes and the boasting of what he has and does—comes not from the Father but from the world. The world and its desires pass away, but the man who does the will of God lives forever"* (1st John 2:15–16).

We have a duty to avoid worldliness in all of our activities and thoughts.

Then, in these times of great financial uncertainty, volatility, and intense temptations to join the world in the mad rush to build a heaven of material prosperity on earth, just how should we manage our savings and investments?

Investing in today's financial markets is a very dangerous game that will ultimately end very badly. It's a high stakes game that has little to do with sound stewardship. It's all about brinkmanship and gambling, playing the world's frenzied and unprincipled game of wealth maximization. The fruits of this game are obvious: anxiousness, greed followed by fear, with peace nowhere to be found. In the meantime it is luring many investors into the belief that wealth can be created from magic.

For those of us who do have money invested in longer-term financial assets such as stocks and bonds, how should we manage them? Actually, almost everyone will be exposed to financial market trends in one way or another. Even though we may not invest in stock and bond markets directly ourselves, our insurance policies and future pensions claims are backed by such investments. Government pension systems are also dependent upon financial and economic conditions. Whether we are direct investors or not, our lives are inextricably tied up with the world's financial system. Even though we may have overcome the ensnarements of a materialistic world system with our hearts, the global financial/commercial colossus has become so pervasive and invasive, that we must still take account of its dangers to our physical livelihoods.

Here are some approaches to consider when stewarding our savings, beginning with the basics:

1. **Always examine motives:** Why are you investing? Is a humble and balanced stewardship ethic governing your financial savings activities? Or, is it purely the lure of high financial returns — yours, or those others are bragging about — and the intoxication of past gains that is pushing your thinking? If so, disappointments will be ahead ... perhaps sooner than we may even think. Those are precisely the emotions that conspire to pull you into the maws of the *Endtime Money Snare.* We are reminded: *"For where your treasure is, there your heart will be also"* (Matthew 6:21). Those who are rich are commanded, *"...not to be arrogant nor to put their hope in wealth, which is so uncertain, but to put their hope in God, who richly provides us with everything for our enjoyment"* (1st Timothy 6:17). We are further warned that, *"People who want to get rich fall into temptation and a trap and into many foolish and harmful desires that plunge men into ruin and destruction"* (1st Timothy 6:9).

2. **Be a steward, not a hoarder:** I believe that God's economy is mainly composed of flows, not overstuffed storehouses of idle money. Just as God is love in motion — love lived — so it should be with money. Of course, we need to save for our future anticipated needs and to fund the activities of our businesses and livelihoods. However, there comes a point where the act of saving becomes hoarding. In this sense, for the saints, all savings must be done in a spirit of stewardship. In contrast,

the world promotes the spirit of hoarding; the pursuit of earthly wealth as a measure of success; a bulwark of security; to satisfy boasts. Be a flow-person, not a hoarder. Most all of God's gifts to us, whether the gifts of the Spirit or material resources, are meant for sharing and blessing others through our giving in turn.

3. **Trust God and live humbly**: Let the world go by in its frenzied hunt for wealth and prosperity. These days, that means high caution is in order with respect to most stock and bond markets. They are objects of a crazed lust for wealth. Rather, I think it is better to store one's savings in safer investments that are not the object of greedy affections. In my estimation, such investments would include short-term treasury bonds and treasury bills as well as investments in solid, private businesses.

4. **Gain control of your savings**: Gain as much control of your savings as possible so that you can determine how they are invested. The investment recommendations of so-called professionals — pension fund consultants, actuaries, and mutual fund managers — may be well-meaning, their recommendations can still be harmful. Many are simply unknowledgeable and deceived — a case of the blind leading the blind — who, like all of us, need to put bread on the table. Sadly, there are others who do know better, who consciously recommend hollow solutions in the pursuit of their own self interests. So, as a rule, wherever you can, seek control of your own investments. And where you can't do so (such as may be the case in a company defined-benefit pension plan or an endowment insurance policy), or in the case of a complex investment which requires professional help (a real estate part-

nership or a specialized mutual fund) scrutinize, scrutinize, and again, scrutinize. In the end, how your savings are invested is still your responsibility.

5. Follow common sense: If an investment or financial deal sounds too good to be true, it probably is. High returns usually require a measure of speculation.

6. Investigate risk: Whenever a promised interest rate (for a given time-frame) is substantially higher than a competing investment, beware. There must be a reason. The financial institution that is offering this interest rate must earn enough on the money that you invest with them in order to pay you the promised return. Given the competitive financial systems we have today, the only way a financial institution can offer a substantially higher interest-rate return is to take on more risk. Determine why one financial institution is able to offer substantially higher returns than another.

7. Research Extensively: When researching an investment option, seek information from sources other than the firm or person offering the opportunity. The promoter of an investment is likely to have a one-sided perspective. Even better, seek financial knowledge from an alternative source that has no obvious biased interests ... in other words, an incentive in having you buy the investment from them. Sources for such information are newsletters or financial counseling services that do not derive any support or income from the sale of investments.

8. Don't make exceptions because of religious affiliations: If you are approached by a self-proclaimed Christian financial advisor, hold him or her accountable to the same standards you would apply to anyone from whom you would seek investment advice. To date, I have come across no evidence that suggests that people with religious connections are more successful investors than others. Why should Christians be more adept at beating the odds in godless investment markets than the wicked? All too often, Christian investors are fleeced by con artists. They like to prey on the faithful because they are quick to drop their guard the moment a religious association is implied.

9. Save More: Even though it will be difficult to find a good storehouse for your retirement nestegg — one that will remain secure for a long period of time until you pass on — you must continue to save. In fact, you must save more than other people if you wish to claim a higher-than-average income when you retire.

10. Get a claim upon income: When all the dealing is done and the first down phase of this new age of financial wealth sets in or your retirement age arrives, make absolutely sure that you have a claim on investment earnings — quality interest and dividend income. Along with liquidity, it's these things that are scarce these days. Ultimately — especially so in a world of declining population growth — all financial values must rest on basic income. That aspect of the human economy will always remain true, no matter how sizzling and futuristic the world may seem. Pay less attention to capital appreciation alone. Whenever opportunities avail, invest your savings in securities or ventures that have a strong prospect of continuing to deliver income — whether markets rise or collapse.

11. Avoid assets that can be manipulated: Choose investments that are least subject to manipulation. Securities markets are notoriously easy to manipulate by monetary authorities and owners or managers of large pools of financial wealth. For the long haul, minimize the type of investments whose value can fluctuate suddenly and wildly with supply and demand. As much as practicable, avoid securities markets.

12. Seek other types of savings: Invest savings in stores of value other than in financial securities markets. Direct ownership of businesses and real property with good income prospects and/or real estate would be recommended ways of diversifying future income potential.

13. Invest in your extended family: Remember, in times past, one's retirement lifestyle depended on the amount of children and the size of the future extended family — at least in the sense that one could access the income potential of this group at retirement. It's no different today, though mainly in a socialized form in developed countries. Here finances intersect families. Both are about developing future income potential and are actually directly related. So what to do? At the very least, it makes good sense to invest in relationships with your children. You never know. You may need to live with them someday as do more than two-thirds of the world's elderly. Encourage them to be productive future citizens and hope that it will translate into superior income power for your extended family.

The above list, while intended to be a comprehensive stewardship guide, if followed along with the plan laid out in 2nd Peter 1:4–7 (presented in Chapter 18 of this book) should indeed result in true wealth with eternal value — godliness with contentedness.

⫸ *The author publishes the free newsletter*

Readers wishing to receive regular updates on global perspectives and financial trends are invited to subscribe. Please visit the website www.eternalvalue.com and sign-up for a free e-mail distribution, or for further information, please write:

Mulberry Press Inc.
P.O. Box 903, Smithville, Ontario, Canada L0R 2A0
Telephone: 888-957-0602 • Facsimile: 905-957-5263

*T*ap into the Bible analysis of top prophecy authorities...

Midnight Call is a hard-hitting Bible-based magazine loaded with news, commentary, special features, and teaching, illustrated with explosive color pictures and graphics. Join hundreds of thousands of readers in 140 countries who enjoy this magazine regularly!

➡ *The world's leading prophetic Bible magazine*

➡ *Covering international topics with detailed commentary*

➡ *Bold, uncompromising biblical stands on issues*

➡ *Pro-Bible, Pro-family, Pro-life*

12 issues/1 yr. $28.95
24 issues/2 yr. $45